Fetal Protection
in the Workplace

Fetal Protection in the Workplace

*Women's Rights,
Business Interests,
and the Unborn*

Robert H. Blank

Columbia University Press
New York

Columbia University Press
New York   Chichester, West Sussex
Copyright © 1993 Columbia University Press
All rights reserved

Library of Congress Cataloging-in-Publication Data

Blank, Robert H.
    Fetal protection in the workplace: women's rights, business
interests, and the unborn / Robert H. Blank.
        p.   cm.
    Includes bibliographical references and index.
    ISBN 0-231-07694-0
    1. Pregnant women—Employment—Law and legislation—United States.
    2. Unborn children (Law)—United States.
    3. Fetus—Abnormalities.
    4. Pregnancy—Complications.   I. Title.
KF3467.B57   1993
344.73'0144—dc20
[347.304144]
92-42906
    CIP

Casebound editions of Columbia University Press books are printed on
permanent and durable acid-free paper.

Printed in the United States of America

c 10 9 8 7 6 5 4 3 2 1

to
my daughters
Mai-Ling and Maigin
and their freedom of choice

Contents

Contents

Fetal Protection
in the Workplace

1 | Introduction: Changing Views of Maternal Responsibility

We are in the midst of a revolution in biomedical technology, especially where that technology affects human genetics and reproduction. Rapid advances in prenatal diagnosis and therapy are joined with new reproductive-aiding technologies such as in vitro fertilization and more precise genetic tests. Combined with the burgeoning knowledge of fetal development and the causes of congenital illness, these technologies are altering our perception of the fetus. As a result prevailing values are being challenged by the new biology and the courts are being confronted with novel, onerous cases that require a reevaluation of established legal principles.

One critical set of values undergoing reevaluation centers on the relationship between mother and fetus. The technological removal of the fetus from the "secrecy of the womb" through ultrasound and other prenatal procedures gives the fetus social recognition as an individual separate from the mother. The emergence of in utero surgery (see Harrison et al. 1990) gives the fetus potential patient status, which might at times conflict with that of the pregnant women who carries it. Moreover, conclusive evidence that certain maternal actions during pregnancy such as cocaine (Chasnoff 1988) and alcohol (Wagner 1991) abuse can have devastating effects on fetal health challenges conventional notions of maternal autonomy. Together these scientific trends are producing a context in which women's procreative rights achieved only recently after decades of struggle are threatened. In the words of legal scholar George Annas, "Bodies of pregnant women are the battleground on which the campaign to define the right of privacy is fought. The ultimate outcome will likely be shaped at least as much by new medical technologies as by politics or moral persuasion" (Annas 1989). No applications of medicine promise more acrimonious and intense legal debate in the coming decades than the impact of these technologies on the maternal-fetal relationship and on our notions of individual rights.

On the one hand proponents of fetal rights contend that the health of the unborn fetus must be protected even at the expense of maternal rights (Balisy 1987). They argue that the state's interest in protecting fetal health must take precedence over the maternal right to privacy. In contrast proponents of maternal autonomy argue that no one but the pregnant woman can make such intimate decisions (see Gallagher 1987, Johnsen 1986, 1989). Any attempt at state or third-party intervention, therefore, represents unjustifiable constraints on women and is a return to the days when enslavement of women was justified as biological destiny.

In the last decade there has been a persistent intensification of policy issues surrounding attempts to define maternal responsibility (Losco 1989). Unfortunately the current policy context and the government response to date have been inconsistent, haphazard, and often contradictory. Considerable interest has focused on the development of case law and the activity of the courts in redefining responsible maternal behavior and the standard of care owed the unborn (see Blank 1992a). It is clear that the courts are already heavily involved in revising conventional views of maternal autonomy and discretion during the prenatal period. Trends in both tort and criminal law appear to be on a collision course with the recently established predominance given maternal autonomy.

A major influence on the way the courts as well as the public views the maternal-fetal relationship is technology. Rapid advances in biomedical science as reflected in prenatal diagnosis and therapy, reproduction-aiding techniques such as in vitro fertilization, and a growing array of ever more precise genetic tests are inalterably changing our perceptions of the fetus. In combination with a heightened understanding of fetal development and the potentially deleterious impact of a broad range of behavior by the pregnant woman these technologies force a reevaluation of maternal responsibility for fetal health.

Constitutional Rights of Pregnant Women

Reproduction has always been a sensitive topic in the United States and has elicited controversy as well as conflict between social values and social practice. Controversy often centers on how and to what extent the state can intervene and limit individual freedoms of reproduction. Most recently it has centered on debate over limiting the procreative choice of women to protect the life or health of the developing fetus. It is important that this debate be placed in the proper constitutional context that has developed over the last century. Three basic constitutional rights limit the power of the states to intervene in the health care decisions of pregnant women: the right to bodily integrity; the right to make intimate family decisions; and the right of parents to make decisions about how to raise their child. Any attempts to control women's actions during pregnancy must face constitutional challenges on these grounds.

The Right to Bodily Integrity

The Supreme Court in *Union Pacific Railway v. Botsford* (1891) held that "no right is held more sacred or is more carefully guarded . . . than the right of every individual to the possession and control of his own person, free from a restraint or interference of others, unless by clear and unquestionable authority of law" (p. 251). The origins of the right to bodily integrity lie in the Fourth Amendment "right of the people to be secure in their persons, houses, papers and effects against unreasonable searches and seizures" and in the due process clause of the Fourteenth

Amendment. This right to self-determination and bodily integrity has long been applied to decisions involving medical treatment: a doctor who does not obtain consent before treating the patient can be charged with battery (*Schloendorff v. Society of New York Hospitals* 1914). Since that time consent has come to be interpreted as informed, thus allowing the individual to weigh the risks and benefits of a proposed treatment (*Canterbury v. Spence* 1972). Implicit in the concept of informed consent is the right to refuse treatment, even if it might lead to the patient's death (*Bouvia v. Superior Court* 1986).

Although the right to bodily integrity is basic, it is a qualified right. The courts have not prohibited all state action interfering with the right but have applied a balancing test weighting the invasion of bodily integrity against the legitimate state interest in taking that action. The Constitution, then, allows state to intrude into an individual's bodily integrity only if the intrusion is essential to achieve a legitimate state goal more important than the individual's bodily privacy. For instance, in some cases the courts have held that the state's compelling interest in protecting the life and health of dependents outweighs the mother's right to bodily integrity (see *In re President and Directors of Georgetown College, Inc.* 1964, where the court ordered a blood transfusion for a women against her will when it found that her death would jeopardize the welfare of her minor children). The state's interest in taking the intrusive action, however, must outweigh the individual's privacy interest. Furthermore, the state must not be able to achieve its goal through any less intrusive means. Additionally, the state must grant the individual adequate procedural rights if his or her rights are adjudicated.

The Right to Make Intimate Family Decisions

The Supreme Court in *Griswold v. Connecticut* (1965) enunciated a right to marital privacy that protects couples from governmental efforts to prevent their use of contraceptives. In *Griswold* the Court struck down a Connecticut statute proscribing all individuals and couples from using birth control. The Court held that the Bill of Rights implicitly protects a "zone of privacy." While there is no explicit mention of the term "privacy," the Court forged this right in the "penumbra" of rights emanating from the First Amendment right of association, the Third Amendment prohibition against quartering soldiers in peacetime, the Fourth Amendment prohibition against unreasonable searches and seizures, the Fifth Amendment protection against self-incrimination, and the Ninth Amendment vesting in the people those rights not enumerated in the Constitution (p. 484).

In *Eisenstadt v. Baird* (1972), the Court extended the right to use contraceptives to nonmarried couples by applying the equal protection clause of the Fourteenth Amendment. The right to autonomy in intimate decision making rests on two principles: a person should be free from governmental intrusion into his or her home or family, and a person has a right to autonomy in making certain personal decisions. The second principle led to the *Roe v. Wade* (1973) decision invalidating the Texas statute prohibiting abortion. The *Roe* Court elaborated on the principle of autonomy, holding that it prevents a state from interfering in fundamental intimate decisions in the absence of a compelling state interest. The right to terminate pregnancy involves rights "implicit in the concept of ordered liberty" (p. 162) and falls within the zone of privacy protected by the Constitution. To deny a woman the right to make this decision would cause distress and the risk of harm inherent in imposing an unwanted child on the woman. Only after viability of the fetus could the state demonstrate a compelling interest to intervene.

The Court has been willing to apply less demanding scrutiny of state actions that fall short of denying the woman the right to decide, however. In *Harris v. McRae* (1980), for example, the Court held that the denial of Medicaid funding even for medically necessary abortions does not interfere unduly with the freedom of choice protected in *Roe*, even though it makes "childbirth a more attractive alternative, thereby influencing the woman's decision" (p. 2687). Freedom of choice does not impose an obligation on the state to subsidize all alternatives equally for the *Harris* Court. Although the Court is adamant in prohibiting any absolute denial of the constitutional right to make autonomous procreative decisions, it is willing to apply a balancing analysis for lesser intrusions varying in intensity according to the means employed and the extent of intrusion on privacy rights. It requires considerable care on the part of the state in framing any regulations that affect childbearing decisions, but upon a compelling state interest the Court is willing to permit lesser forms of interference with procreative rights (*Webster v. Reproductive Health Services* 1989).

The Right to Parental Autonomy in Childbearing

There is a traditional preference in U.S. society for minimal state intervention in childbearing decisions. This preference is based on the assumption that parents are able and willing to pursue the course of action that is in their child's best interest. According to the Supreme Court

> The law's concept of the family rests on a presumption that parents possess what a child lacks in maturity, experience, and capacity for judgment required for making life's difficult decisions. More importantly, historically it has recognized that natural bonds of affection lead parents to act in the best interests of their children.   (*Parham v. J.R.* 1979:602)

The parent-child relationship, then, is special, and comprises deep psychological and social bonds as well as physical and material dependence. When in doubt the courts have chosen to err on the side of nonintervention in order to preserve the stability of the parent-child relationship. "The state should usually defer to the wishes of the parents, it has a serious burden of justification before abridging parental authority by 'substituting its judgment' for that of the parents" (*In re Phillip B.* 1979:51). In a challenge to the law that mandated aggressive treatment of ill newborns over the refusal of parents (*Bowen v. American Hospital Association* 1986), the Supreme Court held that the state should intervene only in "exceptional" cases. In the Court's words: "Traditional law concerning the family, buttressed by the emerging constitutional right of privacy, protects a substantial range of discretion for parents" (p. 2113). Furthermore, the courts have been hesitant to allow state intervention in childrearing decisions because such actions might undermine the diversity of views and life styles promoted by allowing families to raise children in a wide variety of living situations. There is an implicit grounding of this right to the autonomy of parents' decisions in the First Amendment freedom of religion, which has played prominently in many of the cases involving medical decisions (*Jehovah's Witnesses v. King's County Hospital* 1967).

Limiting Parental Choice in Procreation

The prevailing value orientation in the United States continues to give preeminence to the right to procreate without restriction as an interest so fundamental that society should not interfere. However, technological advances are shifting emphasis gradually to a less rigid viewpoint. There has been a serious questioning of the heavy reliance on the parent-child relationship, especially the assumption that parents will make good faith efforts to act in the best interests of their children even if they are incapable of knowing what is best. Issues in child abuse, state support of dependent children, medical decision making, and lack of fertility control by those often least able to raise their children heighten this concern. As this book demonstrates, there is increased emphasis in both case law and literature on the parental duty to provide an adequate environment so that children have a chance to succeed; a growing view is that a child has a corresponding right to as sound a body and mind as possible. Although procreative rights are still fundamental under the Constitution, there is considerable new pressure for setting limits when exercise of these rights conflicts with the health and life of children, including the unborn under some circumstances.

Within the context of emerging technologies for procreative control there exists an alternative view that society has not only the authority but also the duty to intervene in reproductive decision making. Whether out of concern for affected children, future generations, the health of the gene pool, or some other general or societal good, there appears to be a growing agreement that some constraints ought to be placed on human reproduction when persons abuse those rights. Many advocates of this approach contend that even if procreation is an inalienable right it can be regulated by a society concerned with the existence of the child to be born and with its own survival as a society. Reproduction in these terms is a right shared with society as a whole and is but part of a larger complex of rights, responsibilities, and obligations. State intervention might be justified under certain circumstances, although each case must be addressed with caution.

Social Recognition of Fetus as a Person

In discussing criteria of selfhood used by a society, Grobstein (1981:89) declares that "the social status of personhood is accorded through recognition and acceptance by others. Recognition and empathy registered by observers are especially important criteria for assessing levels of selfness when policy issues are at stake." Even Baron (1983:122), who suggests that we are perfectly capable of refusing to grant personhood on the basis of empathy where that status would exact a result we are unwilling to accept, agrees that in close cases the force of empathy may carry the day. Social recognition in addition to behavioral manifestations and evidence of functional capabilities is a critical sign that rudiments of personhood might be present.

Until the recent decade the fetus in utero could not take on the social recognition of a human except conceptually. Hidden in the womb, the first evidence of life was the movement detectable to the mother at quickening, around the eighteenth week of pregnancy. Even here, however, the evidence was only of life, not of recognition as a human form. Since the late 1960s a number of biomedical innovations have significantly altered the perception of the fetus. Ultimately these innovations promise to result in recognition of human qualities at progressively earlier stages of fetal development. One of the most critical elements of recognition is visualization. Only in the last ten years has it been possible to visualize the fetus in utero through sophisticated electronic equipment. As ultrasound technology has advanced to produce more explicit real time images of the fetal limbs and movement, it is reasonable to expect a tendency to perceive the fetus as a small baby instead of an unseen organism residing in the womb. According to John Fletcher,

> I think this technology itself has had a tendency to allow us to identify fetuses as persons much earlier if we decide to. My point is that there may be a socio-biological force working here. If you identify with a person when you see the fetus this imprints on you the idea that there is one of us here that we can't neglect. The technology itself has a powerful logical grip in terms of identifying personhood.   (1983:305)

Ultrasound technology allows presentation of a humanlike form as early as twelve weeks. Also, ultrasound observations give evidence of spontaneous fetal movements as early as nine weeks, at least two months before quickening. The most discernible impact of ultrasound on one's perception of the fetus, however, occurs during the second trimester when the fetus exhibits miniature yet unmistakable human features. Apparently it is not uncommon for women undergoing ultrasound monitoring to refer to their "baby" when discussing the fetus, particularly after they obtain their videotape of the imaging procedure to take home. Fletcher (1983:95ff.) discusses the more evident closeness of a pregnant woman to the fetus and her identity with the fetus as a person after seeing ultrasound pictures and prenatal diagnosis karyotypes. The capability of determining the sex of the fetus through chorionic villus sampling by the tenth week or so introduces yet another human attribute to fetal identity. The unborn "baby" now takes on the identity of "he" or "she," often with naming accompanying discovery of the sex.

Fetoscopy foretells even greater opportunities to "humanize" the fetus through direct observation of the fetal body. Although fetoscopy is limited currently by technical restrictions, which enable visualization of only sections of the fetus at a time, couples are able to see minute details of the fetus. Without doubt this capability accentuates social or at least parental recognition of the fetus as an individual human entity. Although Glass (1983:349) questions at what precise time the gradual emergence of consciousness and awareness of the fetus will confer the status of personhood, the appearance of sensory activity and pain provided by technology is critical.

Perhaps the most consequential challenges to prevailing impressions of the fetus as something "prehuman" are the result of recent successes in fetal surgery. Although corrective prenatal surgery promises renewed hope for many fetuses that otherwise would have been born with severe handicaps or not born at all, it is likely to produce conflict between the right of the woman to her privacy and the right of the fetus to whatever society deems to be proper medical care. King (1980:190) suggests that "recent research has garnered so much knowledge about the fetus and its environment that we can view the fetus as a 'second patient.' " Should this view progress it would represent a dramatic reversal of the notion that the woman is the only patient. If the fetus becomes a "patient" in its own right, it adopts characteristics that before were impossible and thus diminishes the corresponding rights of the mother.

The term *fetal rights* is a distortion of the real issue and obscures what ought to be the primary concern—the health of the child when born. It is not the fetus that has rights; rather it is the child once born that must be protected from avertable harm during gestation. The goal of any policies designed to make the fetal environment as safe as possible should be to maximize the birth of healthy children. The unfortunate but conscious focus on fetal rights instead of the rights of the newborn intensifies opposition without contributing to resolution of the problem. Although the fetus may have "interests" to be protected that will materialize after birth, it is clear under *Roe v. Wade* (1973) that fetuses do not even have a "right" to be born, at least throughout the first two trimesters. The term "interests" will be used here in order to avoid getting bogged down in the continuing debate over fetal rights (for good discussions of the problems of the rights context as applied to the fetus see Condit 1991 and Gonen 1991). Although some critics might further argue that the fetus has no interests, I agree with Feinberg (1984:96) that even though a fetus presumably has no actual interests, it can correctly be said to have future interests on the assumption that it will at some point in its normal development (at birth and subsequent to it) become a person and the possessor of actual interests.

Despite the uncertainties as to whose "interests" ultimately will be predominant, the rapidly evolving advances in a variety of in utero treatments including fetal surgery accentuate a subtle but real shift toward a recognition of the fetus as an independent self. Technologies that help visualize the growing organism as human, prenatal diagnosis labeling that entity as "boy" or "girl," and prospects of a wide variety of direct surgical interventions certainly provide the developing fetus with recognition as a person. Although it does not seem feasible to speak of the fetus as a fully autonomous person, these technologies give the fetus broader human characteristics, which lead to a redefinition of parental responsibility to the "unborn" patient.

The Impact of New Technologies and Knowledge on Maternal Rights

In addition to the impact of technology on society's perceptions of the fetus other advances in reproductive technologies and knowledge of fetal development are forcing increased consideration of fetal interests in the rights equation. Figure 1 illustrates the complex set of factors where there is evidence of potential harm for the fetus. Although these factors have been categorized as either maternal or extramaternal, in fact they are overlapping and interrelated. The major distinction, perhaps, is the extent to which the pregnant woman has control, but most of the hazards eventually must pass through the woman to reach the fetus. Although this book focuses only on one factor, that of workplace hazards, the remainder of chapter 1 outlines some of the other areas in which emerging knowledge and technology are threatening to redefine the rights and responsibilities of pregnant women.

Pressures for Constraints on Maternal Behavior During Pregnancy

Despite the complex nature of the fetal environment and the variation of effects any single stimulus might have on a specific fetus, growing medical evidence demonstrates that there are many ways in which maternal behavioral patterns and health status can impair the proper development of the fetus, causing irreparable

FIGURE 1
Hazards for Developing Fetus

Extramaternal Factors

Maternal/Paternal
exposure to
workplace hazards

Inadequate   Economic
prenatal   deprivation
care

Stress   Physical abuse/
                                                    violence

Noise pollution   Secondary smoke

Environmental   Exposure to
toxins   radiation

FETUS

Sexually transmitted   Vehicular
diseases   accidents

Smoking   Prescribed
                                                    drugs

Street Drugs   Poor nutrition

Alcohol   Infections
abuse

General
health

Maternal Factors

harm in some cases. Although data remain inconclusive there is evidence of the importance of providing as risk-free a fetal environment as possible. Maternal smoking, drinking, eating, and general lifestyle can and do have an effect on the fetus. As more is known about the specific deleterious effects of certain maternal behavior it is likely that increased attention will be directed toward the responsibility of the mother to assure the fetus as healthy as possible an environment throughout the gestation period. Unlike most other prenatal disorders, many of these threats to the fetus and newborn are completely avoidable. For law professor Patricia King this "increasing awareness that a mother's activities during pregnancy may affect the health of the offspring creates pressing policy issues that raise possible conflicts among fetuses, mothers and researchers" (1980:81).

Within the context of the growing knowledge of these hazards the question reemerges as to what right a child has to a safe fetal environment and as healthy as possible start in life. In turn this question illuminates the potential conflict of rights between the developing fetus and the mother. It is certainly a tragedy that in an affluent country such as the United States children continue to be born with birth defects caused primarily by a lack of proper nutrition or the behavior of the mother during pregnancy. However in a democratic society the primary responsibility remains the woman's. She alone is the direct link to the fetus and she alone makes the ultimate decision as to whether or not to smoke, use alcohol or other drugs, maintain proper nutrition, and so forth.

Until recently the courts were hesitant to recognize causes of action for prenatal injury because of the difficulty of demonstrating proximate cause and determining reasonable standards of care. Advances in medical technology and in knowledge of fetal development, however, are rapidly altering this situation. In addition to increasing social recognition of and empathy for the fetus innovative diagnostic and therapeutic technologies make prenatal injury cases increasingly similar to more conventional liability or injury torts.

As a result of these technological developments there is a discernible trend in tort law toward recognition of a maternal responsibility for the well-being of the unborn child. Despite many inconsistencies across jurisdictions, there is an unmistakable pattern toward finding a cause of action against third parties for fetal death or prenatal injury even if it occurred at the previable stage. The abrogation of intrafamily immunity and the willingness of some courts to hold parents liable for prenatal injury opens the door for increased judicial involvement in defining parental responsibilities. In a short time span torts against parents for prenatal injury caused either by commission or omission have been recognized by some courts (see *Grodin v. Grodin* 1980).

One of the most troubling legal trends is criminal actions taken against pregnant women. One of the most publicized legal developments in the late 1980s was the increasing number of jurisdictions that tried to impose legal sanctions to deter illegal drug use by pregnant women. Women have been charged under statutes against child abuse and neglect, delivery of a controlled substance to a minor, and involuntary manslaughter. In an early case a Michigan appeals court convicted a heroin addict of child abuse after she gave birth to an addicted baby (*In re Baby X* 1980). Similarly a Florida woman was convicted of delivery of a controlled substance when tests confirmed traces of cocaine in her newborn daughter's system (*Florida v. Johnson* 1989). A Washington, D.C. pregnant woman who pled guilty to a charge of forgery was sentenced to prison because she tested positive for cocaine and the judge wanted to ensure she would not use cocaine for the duration of her pregnancy (*United States v. Vaughn,* 1989). These and many other similar cases raise serious questions concerning the extent to which the state can punish women for harm to the fetus.

Although a major argument for legal sanctions is deterrence, there is no evidence that prosecution of pregnant drug abusers has any deterrent effect. To the contrary, there is some evidence that a major effect of such high publicized cases is to discourage other pregnant women from obtaining proper prenatal care out of fear of criminal prosecution, thus potentially exacerbating the problem (Johnsen 1986). It seems reasonable that pregnant women who are substance abusers would avoid any medical treatment for fear that their physician's knowledge of their abuse might result in a jail sentence. Moreover, imposing criminal sanctions on pregnant women for potentially harmful behavior could provoke other women to seek abortions in order to avoid legal repercussions. Finally, evidence to date demonstrates that criminal prosecution of pregnant women has a clear bias against minority and low socioeconomic status women (Chavkin and Kandall 1990). Although criminal sanctions might be successful in punishing a few women, the lack of deterrence and its likely inequitable application make it unattractive as a policy for assuring the birth of healthy children.

The relationship between the pregnant woman and the developing fetus is a special one, one that is culturally as well as biologically unique. While there exist strong pressures to make this relationship potentially adversarial, generally this approach serves neither party well. The fact is that the fetus—more than a born child—needs the mother for its health and life and that many acts of commission and omission by the woman can be injurious to the fetus. Any feasible strategy for dealing with the problems raised here must, therefore, place emphasis on the common, shared interests of the mother and fetus, not on the conflicts between them. Unfortunately, the dominant emphasis on individual rights in our society continues to exaggerate the potential conflicts.

The problems in the mother-fetal relationship, then, cannot be separated from the broader social context. Drastic socioeconomic inequities and the resulting lack of adequate primary care for a large segment of the population continue to contribute to the risk for women and the fetuses they carry. Although large numbers of women who lack proper health care and education live in isolated rural areas, it is paradoxical that the most vulnerable women are congregated in urban areas, often within sight of the most impressive concentrations of medical technology in the world.

In addition to the macro social context one cannot explain an individual pregnant woman's behavior without knowledge of her personal experiences. The emphasis on punishing a pregnant woman diverts attention from the root causes of the woman's often self-destructive behavior that also threatens the fetus. How many of these women were victims of sexual abuse, incest, and other attacks on their self-esteem? In the long run, only by understanding why particular women act in ways dangerous to the health of their fetus and ameliorating these causes can a policy succeed.

Although no individual ultimately can escape responsibility for her or his actions, the social and personal plight of an increasing number of young women makes rational choice problematic and elusive. The birth of addicted, very premature, or otherwise ill babies to these women, however, only extenuates the problem and continues the dreadful cycle into another generation. For all the stated concern of elected officials with the health of the children and their right to be born with a sound mind and body, they have consistently come up short on action. Unless we are willing to expend considerable resources to overcome the problems of poverty, illiteracy, housing, and lack of access to good prenatal care and meaningful employment for women of childbearing age, the future looks bleak for many children.

An Emerging Maternal Duty to Utilize Prenatal Technologies?

Despite many inconsistencies recent case law clearly demonstrates a cause of action against third parties for negligence in informing the parents about available prenatal diagnostic technologies. Physicians have been held liable to substantial damage claims for wrongful birth of children born with defects that would have been identifiable if proper techniques had been recommended to the parents by the physician. Also, various legal trends demonstrate that parents are likely to be held liable for prenatal injury or wrongful death torts in the near future (Blank 1992a:91–123). Furthermore, as prenatal technologies move from primarily diagnostic in scope to therapeutic the courts are even more likely to extend their notions of prenatal injury to include acts of omission as well as acts of commission. This may well place increased pressure on parents to exercise "responsibility" to the unborn child by availing themselves of the rapidly expanding selection of prenatal diagnostic and treatment technologies. If they choose not to use technologies recommended by their physician, their decision is likely to be viewed in the least as "irresponsible" and at the extreme as illegal.

Over the last two decades there has been a continual expansion of the prenatal diagnostic techniques available to women to identify fetal defects. In the past few years many of these, including amniocentesis, chorionic villus sampling, and ultrasound, have become standard clinical procedures. In most instances these technologies enhance a woman's reproductive freedom by providing information that helps her decide how to manage her pregnancy. However, as with all reproductive technologies, anything that can be done voluntarily can also be coerced. If prenatal diagnosis were to become legally mandated by imposing tort liability on those persons whose failure to use it resulted in the birth of a fetus with injury, then its very availability could limit the freedom of a woman who would choose not to use it. What if a physician recommends that a woman at high risk for a Down Syndrome infant have amniocentesis, she refuses and bears a child with that chromosomal abnormality? Will she be legally liable for the wrongful life of the affected infant? Will her action be seen by the community as irresponsible? What if she undergoes amniocentesis, finds out the fetus is affected, but because of religious objections refuses to abort the fetus?

One dilemma surrounding current use of these techniques is that while they give us the ability to reduce the incidence of genetic disease, they do so primarily by eliminating the affected fetus through selective abortion, not by treating the disease. Future developments in gene therapy might shift emphasis toward treatment, but prenatal diagnosis will continue largely to expand parental choice only to the extent it allows parents to terminate the pregnancies of affected fetuses. Thus it will continue to be a policy issue congruent with abortion.

The dilemma becomes more immediate, however, if therapy is available in conjunction with the diagnosis, for instance in the case of Rh incompatibility. In *Grodin v. Grodin* (301 N.W. 2d 869, 1983) a Michigan appellate court recognized the right of a child to sue his or her mother for failure to obtain a pregnancy test. The logic of this ruling implies that a child would also have legal recourse to sue his or her mother for failing to monitor the pregnancy and identify and correct threats to his or her health during gestation. As Robertson (1983:448) points out, "The issue in such a case would be whether the mother's failure to seek a test was negligent in light of the risks that the test posed to her and the fetus and the probability that the test would uncover a correctable defect." Of course, prenatal diagnosis could be directly mandated by state statute with criminal sanctions for women who fail to comply with the law. According to Robertson (1983:449), state authorities could justify such a statute on public health grounds. Despite constitutional questions of invasion of bodily integrity and privacy, it would probably meet a compelling state interest standard.

Even more problematic is the duty of prospective parents in

high-risk groups to be tested for carrier status prior to having children. This involves screening for carriers of particular recessive genetic diseases. The primary clinical objective of this type of testing is to identify those individuals who, if mated with another person with that same particular genetic trait, have a 25 percent chance of having offspring with the disease. Once identified couples with carrier status can be offered prenatal diagnosis if it is available for that disease or at least be educated as to the risk they take in having children.

Carrier screening programs have been in effect in many states and localities for Tay-Sachs disease and sickle-cell anemia since the early 1970s. The sickle-cell programs have been especially controversial because the trait is concentrated in the black population and—unlike Tay-Sachs screening, which has always been voluntary—sickle-cell screening started out as mandatory in many states. Carrier screening tests for many recessive genetic diseases and even more precise genetic trait markings will be available in the near future. The most rapid developments have been in the area of DNA probes to identify polymorphisms (genetic variations) that mark a particular trait. Following the discovery of such a molecular probe for the Huntington's disease gene in 1983, efforts have been initiated to identify genetic markers for Alzheimer's disease, manic-depression, malignant melanoma, and a host of other conditions. Out of this research a gene for cystic fibrosis was found in 1989 (Marx 1989). In addition, considerable attention is being directed to the genetic bases of alcoholism and drug addiction (Holden 1991).

Ironically these new capabilities accentuate rather than reduce the political-legal-ethical issues of genetic counseling and screening. When screening leads to aversion or treatment of genetic disease the issues, though often controversial, are reasonably straightforward. However, when screening involves identifying heightened risk or susceptibility for particular conditions it becomes considerably more problematic. As new diagnostic tests and genetic probes emerge, public expectations will intensify and the demand for accessibility to information derived from such efforts will be heightened. Once policy makers accept the tests' legitimacy legislatures and courts will probably recognize professional standards of care that incorporate them. Legislation in California that requires physicians to inform pregnant patients of the availability of alpha-fetoprotein tests and similar court pressure involving a variety of prenatal tests attest to the public policy dimensions inherent in these applications.

Is there a responsibility of prospective parents to be familiar with and utilize tests that are warranted for their particular family background in order to avoid propagating offspring with the disease? Furthermore, if a testing program is available and parents are advised by their doctor to use it but refuse, are they liable for a preconceptual injury tort or wrongful life tort for a child born with the disease? Although the relevance of these questions seems distant now, rapid advances in genetic screening, combined with those in prenatal diagnosis advise attention to the social and ethical issues they raise concerning parental duty to their offspring.

The new knowledge concerning transmission of genetic disease along with the capability to identify carriers of a growing number of deleterious traits raise another question. Is there a duty of carriers of genetic disease or genes that make their children more susceptible to ill health to either refrain from procreating or utilize collaborative conception technologies such as artificial insemination or embryo transfer so that these deleterious genes are not transmitted to their offspring? If there is such a duty, where are the lines to be drawn: a genetic disease like Huntington's or sickle-cell anemia, a heightened risk for manic depression or alcoholism, susceptibility to early heart disease?

With current techniques in artificial insemination, cryopreservation, and embryo transfer, no longer need these individuals necessarily refrain from conception in order to protect their offspring. Now, for instance, if a husband is suspected of carrying a dominant gene for Huntington's disease he can use the services of a sperm bank or donor. Although this process eliminates his biological contribution to the child, it also eliminates the 50 percent risk of transmitting the disease to his progeny. Similarly, if both persons in a couple are identified as carriers of a recessive disease, they can: (1) take a 25 percent chance that a child will have the disease and live with it; (2) undergo prenatal diagnosis if available for that disease and abort the one-in-four fetus that is identified as having the disease; or (3) use reproductive technology such as artificial insemination or egg donation and be content with a healthy child, albeit one that is not genetically both of theirs.

Although these options are currently open to couples the key question is whether any couple has a legal responsibility to take option 2 or 3 and thereby reduce the chance of bearing a child with an avertable genetic disease. Does the child born with Tay-Sachs disease have a cause of action against a physician who fails to advise the use of artificial insemination in case of a disease that cannot be diagnosed prenatally? If the physician or genetic counselor recommends such action and the parents refuse, should the parents be liable for the "wrongful" life of their child? Again, the availability of technologies shapes the options available as well as the alternative perceived by the community as most responsible.

The Fetus as a Patient: In Utero Surgery

Technologies in prenatal diagnostics have given us the capacity to discern an array of fetal defects in utero. The newer generation of prenatal technologies, however, is shifting emphasis to treatment and correction of these defects before birth. Fetal therapy and surgery, although still in the formative stages, promises to aggrandize concern for the fetus significantly. As we rapidly move from the sad choice between aborting or carrying to term an identified affected fetus toward surgical treatment of the defect, situations will arise where the benefits to the fetus may far outweigh negligible or minimal risks to the mother (Fletcher 1983:307). Although the interests of the mother in having a healthy child and those of the fetus are likely to be congruent, in some cases their interests will be perceived to be in conflict.

One of the most difficult legal issues to be faced in the near future will be how to balance the rights of the mother and the medical needs of the fetus when they conflict. The basic issue here is whether, in cases where the fetus can be treated either medically or surgically, the fetus is a patient separate from its mother. Prior to recent developments in fetal surgery the fetus was generally considered a medical patient and certain problems were treated with medicines administered to the mother or directly into the amniotic fluid. Although these procedures required the cooperation of the pregnant woman they were not as physically intrusive as surgery. The difficulty with fetal surgery is that any treatment of the fetus can be accomplished only by invading the physical integrity and privacy of the woman. She must consent to surgery, not only for her unborn child but also for herself.

Although many obstetricians prefer to view the mother and fetus as a single biological entity sharing interests that are furthered by proper maternal care during pregnancy, this perception is bound to be altered in light of advances in fetal care, which clearly contrast the fetus from its mother for treatment purposes (Harrison et al. 1990). Moreover, as neonatology burgeons as a field the fetus will gain more advocates within the medical community (Bolognese 1982). Due to this potential conflict between obstetricians representing maternal interests and neonatologists representing fetal interests judicial deference to the medical profession's determination of viability may be problematic. However these issues are resolved the remarkable advances being made in fetal surgery are certain to accentuate potential conflict between maternal interests and the fetus as patient.

Rosenfeld (1982:22) declares that when the applause over the successes in fetal surgery dies down "one must quietly consider the consequences." As fetal surgery becomes more commonplace, which it is certain to do, and as it is performed earlier in gestation, the status of all fetuses as potential patients will further complicate the issue of fetal rights. John Fletcher (1983) feels that "improvements in fetal therapy will establish a stronger ground to protect the affected fetus' right to life" and that this will collide with the established ground for the woman's right to choice concerning abortion. Ruddick and Wilcox (1982:11) agree that "fetal therapy, especially lifesaving surgery, would seem to make it easier to respect" the fetal claim to the right to life. While Elias and Annas view forcible medical treatment as "brutish and horrible," they concede the following:

[W]hen fetal surgery becomes accepted medical practice, and if the procedure can be done with minimal invasiveness and risk to the mother and significant benefit to the fetus, there is an argument to be made that the woman should not be permitted to reject it. Such rejection of therapy could be considered "fetal abuse" and, at a late stage in pregnancy, "child abuse," and an appropriate court order sought to force treatment.   (1983:811)

The unique feature of fetal surgery is that it requires violation of the mother's rights of personal autonomy if she does not consent to have the surgery. No new legal problems arise unless the mother refuses to consent, in which case the legal dilemma is agonizing, especially if she desires to carry the fetus to term. In our society the status of patient usually carries with it the notion of autonomy. But in these cases whose rights take precedence, those of the fetus or those of the mother whose body must be "invaded" in order to facilitate the surgery? Although case law is primitive in this area, some precedents exist in which the courts have ordered surgical procedures over the objections of the mother solely to provide medical care for her unborn child (see *Jefferson v. Griffin Spaulding City Memorial Hospital,* 274 S.E.2d 457, Ga. 1981; *Taft v. Taft,* 146 N.E.2d 395, Mass. 1983; *In re: A.C.,* 539 A.2d, 1988, en banc, D.C. Ct.App., April 26, 1990, reversed).

The Technological Imperative and Pregnant Women

The issue of maternal responsibility for fetal health is framed by the broader social value system in the United States. Our great faith in technology and medical knowledge and overdependence on the technological fix has not only medicalized pregnancy but created a perfect child mentality. This is clearly reflected in many courts' acceptance of medical "fact" in cases of forced cesarean sections, even when "fact" is uncertain and probabilistic. Significantly, the public's view of responsible maternal behavior is shaped by the rapidly changing technological context.

As a result of society's reliance on medical technology when new "choices" become available to women they rapidly become obligations to make the "right" choice by "choosing" the socially approved alternative (Hubbard 1990:156).

> The "right to choose" means very little when women are power-less. . . . Women make their own reproductive choices, but they do not make them just as they please; they do not make them under conditions which they themselves create but under social conditions and constraints which they, as mere individuals, are powerless to change.   (Petchesky 1980:685)

Furthermore, these technologies contribute to the medicalization of reproduction, which threatens the freedom and dignity of women in general. By requiring third-party involvement and dependence on medical expertise new technologies force the woman to surrender her control over procreation. Ruth Hubbard (1985:567) decries the practice of making every pregnancy a medical event and sees it as a result of the economic incentives for physicians to stimulate a new need for their services during pregnancy in light of declining birth rates and increasing interest in midwifery and home birth. Barbara Katz Rothman (1986:114) adds that the new images of the fetus resulting from prenatal technologies are making us aware of the "unborn" as people, "but they do so at the cost of making transparent the mother." Furthermore, diagnostic technologies that pronounce judgments halfway through the pregnancy make extraordinary demands on women to separate themselves from the fetus within.

> The medical status of the fetus as distinct from the woman who is pregnant is becoming a star criterion to judge a woman's behavior before, during, and after pregnancy. It is no longer only our sexuality or marital status which defines us as good woman-mothers; now, we must not smoke or drink or deny medical intervention when we are pregnant, or else we are not acting in the "best interests of the fetus". Meanwhile, obstetricians have authorized themselves to act against the wishes of the pregnant woman if necessary to "protect" the interests of the fetus.
> (Spallone, 1989:40)

Some feminists rightly argue that women bear most of the risks of any reproductive research and technological application.

The history of human reproduction has been, in large measure, a story of control of women, their fertility, and fecundity by society. This control, whether self-imposed or inflicted by others in a given society, has resulted in a significant loss of freedom to women and their exclusion from many activities, including intellectual creativity, waged work, and training for self-support (Oakley 1984:84). Women, it is alleged, have been held hostage to the reproductive needs of society throughout history. The new prenatal technologies in many ways reinforce this condition. As persons whose self-identity and social role have been defined historically in relation to their procreative capacities, then, women have a great deal at stake in questions of reproductive freedom (Ryan 1990:6).

There is little doubt that the status of women is intimately related to prenatal technologies. Technology is never neutral—it both reflects and shapes social values. Because of women's critical biological role as the bearers of children, any technologies that deal with reproduction affect their social role directly. Moreover, because these technologies focus on the role of women as mothers, they could lead to diminution of other roles. Some feminists argue that too much emphasis is already placed on women as only mothers in this society. Robin Rowland (1985:39) insists that women must reevaluate this social overstatement of the role of motherhood. "The catchcry 'but women want it' has been sounded over and over again by the medical profession to justify continuing medical advances in this field. Women need to reevaluate just what it is they want and question this justification for turning women into living laboratories."

While prenatal diagnosis, genetic screening, gene therapy, and new knowledge of fetal development expand options and will be used by women, as argued earlier, their existence carries with it a causal logic that could label as "socially irresponsible" women who fail to make use of them under certain circumstances. As Ruth Hubbard (1985:567) cogently states: "The point is that once such a test is available and a woman decides not to use it, if her baby is born with a disability that could have been diagnosed, it is no longer an act of fate but has become her fault." Mies (1987:334) adds that the emphasis on quality control means for most women a loss of confidence in their own bodies and their childbearing competence. She argues that the social pressure on women to produce perfect children is already enormous today.

Although the technologies that allow for the conscious design of children do not necessarily result in the denigration of the role of women or the restriction of their reproductive rights, within the context of a social value system sympathetic to that end that danger clearly exists. A full policy assessment of these technologies, therefore, requires close attention to their cumulative impact on women as well as to women's actual experiences as reproductive beings (Overall 1987). This requires a widened commitment of policy makers to fund extensive behavioral research on women who are parties to these reproductive applications or who are contemplating using those services.

Despite many inconsistencies among court decisions, there is a perceptible trend in tort and criminal law toward recognition of a maternal responsibility for the well-being of the unborn child. Although viability remains a crucial distinction in some jurisdictions, the pattern clearly is to find a cause of action against third parties for fetal death or prenatal injury at the previable stage. The abrogation of intrafamily immunity and the willingness of some courts to hold parents liable for prenatal injury opens the door for increased action in this area. In a short time span torts against parents for prenatal injury caused either by commission or omission have been recognized as a legitimate cause of action. A major reason for this shift has been the recent advances in medical science.

Workplace Hazards: Plan of the Book

This book explicates the legal-policy dimensions of women in the workplace within the context of this heightened concern for fetal health. No set of issues more cogently contrasts the rights of women with the supposed concern for fetal interests. Although the primacy given individual rights in U.S. political culture has often worked to protect the interests of the most vulnerable persons in the past, it creates inexorable dilemmas when strictly applied to the maternal-fetal relationship in the workplace. The place of women in the workplace has always been characterized by discriminatory policies, often explicitly established by the states.

As with other issues surrounding the relationship between the pregnant woman and the fetus summarized here, the debate over workplace hazards unfortunately has oversimplified what is a very complex set of policy problems. More important, the focus on fetal hazards has diverted attention from critical broader problems of the reproductive health of women and men in the workplace. The rapid increase of women in the workplace has raised a wide array of reproductive risks, many in women-dominated professions. Furthermore, fear of recrimination through exclusionary policies to protect fetuses has forced women to abandon or at least downplay very real concerns for women's reproductive health and special needs that arise during pregnancy and childbirth. By dominating attention in the 1980s the debate over fetal protection policies has obscured the need for alternative public policies designed to protect the health of potential children, such as the provision of prenatal care, pregnancy disability leave, and parental leave. One objective of this book is to redirect the policy focus toward these more meaningful strategies for meeting the twin goals of protecting women's rights and the interests of unborn children.

Chapter 2 puts recent actions into perspective by describing the history of sex discrimination in the U.S. workplace. It analyzes the impact of legislation designed to eliminate such discrimination and outlines the inherent difficulties of protective workplace policies.

Chapter 3 describes the current state of medical knowledge of workplace hazards to reproductive health with an emphasis on evidence of potential risks for the developing fetus. It stresses that although we have a considerable amount of preliminary data, we lack conclusive human evidence in most areas. This chapter also looks at the potential harm to the fetus through paternal exposure to workplace hazards.

Chapter 4 describes fetal protection policies established in the last two decades. It analyzes the rationale behind exclusionary policies and the criticisms of such policies. Chapter 5 continues this analysis by examining the response of U.S. courts and regulatory agents to fetal protection policies. It argues that the fragmented and often contradictory response of the various jurisdictions makes the development of national standards necessary.

Chapter 6 describes the current means of compensating victims of occupational related injuries—workers' compensation systems and civil torts—and demonstrates why they fail to adequately compensate for reproductive injuries. Chapter 7 looks at alternatives to exclusionary policies that are more likely to ensure the birth of children with sound minds and bodies. Adequate paid pregnancy disability and paternal leaves with job and benefits protections, while commonplace in other nations, are rare in the United States. Current U.S. statutes are analyzed and found seriously lacking both in resolve and in effectiveness. The final chapter attempts to design a workable strategy that will maximize women's employment choices and reproductive health while at the same time reducing to a minimum the risks associated with fetal harm.

2 | History of Sex Discrimination in the U.S. Workplace

Traditionally, societal attitudes defined the role of women almost exclusively as wife and mother. Women were not supposed to work outside the home, and if they did, usually prior to marriage, they did "women's work," such as serving, weaving, housecleaning, and cooking. The labor market was, therefore, overtly segregated by sex with women confined to the same low paying job categories that were reserved for children. Despite their marginal status in the nonagricultural labor force women came to represent a reserve of inexpensive labor available to replace higher paid males. As a result women were viewed as threats to men's jobs and wage levels, thus leading to heightened steps to keep them in the home and out of the workplace, particularly in male-dominated occupations.

As women began to enter the workplace in greater numbers toward the end of the nineteenth century they faced heightened discrimination by labor unions. Some union constitutions explicitly excluded women from membership, others set quotas on female membership or limited women to positions as apprentices or helpers (Office of Technology Assessment, hereafter OTA 1985:234). Furthermore, unions frequently negotiated separate contracts for women through which they were paid less than men and were excluded from jobs reserved for men, thus solidifying the segregated workplace.

During the latter half of the nineteenth century and early decades of the twentieth century women who were discriminated against had little legal recourse. For instance, in *Bradwell v. Illinois* (1873) the U.S. Supreme Court rejected Myra Bradwell's claim that the Illinois Supreme Court had unconstitutionally denied her admission to the Illinois bar under the equal protection clause of the Fourteenth Amendment. Although Bradwell passed the qualifying exam she was denied admission simply because she was a women. In rejecting her claim the Court concluded that the "paramount destiny and mission of women are to fulfill the noble and benign offices of wife and mother. This is the law of the Creator" (at 1130). The "natural and proper timidity and delicacy" of the female sex precluded women from many of the occupations of civil life, according to the Court. This view proved to be very representative of judicial thinking for many decades after the *Bradwell* opinion was written.

Another trend during this era reinforced discrimination against women in the workplace. Concern over unhealthy working conditions brought on by the early industrial revolution led the states to enact protective labor laws, many of which applied only to women or required different work for women. Although social reformers initially lobbied the states for protective laws that would cover women, children, and men, they gradually focused their attention on women. In part this shift was an attempt to bring women workers under regulatory standards that men had secured through union action and in part it was a continuation of the paternalistic belief that women who worked for wages outside the home needed protection (Maschke 1989:7–8). These statutes limited the number of hours women could work, the number of days in a row they could work, the weights they could lift, and the jobs they could perform. Some protective statutes required that women be given time off for rest periods and lunch, established minimum wages, and attempted to protect the health and safety of women in the workplace. Others prohibited the employment of women in specific industries or limited women to daytime work.

By 1908 twenty states had enacted laws setting maximum hours or prohibiting night work for women. The constitutionality of these statutes was upheld by four state courts and struck down by two state courts. Although whether protectionist statutes helped or hurt women in the aggregate is unknown, many supporters of the legislation were women and men sympathetic to the needs of working women who bore the risks of low paying jobs.

> Many of those who promoted women's causes, including the social feminists led by the National Consumers' League (NCL), considered work to be harmful to woman, especially in her maternal function. . . . The onerous conditions of factories and sweatshops threatened women's health and their ability to have healthy children. Laws were necessary to prevent employers from hurting women and potential offspring.   (Stetson 1991:407)

Many women's organizations who were unable to secure voting rights for women lobbied in favor of protective legislation. The impact of the actual legislation, however, often proved to "protect" women only from more lucrative jobs. For example, women were "protected" from high paying night shifts in factories but not night work as waitresses or domestic services (Kessler-Harris 1982:188). Moreover, in California the maximum hours law for women was suspended during harvest season when women workers were needed for low-paying jobs (OTA 1985:236). As a result of these consequences and in spite of the initial support of women's organizations these statutes were challenged in the courts, often by employers who claimed that they violated their rights and those of women to contract freely (Baer 1978).

Reaction by the state courts to these protective statutes uniformly upheld them. In *Commonwealth v. Beatty* (1900) the Pennsylvania Supreme Court upheld a twelve-hour law for women workers, concluding that adult females are as distinct a class as minors and therefore could be protected by the state. Similar reasoning was used by a Nebraska court (*Wenham v. State* 1902) in upholding a maximum work hours law for women, "who like children" are to a certain extent "wards of the state." In that same year a Washington court (*State v. Buchanan* 1902) upheld an hours law for women on the grounds of protecting succeeding generations, thus assuming that all women are potentially and primarily mothers. The number of cases challenging protective laws in the state courts soon led to appeals to the federal courts on constitutional grounds.

In 1905 the U.S. Supreme Court (*Lochner v. New York*) struck down a New York law that established maximum hours covering both male and female bakers. Three years later, however, a unanimous Court (*Muller v. Oregon* 1908) upheld an Oregon statute that prohibited the employment of any women for more than ten hours a day in any factory or laundry. The *Muller* decision resolved this discrepancy by stating that a woman "is properly placed in a class by herself, and legislation designed for her protection may be sustained, even when like legislation is not necessary for men and could not be sustained" (at 419). In this first case involving a sex-based protective law to reach the U.S. Supreme Court the Court soundly endorsed laws restricting only the employment of women as permissible for the "benefit of all."

> That a woman's physical structure and the performance of maternal functions place her at a disadvantage in the struggle for subsistence is obvious. This is especially true when the burdens of motherhood are upon her . . . as healthy mothers are essential to vigorous offspring, the physical well-being of women becomes an object of public interest and care in order to preserve the strength and vigor of the race. (at 421)

The *Muller* case was one of the first in which suspected reproductive harm caused by working conditions was advanced as a justification to limit the employment of women (OTA 1985:237). The woman's central biological role in procreation, therefore, made her a justifiable target of discrimination in the workplace for the Court. Moreover, the Court failed to discuss the economic consequences of such a policy for women but instead emphasized women's dependence upon men and their need for protection (at 421).

This rationale was also reflected several years later in a 114-page brief submitted to the Supreme Court by Louis D. Brandeis in a New York case. At issue in *People v. Charles Schweinler*

Press (1915) was a New York statute that forbade employment of women for night shift work in factories and laundries. Brandeis argued that the state was justified in resolving any conflict between the woman's interest in wage work and society's interest in her domestic and reproductive responsibilities in favor of society's interests. Despite evidence presented in his own brief that night work had detrimental effects on male reproductive capacity (see Becker 1986:1223), Brandeis did not acknowledge the possibility that a woman might be able to make a competent decision about night shift work. In 1924 the Court (*Radice v. People*) again upheld a state night work protective law for women.

After the *Muller* ruling reform groups turned their attention to the establishment of minimum wage laws for women. Supporters of women's minimum wage statutes submitted briefs that clearly demonstrated the impact of poverty and malnutrition on the health of women workers and their children. If, as argued in *Muller*, the Court was so concerned about protecting women and their offspring and thus the interests of society in preserving the strength and vigor of the race, then a minimum wage seemed an essential aspect of that protection. In *Atkins v. Children's Hospital of the District of Columbia* (1923), however, the Supreme Court rejected arguments about the relationship between women's wages and the health of future generations and found the minimum wage law for women unconstitutional. The courts continued to hold minimum wage laws for both women and men to be unconstitutional until 1937, when the Supreme Court reversed itself in *West Coast Hotel Co. v. Parrish* and upheld a minimum wage law for women.

As a result of the Court's indifference to the rights of women in the workplace, up until World War II few women worked outside the home. When they did it was often assumed that they would work only until marriage or childbearing responsibilities took them out of the workplace. Even many school systems barred women from employment or dismissed them if they married, which meant that only committed spinsters could have teaching professions. For instance, a National Education Association study conducted in 1930–31 found that 77 percent of the surveyed districts refused to hire married women and 63 percent dismissed female teachers if they married (Gelb and Palley 1987:163). In addition, women were discriminated against by many companies, which allowed them fewer fringe benefits than male colleagues or excluded them fully from being eligible for such benefits.

During World War II and the domestic manpower shortage over four million women entered the workplace to take jobs previously held by men (see Milkman 1987). At the completion of the war, however, most of these women were terminated without regard to seniority or their desire to continue and their jobs were "given back" to returning veterans (Stolz 1985:37). Often these terminations were justified on grounds of protection of mother and fetus as well as a fear of liability for miscarriage, a concern that was not expressed as long as women were needed in the workplace. Studies by the War Manpower Commission and Children's Bureau that demonstrated the need to reassess employment practices and policies were largely ignored as the nation returned to prewar patterns of excluding women on biological grounds. Women could now work, but only in "women's occupations" such as teaching, nursing, and domestic services. By the mid-1960s twenty-six states had laws prohibiting women from working in certain jobs and nineteen had regulations on the hours women could work (Maschke 1989:5). It was inevitable that the transition back to prewar employment patterns for women would lead to action for change after women had proven themselves capable of working "men's" jobs during the war years.

Equal Protection Clause: Constitutional Context

Throughout this period the courts had at their disposal one means of eliminating sex discrimination emanating from state protective laws. The equal protection clause of the Fourteenth Amendment is the primary constitutional limiting factor on legislating biased classifications. Until the late 1960s, however, the courts generally were reluctant to place sex-biased classifications in the same category as classifications based on race, religion, or ethnic origin. The courts interpreted the equal protection clause as permitting a wide range of state imposed restrictions on the rights of women in the workplace, because, as noted earlier, women were considered to be persons in need of protection in part due to their childbearing capacity.

To distinguish between different levels of discrimination the courts created a conceptual framework that labels legislative classifications as either suspect or nonsuspect. Classifications are suspect if they identify for special treatment groups who historically have been victims of discriminatory treatment, especially if they are easily identifiable by physical characteristics, race being the prime example. Conversely, classifications are nonsuspect if they do not apply to previously victimized groups. The courts historically placed sex-biased classifications in the nonsuspect category, but now rank them somewhere between suspect and nonsuspect.

How the courts interpret particular classification categories is critical because the degree of scrutiny in each case varies significantly. On the one hand suspect classifications are subject to a "strict scrutiny test." State laws will be upheld only if (1) it can be demonstrated by the state that it has a compelling interest, that its goal is of overwhelming public importance overriding the interests of those persons discriminated against, *and* (2) that the legislative purpose cannot be achieved with a less drastic or burdensome classification. On the other hand for nonsuspect classifications the courts require only that a rational relationship exist between the classification and a valid state interest. The "rational basis test" is met if (1) sufficient data demonstrate that the classification is not arbitrary and (2) that the legislative purpose is constitutionally permissible. The state does not have to show a compelling interest nor prove the absence of a more rational classification. Importantly, the full burden of proof in a suspect classification is on the state while in a nonsuspect classification it is on the person challenging the law. In the latter applications the courts ordinarily presume the legislature has acted rationally and accept its version of the facts.

In addition to the different degrees of scrutiny the courts also make distinctions based on the doctrine of "reasonable classification." This doctrine requires that legislative classifications be reasonably related to achieving a constitutionally permissible or, in the case of strict scrutiny, a compelling purpose. This doctrine assures that while people with different characteristics need not be treated as if they were all the same, similar things be treated similarly. The extent to which a legislative classification is reasonable and thus acceptable to the court is determined by its success in treating similarly those people who are similarly situated and excluding those who are not. An "overinclusive" classification would include those who are different while an "underinclusive" classification would exclude some who are the same.

> For example, if a legislature wants to prevent birth defects caused by developmental hazards in the workplace (a constitutionally permissible purpose), it might decide to exclude from the workplace persons at risk. If the legislature excludes "all women," this classification might be overinclusive because it includes infertile women, who do not need protection from the risks of reproductive health hazards. However, excluding all women might also be underinclusive if men are subject to the same risk but have not been excluded. "All women" might also be considered overinclusive because it lumps together both women who are, or plan to be, pregnant with women who are practicing birth control or are abstaining and those who are no longer of reproductive age.
>
> (OTA 1985:238)

In 1971 the Supreme Court began to accept an equal protection analysis to sex discrimination. In *Reed v. Reed* the Court unanimously invalidated a state law that gave mandatory preference to males as estate administrators. The Court held that preference for males was arbitrary and wholly unrelated to the state's objective of reducing the workload on probate courts. For the first time the Court recognized that a classification based on sex was subject to scrutiny. Although this approach did not require the legislature to have a compelling state interest or even to show that the classification was the least drastic way of achieving the legislature's goals, sex was no longer a nonsuspect category.

Five years later in *Craig v. Boren* (1976) the Court went further and articulated a new standard for evaluating sex discrimination claims under the equal protection clause. Classifications by sex must be "substantially related" to an "important" government objective. Although less stringent than the compelling state interest required under the strict scrutiny standard used for race and national origin, this "heightened scrutiny" test is stricter than the "valid government interest" of the rational basis test used prior to this case. Although this test continues to be the standard against which most sex-based classifications are measured when challenged on constitutional grounds, the courts have generally agreed that the gender equality principle can be applied only where men and women are treated differently with respect to a shared characteristic. Discrimination on the basis of pregnancy has not been considered sex discrimination per se under constitutional analysis. (OTA 1985:240). Therefore, a statutory ground was necessary to deal with such applications.

Court Reaction to Title VII of the 1964 Civil Rights Act

Passage of the far-reaching Civil Rights Act of 1964 promised to eliminate a wide array of discrimination including sex discrimination in the workplace. Title VII of the act prohibits sex discrimination by an employer of fifteen or more employees engaged in any industry affecting commerce. According to this title it is unlawful for an employer to:

1. fail or refuse to hire or to discharge any individual, or otherwise to discriminate against any individual with respect to his compensation, terms, conditions, or privileges of employment, because of such individual's race, color, religion, sex, or national origin; or

2. limit, segregate, or classify his employees or applicants for employment in any way which would deprive or tend to deprive any individual of employment opportunities or otherwise affect his status as an employee because of such individual's race, color, religion, sex, or national origin.

Although Title VII forced the courts to scrutinize more carefully states' justifications for differential treatment of women in the workplace, because it failed to provide clear legislative guidance for defining discrimination "because of sex" it led to inconsistent judicial interpretations of its requirements regarding sex-based exclusionary policies.

Several courts applied Title VII to sex discrimination in the workplace. In *Rosenfeld v. Southern Pacific Co.* (1971), for instance, the Ninth Circuit ruled that a California law prohibiting the employment of women for more than ten hours per day or to lift weights over 50 pounds was in violation of Title VII. Similarly, in *Cleveland Board of Education v. La Fleur* (1974) the Supreme Court held that mandatory maternity leaves for schoolteachers were unconstitutional under the due process clause of the Fourteenth Amendment. The Court held that the arbitrary cutoff dates (five months before expected childbirth to three months after birth) are violative of due process because they create a conclusive presumption that every teacher who is four or five months pregnant is incapable of continuing her duties, whereas any such teacher's ability to continue past a fixed pregnancy period is an individual matter. In *Nashville Gas Co. v. Satty* (1977) the Court held that the petitioner's policy for forfeiting accumulated seniority for female employees during unpaid mandatory pregnancy leave, although not constituting disparate treatment did have a disparate effect on women and did therefore violate Title VII.

In *Geduldig v. Aiello* (1974), however, the Supreme Court determined that exclusion of pregnancy from disability insurance plans was not in violation of the equal protection clause of the Fourteenth Amendment because pregnancy is a "condition" and the issue is not one of gender discrimination. The Court ruled that California is not required by the equal protection clause to sacrifice the self-supporting nature of the program, reduce the benefits payable for covered disabilities, or increase the maximum employee contribution rate just to provide protection against another risk of disability such as normal pregnancy. According to the Court the plan

> does not exclude anyone from benefit eligibility because of gender but merely removes one physical condition—pregnancy—from the list of compensational disabilities. . . . Absent a showing that distinctions involving pregnancy are mere pretexts designed to effect an invidious discrimination against the members of one sex or the other, lawmakers are constitutionally free to include or exclude pregnancy from the coverage of legislation such as this on

any reasonable basis, just with respect to any other physical
condition.   (at 496–497)

In a controversial decision that was destined to produce a
legislative response the Supreme Court in December 1976 (*General Electric Co. v. Gilbert*) accepted the *Geduldig* rationale that
disparate treatment of pregnant women did not always constitute
sex discrimination. In reversing both the district and appellate
courts' finding of sex discrimination on the basis of pregnancy,
the majority opinion, authored by Justice Rehnquist, found that
the exclusion of pregnancy and pregnancy-related disabilities from
coverage under an otherwise comprehensive disability plan was
not in violation of Title VII. According to *Gilbert* General Electric's policy was facially neutral and did not constitute disparate
treatment since not all women become pregnant. Because the
nature of exemption was pregnancy and not pregnant women
there was no sex discrimination—this despite the fact that approximately 80 percent of all women become pregnant at some
time during their working lives (Gelb and Palley 1987:165) and
presumably no men do. The stage was set for political action.

Pregnancy Discrimination Act

Within several days of the *Gilbert* decision a broad coalition of
over three hundred feminist, labor, and religious groups formed
the Campaign to End Discrimination Against Pregnant Workers
in order to lobby Congress to rectify the situation. The reaction
of Congress to this well-organized lobbying effort as well as to
dramatic media coverage of purported violations was swift. In
March 1977 the Pregnancy Discrimination Act (Senate 995) was
introduced, which would amend Title VII to specify that "because
of sex" include pregnancy-related disability and prohibit discrimination of pregnant women in all areas of employment.

Despite internal conflict within the coalition, particularly from
pro-life forces who called for the addition of language eliminating
elective abortions from the definition of covered conditions, in
October 1978 a compromise wording was approved by the conference committee (see Gelb and Palley 1987:168–172). Although

the final version allows employees to exempt elective abortions from medical coverage, except if the life of the mother is threatened or medical complications arise from the abortion, it does not prohibit employer provision of abortion benefits.

On October 31, 1978 President Jimmy Carter signed the Pregnancy Discrimination Act (Public Law 95-555), which included the Pregnancy Amendment to Title VII of the Civil Rights Act. This amendment left no doubt that the intent of Congress was to include discrimination on the basis of pregnancy as a clear case of sex discrimination. The act states that "women affected by pregnancy, childbirth, or related medical conditions shall be treated the same for all employment-related purposes . . . as other persons not so affected but similar in their ability or inability to work." The act took effect immediately upon passage, with the exception of the fringe and insurance benefits, which took effect one hundred and eighty days after passage. Not surprisingly, enforcement of this act pitted the law against two sets of interest parties: employers intent on excluding pregnant women from particular jobs and pregnant employees who wished to be excused from particular jobs temporarily. Furthermore, the act was criticized for disregarding "the potential for harm to the unborn in certain working environments" (Mattson 1981:33). Although the Pregnancy Discrimination Act extended the scope of Title VII to the whole range of matters concerning the childbearing process, it gave virtually no consideration to the issue of fetal vulnerability to workplace hazards.

While the Pregnancy Discrimination Act put pregnancy on a par with other forms of sex discrimination under Title VII, it must be understood that Title VII provides exceptions to the prohibition against discrimination. In each case, however, the burden of proof is on the employer to defend the exception. There are two defenses available to employers in Title VII challenges. The Bona Fide Occupational Qualification (BFOQ) defense against facially discriminatory treatment can be advanced only if two conditions are met:

1. the qualification invoked must be reasonably necessary to the essence of the employer's business; and

2. the employer must have a reasonable factual basis for believing that substantially all women would be unable to safely and efficiently perform the duties of the job.

The BFOQ exception has generally been interpreted very narrowly by the courts (see chapter 5 for pregnancy cases). Sex is a bona fide occupational qualification only where it is essential to the performance of particular job duties. Examples include purposes of successful job performance (e.g., sperm donors to be men), authenticity (e.g., male character to be played by male actor), and safe operation of a business where safety is essential (e.g., requiring violent male prisoners to be supervised by male guards). Conversely, the BFOQ exception does not allow sex discrimination because of customer preferences, assumptions about the comparative employment characteristics of women in general (e.g., higher turnover rates of women), or because of stereotypical characteristics of the sexes. Moreover, if the job requires a particular physical task, i.e., lifting heavy boxes, an employer cannot refuse to consider women applicants even though most men can perform the task more safely and efficiently than most women. Unless the employer can prove that all or substantially all women are unable to safely and efficiently perform the duties, the employer is required to test every job applicant, male and female, to determine whether that particular individual is capable of performing the task. Finally, the increased economic cost of testing women may not be used to justify discrimination (OTA 1985:243).

The second defense for making employment distinctions, applied only to conditions of disparate impact (where the plaintiff admits that the employer's policy is sex-neutral but that it has a disproportionately adverse affect on women) is the "business necessity" exception. This defense is significantly broader than BFOQ because it focuses on the general business enterprise and job-relatedness and not on the narrower concept of comparative job qualifications. Under this defense three conditions must be met:

1. the business purpose must be "sufficiently compelling" to override any discriminatory impact;

3 | Evidence of Reproductive Hazards in the Workplace

The "new protectionism" that would exclude women from certain high-risk workplaces out of concern for the unborn fetus cannot be analyzed objectively without an understanding of the biological context of workplace hazards. After describing the broad range of potential reproductive hazards in the workplace this chapter focuses on current knowledge of environmental effects on the fetus. Problems in identifying teratogenic agents in humans are explained, specifically relating to experimental data and interspecies variation. The difficulties of isolating the impact of any particular agent and the problem of ascertaining susceptibility of males and females are also discussed. Last, a review of known workplace hazards for the developing fetus is presented.

Reproductive Injury and the Workplace

All organ systems and functions of the human body are potentially affected by a broad range of occupational hazards (see Proctor, Hughes, and Fischman 1988). The reproductive system is no exception. Successful reproduction requires a complex series of physiological, cellular, and molecular events. The reproductive cycle is vulnerable to workplace hazards at many junctures in both males and females and virtually all of its phases have been shown to be affected by an array of environmental agents (Legator and Ward 1984). Table 3.1 indicates which reproductive organs and functions are vulnerable at each stage in the process and the possible effects of injuries at that point.

Despite the numerous reproductive processes that might be affected by workplace hazards, however, we are able to detect the effects in only a few observable outcomes. Preconception injuries include infertility, which is estimated to affect 15 percent of American couples, impotence, sperm and ova abnormalities, and sexual dysfunction. Injuries during pregnancy include a variety of complications and problems that endanger the health and life of both the pregnant woman and the fetus. Finally, postnatal injuries can occur through exposure of the infant via lactation or absorption/inhalation of hazardous fibers brought into the home on clothing of either parent.

Depending on the stage of life at which a toxicant acts, it might be classified as either "reproductive" or "developmental." Reproductive toxicants are those chemical, physical, or biologic agents that have an adverse impact on the sexual or reproductive performance of a sexually mature person. These toxicants impair reproduction by interfering with or altering normal physiological processes, regulatory mechanisms, organ function, or the genetic integrity of sperm or ova in an exposed person (National Institute for Occupational Safety and Health, hereafter NIOSH 1988:3–4). Importantly, while each sex might have special sensitivity to a particular toxicant because of the fundamental differences in germ cells, in general neither sex can be assumed to be the more vulnerable to reproductive toxicants. Table 3.2 shows how observable disorders of reproduction caused by such toxicants are distributed by sex.

Developmental toxicants, which have unfortunately received undue emphasis in the controversy over women in the workplace, are chemical, physical, or biologic agents that adversely affect the growth and development of an embryo, fetus, or prepubertal child. As Table 3.2 illustrates, development toxicants occur primarily through the pregnant woman. However, recent data discussed in more detail later in this chapter support the contention

TABLE 3.1
Stages of Reproduction, Organs and Functions Affected, and Possible Affect

Reproductive Stage	Organs and Functions Potentially Affected		Possible Effects
	Female	Male	
Germ cell formation	Oogenesis (occurs during fetal development of mother) Gene replication Cell division Egg maturation Ovulation	Spermatogenesis Gene replication Cell division Sperm maturation	Sterility, subfecundity, damaged sperm or eggs, chromosomal aberrations, menstrual effects, age at menopause, hormone imbalances, changes in sex ratio
Fertilization	Oviduct Uterus Nervous system Behavior Libido	Accessory glands Sperm motility and nutrition Nervous system Erection Ejaculation Behavior Libido	Impotence, sterility subfecundity, chromosomal aberrations, changes in sex ratio, reduced sperm function
Implantation	Uterus Changes in uterine lining Secretions Hormonal influence on secretory cells		Spontaneous abortion, fetal resorption, chromosomal aberrations, subfecundity, stillbirths, low birth weight
Embryogenesis	Uterus Placenta formation Embryo Cell division Tissue differentiation Hormone production Growth		Spontaneous abortion, other fetal losses, birth defects, chromosomal abnormalities, change in sex ratio, stillbirths, low birth weight
Organogensis	Placenta Nutrient transfer Hormone production Protection from toxic agents Embryo Organ development and placement Growth Maternal nutrition		Birth defects, spontaneous abortion and other fetal death, chromosomal aberrations, retarded growth and development, transplacental carcinogenesis
Perinatal	Fetus Growth and development Uterus Contractility Hormonal effects on muscle cells Maternal nutrition		Premature births, birth defects (particularly nervous system), stillbirths, neonatal death, low birth weight, toxic syndromes or withdrawal symptoms in neonates
Postnatal	Infant survival Lactation		Mental retardation, infant mortality, retarded development, metabolic and functional disorders, developmental disabilities (e.g., cerebral palsy and epilepsy)

SOURCE: Nisbet and Karch 1983: 18–21.

TABLE 3.2
Observable Disorders of Reproduction Following Exposure to Reproductive Hazards

| | Reproductive Toxicants | | | | Developmental Toxicants |
| | Non-mutagenic | | Mutagenic | | |
Potential Outcome	Male	Female	Male	Female	Female
Infertility	X	X	X	X	X
Spontaneous abortion					
normal karyotype	X	X	X	X	X
abnormal karyotype			X	X	
Prematurity					X
Birth defect			X	X	X
Delayed development					X
Low birth weight					X
Postmaturity					X
Semen abnormality	X		X		X*
Sexual dysfunction	X	X			X*
Dysfunction of other					
organ systems					X*
Childhood cancer			X	X	X*

*Abnormalities in children or adults resulting from utero exposure
SOURCE: National Institute of Occupational Safety and Health 1988:4.

that paternal exposure might also contribute to fetal injury. Furthermore, although reproductive toxicants merit considerably more attention in discussions of reproductive hazards in the workplace, the focus here is on developmental toxicants since the debate over women in the workplace has centered on that dimension.

Environmental Effects on Fetal Development

From the moment of conception a developing human organism is exposed to a multiplicity of environmental factors, all of which are capable of affecting the health of the fetus. These factors include the womb conditions (i.e., the temperature, pressure character, and turnover of amniotic fluid); maternal emotions as expressed in hormonal changes that reach the embryo or fetus; all drugs administered to the mother, prescription and nonprescription; nutrition; infections; and maternal-fetal incompatibilities such as Rh blood factor. The developing human organism is also affected by a range of extramaternal environmental factors such as environmental pollution, radiation, physical violence, motor vehicle accidents, noise, and an array of other potential dangers inflicted upon pregnant women. Any one, or more likely, a combination of these factors significantly affect the developing fetus and can cause congenital deformities, high-risk pregnancies, and numerous other problems.

Recent advances and refinements in biomedical research and data collection have produced growing evidence of the deleterious effects of these environmental factors on fetal development. The behavioral patterns of the mother during gestation and, in some instances, prior to conception have been linked to a variety of congenital disorders ranging from reduced IQ and impaired motor coordination to mental retardation, high-risk premature births, and, in some cases, physical deformation or perinatal death (Harrigan 1980:292). Although the exact causal nature of these environmental factors often remains inconclusive and appears to be interrelated with the mother's physiological constituency, the evidence of fetal damage resulting from the behavior of the mother is mounting.

Stages of Fetal Development

During the two hundred and eighty or so days between fertilization and term birth, the human zygote increases in weight by a factor of several billion and grows from a single cell to a complex organism. Contrary to the beliefs of many individuals and groups, there is no single point at which a fully defined human life begins. Instead, the gestation process presents a continuing, dynamic developmental continuum. Although conception is the point at which the newly fertilized egg contains all the genetic material of a unique individual, many conceptuses never implant, thus naturally precluding their continued development. Quickening and, more recently, viability have been used as critical stages in gestation, but again, they are subjective lines on the continuum. The selection of any point along this developmental progression, although often intuitively attractive, is arbitrary and varies as to the criteria of humanhood used.

On anatomical grounds, however, it is useful to classify stages of development in order to distinguish among the attributes of

TABLE 3.3
Stages of Embryonic and Fetal Development

Period	Weeks After Conception	Stage	Days After Conception
Embryo			
"Preembryo,"	first week	Zygote	1 to 2
"preimplantation		Cleavage	2 to 4
embryo," or		Blastocyst	4 to 6
"conceptus"		Implantation begins	7
Embryonic	2 to 3 weeks	Primitive streak	7 to 8
		Gastrula	7 to 8
		Neurula	20
	3 to 5 weeks	Limb buds	21 to 29
		Heart beat	21 to 29
		Tail-bud	21 to 29
		Complete embryo	35 to 37
	6 to 8 weeks	Body definition	42 to 56
Fetus	9 to 40 weeks	First fetal	56 to 70
		Second fetal	70 to 140
		Third fetal	140 to 280

SOURCE: Office of Technology Assessment 1988, adapted from Blank 1984.

the organism at each stage. It should be noted that every categorization necessarily oversimplifies the complex process that is taking place and obscures significant variation from one individual to the next. Table 3.3 shows just how complex embryonic and fetal development is and lists some of the major stages.

The preembryo period covers the first seven or so days after conception. Following fertilization the egg undergoes a series of cell divisions called cleavage that produce a package of cells. With each division the cells are of diminishing size so that there is relatively little increase in size over this period. After seven cell divisions the blastocyst is formed with about one hundred cells. This period ends with implantation of the blastocyst on the wall of the uterus and beginning of placenta growth.

The embryo period covers the development of the organism from the end of the first week to about fifty-six days after conception. This is a critical phase of development since cell differentiation of the embryo occurs at an accelerated pace. Southgate and Hey (1976:205) state that "partitioning of the heart and its development as a functional organ is virtually complete by 31 days." Furthermore, although the heart increases in size by a factor of about one hundred during the fetal period, as a proportion of the body weight it remains virtually constant after the embryo period. The same holds for the liver, kidney, and other internal organs. During this six- or seven-week period the embryo increases in diameter from about .1 millimeter to approximately 25 millimeters. By seven weeks the embryo manifests primitive limbs and a head with equally crude facial features. By the end of this period of eight weeks human limbs become evident and fingers and toes are present. Facial features, although still crude, become more clearly humanlike. Also, by seven weeks the brain stem has developed and the brain can be seen as a continuous folding tube expanding in the head region to form elementary cerebral lobes. According to Grobstein (1988:31), human embryos by the seventh or eighth week respond to stimuli by slow and weak turning of the head away from the stimulus. For Grobstein this indicates that by this point in development some nerve cells are mature enough to transmit impulses and transfer them from cell to cell. The metamorphosing embryo already has emerged as a highly differentiated organism with some visibly identifiable though primitive "human" features.

The longest period, and, therefore, the least unique, is that of the fetus, which extends from about nine weeks to full term at forty weeks. Because of the duration of this period it is usually subdivided into three stages. The first fetal stage lasts about fourteen days, during which time the eyelids form, the umbilical hernia is withdrawn into the fetus, and external genitalia are differentiated. Spontaneous movements have been observed under ultrasound by the tenth week. Weight of the fetus by the end of this period is approximately five to ten grams. The second fetal period, which extends from about ten to twenty weeks after conception, culminates in a form which is definitely that of a tiny human infant of approximately 45 grams. During this stage the spinal column hardens into bone, the eyelids are sealed, and hair follicles are formed. At about eighteen weeks quickening normally occurs with spontaneous movements of the fetus now detectable by the mother. According to Benirschke (1981:32), at the end of the fifth month the fetus weighs just under 500 grams and has reached one-half the size of its term length. From twelve to twenty-six weeks after conception the biparietal diameter of the head increases from 23 to 74 mm., and the fetus grows "remarkably" in length as well as weight.

The last stage of fetal development extends from twenty weeks to term. During this stage, which encompasses the entire second half of gestation, continuous maturation of function and growth occurs. Weight normally increases from about 45 grams to full birthweight, which averages 3,400 grams. Fetal growth curves indicate that weight gains are fairly consistent across this entire stage. Organs rapidly mature and ready themselves for functioning outside the maternal environment. By the seventh month subcutaneous fat fills out the wrinkled skin. Most crucial is the lung development and the maturation of the respiratory system.

This brief review of the stages of development generally accepted by developmental biologists demonstrates again that there is no single point at which the organism becomes something substantially different than it was at the preceding stage (Biggers 1983). It must be reemphasized that any particular fetus will develop more or less quickly than the norm. When examined within the context of the concept of viability these data imply that choosing any strict cutoff point for defining humanhood is not only arbitrary but also misleading.

Principles of Teratogenic Action

Deleterious agents can act as mutagens, carcinogens, or teratogens. A mutagen is an agent capable of altering the structure of deoxyribonucleic acid (DNA), the genetic material of the cell. They affect the offspring by causing permanent mutations in the germ cells of either parent. Chemicals causing damage are more likely to affect males than females when exposure occurs in adulthood because sperm, unlike ova, are continually being produced. The repeated cell divisions during the sperm cycle maximize the opportunity for mutagenic action. Because a female is born with her full complement of ova, which have developed during her fetal period, her germ cells are more resistant to mutations in adulthood. However, should damage occur to the ova as they develop prenatally, the effects might be carried through to adulthood. On the other hand once adult males are removed from exposure to mutagenic agents recovery of normal sperm activity can occur in a short time, assuming the stem cells were not affected (Barlow and Sullivan 1982:6). Chromosome damage to either the sperm or the ovum (termed a germ cell mutation) might lead to spontaneous abortion of an embryo or defects in fetal development or growth. Moreover, if there is damage to the fetal germ cells the effects might not be detected until reproductive life begins or, in the case of recessive mutations, might not be apparent for several generations.

An agent might also act upon the fetus as a transplacental carcinogen and place a heightened risk on the progeny of the affected person once at reproductive age. Transplacental carcinogens may act either directly on the fetal tissue or indirectly by activation of fetal or maternal enzymes. The identification of carcinogens is difficult because of the long latency period between the original exposure and the time cancer is diagnosed (Sor 1986–87:156). Although only one such agent, the drug diethylstilboestrol (DES), has been identified with certainty as a transplacental carcinogen, animal studies demonstrate that the majority of known carcinogens act transplacentally. Furthermore, often the fetus is more sensitive to the carcinogenic effect of the agents than the adult animal subjects (Barlow and Sullivan 1982:7).

Unlike a mutagen, a teratogen is an environmental agent that acts on the somatic (nongerm) cells or tissues of the developing organism causing structural or functional defects. Therefore, these agents affect only the specific organism where the developmental disruption occurs. Whereas mutagens involve DNA changes, teratogenic changes may be evoked by a number of mechanisms. Moreover, while mutagenic alternations are a common cause of teratogenic changes, the reverse is not true (Council on Scientific Affairs 1985:3432).

Prior to the 1940s it was generally believed that the maternal uterine environment shielded the fetus from external assaults, this despite evidence in the late nineteenth century on the toxic effects of lead on the fetus (Rom 1976). Studies during that period which demonstrated factors such as maternal dietary intake and excessive radiation exposure that could affect fetal development slowly weakened the theory. The thalidomide tragedy in the 1960s brought the problem in sharp focus, although it was still a decade before the myth of the placental barrier fell. Reports in the 1970s from Japan of the birth of children with severe neurological abnormalities in communities living near waters that had been heavily polluted with mercury from industrial waste heightened concern, especially since the data demonstrated that developing embryo/fetuses were more susceptible to methylmercury poisoning than their often symptomless mothers (Koos and Longo 1976).

Congenital anomalies that are severe enough to require some form of treatment occur in approximately 3 to 7 percent of human births. There is general agreement that 3 to 10 percent of these anomalies are caused by chromosomal aberrations and that approximately 20 percent are caused by known recessive and dominant genetic defects. Furthermore, 2 to 3 percent are linked to maternal infections, 1 to 3 percent to maternal disease, and 1 percent to radiation (Hunt 1979:112). This leaves the causes of somewhere between 63 and 73 percent unaccounted for, the result of yet unknown factors. According to some observers, the most logical place to uncover these unidentified causes centers on environmental and occupational exposure to toxic chemicals (Sor 1986–87:151) or to teratogens in general (Council on Scientific Affairs 1985:3432). Considerable research interest now centers on how and to what extent teratogenic agents contribute to fetal death and injury.

Although knowledge of the cause and effect relationship of specific agents and their teratogenic impact remains primitive, the following principles of teratology were proposed to help us understand the mechanisms (Wilson 1977a).

1. Susceptibility to teratogenesis depends on the genotype of the fetus and the manner in which the genotype interacts with environmental factors.

2. Susceptibility to teratogenic agents varies with the developmental stage of the fetus at the time of exposure.

3. Teratogenic agents act through specific mechanisms on de-

veloping cells and tissues, thereby initiating abnormal embryogenesis.

4. The final manifestations of abnormal fetal development are malformation, growth retardation, functional disorder, or death.

5. The access of teratogenic agents to developing tissues depends on the specific nature of the agents.

6. Manifestations of abnormal development increase from no effect to lethal as the dosage increases.

Genotype. The first principle of teratology raises the importance of genetic variation in understanding why teratogens often adversely affect only a portion of exposed individuals. These large individual differences in susceptibility depend on the genotype of the embryo/fetus and the manner in which this interacts with environmental factors, maternal phenotype, and lifestyle variables surrounding both parents. Genetic determinants give individuals as well as species their distinctive similarities and dissimilarities in normal structure and function.

Analogously, variation in susceptibility to a potential teratogenic drug or toxic chemical depends on complex processes, which are at least partially under genetic control, including (1) absorption; (2) biotransformation; (3) distribution; (4) exertion; and (5) interaction with receptor sites. Each of these five processes is controlled by different genes, hence by different proteins.

(Elias and Annas 1987:199)

One key to understanding teratogenic action, therefore, is genotype. Knowledge emerging from the human genome initiatives of the 1990s is likely to contribute substantially to the identification of women who are likely to carry a fetus at heightened susceptibility to specific teratogenic agents.

Stage of Development. As described earlier, although fetal development is a continuous process throughout gestation, discrete periods can be identified in which exposure to potential teratogens may vary substantially in effect. The same toxic agent, therefore, may produce a congenital malformation or be lethal at one stage but merely injure an organ or produce no effect at all at another stage. Prior to implantation and beginning organogenesis (when cells begin to differentiate and form rudimentary organs) the pre-embryo is resistant to certain types of toxins. During this period of approximately two weeks a teratogen can be lethal and lead to spontaneous abortion of the pre-embryo; however, should the embryo survive to implant, no demonstratable adverse effects occur other than perhaps a slight developmental delay (Goldman 1980). Presumably, since early embryonic cells have not yet taken on developmental roles, if one cell is destroyed a surviving cell can normally assume its function unless the insult has produced chromosomal or genetic abnormalities that interfere with the cell's metabolic processes (Elias and Annas 1987:198).

After implantation the organs develop rapidly. This period of organogenesis, characterized by a high rate of cell division and the timed differentiation of primordial cells into organ systems, is the most vulnerable developmental period for induction of congenital malformations. Although functional teratogenesis may act later on, most structural defects occur during this embryonic stage from week two to approximately week twelve of gestation. Furthermore, because teratogens often act in an organ-specific fashion, "a teratogen may affect one organ system at one stage of development and another system at another stage. The precise time at which the insult occurs determines not only whether a malformation will occur, but also the specific spectrum of anomalies" (Elias and Annas 1987:198).

During the fetal stages major functional and tissue maturation occurs. Already formed organs increase in size and mature, thus precluding the production of gross morphological abnormalities or developmental disruptions that may occur in the embryonic period. An agent acting during the fetal period, however, can affect the overall growth of the embryo or the size of specific organs and disrupt the developmental processes essential to a healthy fetus. Moreover, because the brain continues to differentiate throughout gestation, exposure of the developing nervous system to toxic influences may result in lasting behavioral deficits or abnormalities. Ingestion of mercury, alcohol, or other addictive drugs, for instance, can cause such effects even in later fetal stages (OTA 1985:57). Overall, then, while toxins can be deleterious throughout the entire prenatal period, the earlier in the formation of a structure a toxic agent acts, the more complete the damage to that structure is likely to be.

Mechanisms of Action.   The mechanisms through which toxic agents interrupt normal functioning of a cell, tissue, organ, or organism are complex and varied (principle 3). The toxicant acts by interrupting biological processes including the transfer of energy and information necessary for normal reproductive function and development. Some agents may act directly, either through direct chemical action or by structural similarity to endogenous molecules, for instance, hormone mimics. Other agents interrupt the processes indirectly, by either metabolic processing to a direct-acting toxicant or by altering the normal endocrine balance (OTA 1985:62).

Following exposure the toxic agent must be distributed to the target tissue or organ where it exerts its toxic effect. Among the factors that influence the amount of the agent to which the organ is exposed are absorption, penetration, transport, activation, and excretion. Once the toxicant reaches the target organ it interacts with a critical cell or subcellular component, disrupting an event necessary for normal reproductive function. If this interaction goes unrepaired, the toxic effect is produced. Depending on the specific nature of the teratogen (principle 5) the toxic effect may be highly specific and affect only a single function of a single cell type or it may be broad and unspecific affecting multiple sites within the organism (OTA 1985:57). It is also possible for a single toxicant to exert adverse effects through multiple mechanisms. Although knowledge of the specific mechanisms of teratogens is still fragmentary, the following developmental mechanisms can be disrupted leading to defects: (1) faulty cell or tissue differentiation; (2) excessive cell death during development; (3) improper cellular migration; (4) faulty intercellular communication; and (5) disrupted metabolism, manifested as altered respiration, absorption, excretion, or secretion (OTA 1985:59).

Range of Manifestations.   The final outcome of exposure of the fetus to teratogenic agents may vary from no effect to death of the fetus. As discussed earlier, the impact of a particular teratogen on a particular fetus will depend on a complex array of factors including stage of development, duration of exposure, specificity of the agent, and the ability of the agent to alter normal developmental processes. The insult may result from a direct affect of the agent on the fetus or indirectly through toxicity in the mother. The final manifestations of a teratogenic agent include:

o malformation
o growth retardation
o functional disorder
o behavioral disorder
o development of cancer in offspring
o stillbirth or neonatal death
o spontaneous abortion

It is important to note that in many cases the impact of a specific agent will go undetected, particularly in the case of weak teratogens where the manifestations are subtle or delayed.

Dose-Response. Principle 6 states that the manifestations of abnormal development increase in frequency and severity as dosage increases. At any given stage a fetus can respond to a potential teratogen in three ways depending on the dose level: at low dose there is no effect, at intermediate dose a pattern of malformations can result, at high dose the fetus may die. Further increased dosage levels may reach the maternal lethal range (Elias and Annas 1987:202). Although this principle may seem obvious, its implications are significant for efforts to design meaningful policies intended to reduce workplace hazards by setting dose exposure levels.

A problem in attempting to establish "safe" levels of exposure to potentially harmful agents is that tolerance varies substantially from one fetus to the next. The fetus may be considerably more susceptible than the mother to certain toxic environmental agents because of the high rate of cell division and the ongoing process of cell differentiation. Moreover, the fetus unlike the mother is often unable to metabolize and excrete the substance and, thus, bears the entire effect while the mother may suffer no ill effects. Also, as noted earlier, many teratogens pose their greatest danger to the developing embryo during the first several months of pregnancy when the mother is not likely to know that she is pregnant. There is also some evidence that women may absorb some toxicants faster than men and may absorb and circulate them in greatest quantities when pregnant (Buss 1986:580). As a result, it will be difficult to design a policy that responds adequately both to the woman's employment rights and the danger of harm to the fetus.

Multiple Exposures.   A further complicating factor in assessing the mechanisms and effects of potential teratogenic agents is that the impact of exposure to one agent may be altered by exposure of the fetus simultaneously to other agents. Multiple exposures not only raise the problem of identifying the toxic agent responsible but also that of interaction between agents in the expression of toxic effects. "Combinations of agents may give rise to entirely new toxic affects not seen with any of the agents alone or may synergise to produce toxicity at much lower levels than would be caused by any agent alone" (Barlow and Sullivan 1982:23), thus masking the teratogenic potential of the separate agents. This is critical in many workplace settings such as industry, hospitals, and agriculture where workers are exposed to a variety of potential teratogens.

Gender Differences.   With a few notable exceptions the differences in susceptibility to toxic effects of chemicals on male and female animals of the same species are usually slight. Age, weight, and developmental maturity are far more important determinants than sex. Toxic chemicals, then, do not discriminate by sex; they affect both male and female reproductive systems. Both eggs and sperm are susceptible to damage from radiation, viral infection, and chemical insult. These agents may alter the germ cell's genetic material, its membrane or other structures, its response to hormones, or its metabolic pathways (Bellin and Rubenstein 1983:89). However, because their reproductive systems differ, there are significant differences in the ways toxic agents affect the reproductive systems of men and women.

There are two primary mechanisms that may establish a connection between male exposure to teratogenic substances and detrimental reproductive outcomes. First, exposure that damages the sperm may cause either spontaneous abortions or congenital malformations in offspring of the affected male. Because sperm cells are continuously produced and are capable of being replenished, insult to these cells may be reversible depending on the extent of damage. Removal from the toxic producing situation, then, might restore normal sperm production. Until that time abnormal sperm may heighten the risk of damage to progeny. Although there is case report data tying male exposure to vinyl chloride, the pesticide DBCP, and dental anaesthetics, systematic research is needed to clarify the relationship between alterations in male germ cells with specific reproductive outcomes (Hatch 1984:167).

A second mechanism of exposure of the male to teratogens is indirect where his exposure affects the pregnant female and is thus transmitted to the fetus. Here the evidence is even more sparse and anecdotal. Transmission could take place directly through intercourse during pregnancy or indirectly through skin contact, ingestion, or inhalation of teratogens brought home by the male. For instance, there have been reports of elevated levels of neural tube defects in the offspring of men exposed in Vietnam to Agent Orange as well as a relationship between cleft palate and painter-printer fathers (Erickson, Cochran, and Anderson 1979). According to Maureen Hatch,

> the lack of systematic research into the possibility that teratogenic effects, as they are known, can occur through the father reflects the common assumption that the mother is the sole route to the fetus once conception has occurred. This may indeed be the case, but it needs to be proved not assumed.   (1984:169)

The major reason why attention has focused on maternal exposure to teratogenic agents centers on the fact that only females carry the fetus in their uterus through nine months of gestation. Although it might be proven that exposure of males to teratogens can affect fetal development, by far the more direct impact is through the mother. Moreover, while the effects of male exposure may be reversible, because a female is born with her full complement of eggs any damage to them cannot be repaired. Although mutations can be contributed by either parents, female germ cells bear repeated exposure to toxic agents throughout her entire life. This combined with the fact that she carries the fetus has regrettably focused research attention on female exposure to workplace hazards and contributed to the initiation of exclusionary policies. The policy implications of this pattern are discussed later.

Problems in Identifying Human Teratogens

It is not known precisely to what extent congenital malformations are due to (1) genetic damage, (2) tissue injury in the developing embryo, (3) a combination of these two factors, or (4) environment interaction manifested only in those persons genetically susceptible. However, the evidence of the teratogenic effects of a variety of substances is growing. Although thalidomide is the most conclusive example, other drugs including the widely prescribed valium are suspected teratogens. Nonmedical drugs such as caffeine, nicotine, and marijuana are also suspected, although causal evidence is limited. For other factors such as alcohol consumption and cocaine use, however, the data are more conclusive. Also, studies indicate that many of the hundred of thousands of chemicals that now exist in our environment as well as direct radiation from x-rays and other sources cause chromosomal damage (Berg 1979). LSD, cyclamates, methyl mercury, benzene, and vinyl chloride exposure among others have been linked to human chromosomal aberrations.

The deleterious effects of most chemicals on the fetus are not clear, but as Hook and Porter (1980:16) state, "It appears plausible that any agent, operative procedure, or infection which directly affects the structure of the female reproductive system may also influence indirectly the rate of embryonic and fetal death." No chemical is without risk to the fetus, the level of risk depending on dosage, timing, and so forth, because most chemicals will cross the placenta in some form or amount. Furthermore, even a chemical which has low risk for the mother might pose a serious risk for the fetus. For instance, thalidomide produced malformations in the developing fetus at a dose perhaps 1 percent that required for maternal toxicity (NIOSH 1989:6). Likewise, the fetus has greater sensitivity to some carcinogens than adults, thus estimates of doses necessary for transplacental carcinogenisis cannot be accurately predicted from effects in adults (Everson 1987:109). Because the fetus lacks a fully developed liver and kidneys, the placenta takes on the detoxification and excretion functions of the organs that act to protect the adult from the toxic effects of a chemical. If the placenta is unable to accomplish these functions, the fetus will suffer. Even if the placenta is able to detoxify a chemical, what might be a reasonable dose for an adult woman might be an overdose for the developing embryo or fetus.

Shepard (1989) lists over one thousand agents in his *Catalog of Teratogenic Agents.* Only a handful of these are unquestionably associated with human congenital malformations. Care must be taken not to exaggerate available hard data, which is sparse and open to controversy. The complexity of isolating the effect of any chemical is described by Heinonen et al. (1977:1–29). One set of problems arises because some teratogens might be nonspecific producing malformations in general, some might produce recognizable patterns of deformity, and others might be highly specific. Although agents such as thalidomide that are both potent and striking in their effects are relatively easily identified (still, ten thousand babies are born with phocomelia before thalidomide was isolated as the common factor), others that are less potent and cause less obvious or severe teratogenic deformations are extremely difficult to detect.

Epidemiological Studies. Another problem in demonstrating causality is that because human experimental research is precluded (see Lipsett and Fletcher 1983) evidence must come from two types of data, both with inherent constraints. The first source of data on the effects of teratogenic agents are retroactive epidemiological studies of specific populations. Two forms of epidemiological studies are cohort studies and case-control studies. Cohort studies involve the comparison of different groups based on the composition of each group. Case-control studies compare the frequency of exposure to a suspected agent of persons with a particular disease to the frequency of exposure of comparable disease-free persons. Often epidemiological studies are initiated after case reports establishing anecdotal connections between exposure and effect have alerted medical authorities to a potential problem and ecologic studies have uncovered raw correlations between rates of malformation and frequency of exposure.

Epidemiological studies examine a large number of relevant factors, controlling where possible to isolate factors common to particular malformations or to specific patterns of chemical exposure. The results in most every case are a set of statistical associations indicating increased risk related to exposure. In addition to the normal problems of inferring causality from aggregate measures of association, epidemiological studies on teratogens have special problems because the effect of any agent depends on many mediating factors such as dosage, timing of exposure in the developmental process, and constitutional differences among individuals. Moreover, as noted earlier, evidence suggests that the genotype of the fetus can affect susceptibility of a fetus to the teratogenic effects of a particular agent (Phelan et al. 1982). As a result Spielberg (1982:116) cautions against the use of epidemiological risk data in specific cases. "The existence of human genetic polymorphisms in susceptibility to teratogens, however, suggests that we may be dealing with a large population at no risk and a few selected patients with a very high risks." This means that a relative risk factor for an agent derived from epidemiological data could be misleading in that some exposed fetuses would be at high risk and others would be at low risk despite similar timing of exposure, dosage, and so forth.

The most definitive epidemiological study on teratogens to date is the Collaborative Perenatal Project (CPP). This major government-sponsored project studied over fifty thousand mother-child pairs from 1958 to 1965 and focused on the impact of pharmaceuticals. Although many of the drugs examined, including aspirin, were associated with a variety of fetal malformations, Heinonen et al. (1977:420) conclude, "No commonly used drugs were identified whose potency as teratogens could be regarded as even remotely comparable to thalidomide." They caution, however, that less easily identifiable drug teratogens might have escaped detection. Furthermore, they contend that we should not have a false sense of security even though the most commonly used agents were found to be relatively safe. They find it reassuring that the marked secular increase in drug use during the study period was not accompanied by a similar increase in the malformation rate. Conversely, they find it distressing that had a powerful teratogen been made available to the public for some common indications, it would most likely have been widely used. The CPP urged more focused follow-up studies and continued surveillance of all drug exposure, especially during the first forty-five days of gestation.

Animal Experimentation.   Data collected from controlled animal experimentation is generally considered to the best available to predict risk of reproductive damage resulting from exposure to chemical agents and other teratogenic agents. However, because of interspecies differences both in effect and dosage, caution must always be used in extrapolating animal data on teratogens to humans (Dixon and Nadolney 1985:331). Often the predictive value of animal experimentation is hard to measure because most agents found to be highly teratogenic in animal toxicity studies are not administered to humans (Barlow and Sullivan 1982:17). Furthermore, there frequently are conflicting results in studies of different animal species, thus raising questions as to what animal models are most appropriate analogues for humans. Multifactional interaction between genetic and environmental factors determines dose level thresholds, further confusing attempts to generalize across species.

Despite the difficulty of extrapolating animal data on teratogens to humans, for some extensively studied agents significant correlations have been found. In a comparison of animal and human teratogenic effects of ten agents Nisbet and Karch (1983:96) found that with eight there were "close parallels" in the results of the animal and human experiments (table 3.4). Only for warfarin—in which there have been several case reports in humans but negative studies in mice and rabbits—and for anesthetic gases are there differences in effects. It should be noted that in all cases but polychlorinated biphenyls, where effects similar to humans were seen only in rhesus monkeys, dogs, and swine, effects observed in rats were qualitatively similar to the effects observed in humans (Nisbet and Karch 1983:96).

On the other hand some teratogenic agents that act on humans are not evident in other species. A clear case is thalidomide,

TABLE 3.4

Comparison of Reported Teratogenic Effects of Ten Agents in Humans and in Experimental Animals

Agent	Reported Sites in Humans	Reported Sites in Animals
Anesthetic gases	Hemangiomas, hernias, skin, heart	Skeletal defects only
Smelter emissions (lead and/or arsenic)	Multiple malformations	Multiple malformations
Polychlorinated bi-phenyls	Skin discoloration; enlarged fontanelles	Skin discoloration and lesions (monkey); enlarged fontanelles and syndactyly (pig, dog)
Alcohol	Facial, central nervous system	Facial, dermal, neural, extremities
Vinyl chloride	Neural tube?	Various, including encephalocele (rat)
Warfarin	Nose, bones (case reports only)	Negative
Diphenylhydantoin	Cleft lip, cleft palate, other craniofacial, mental deficiency	Cleft lip, cleft palate, syndactyly, other skeletal defects (mouse); minor kidney anomalies (rhesus monkey)
Aminopterin	Multiple malformations	Multiple malformations (sheep, rat)
Busulfan	Eye, cleft palate (1 report)	Skeletal, genital defects (rat)
Methotrexate	Skull, ribs, toes (2 reports)	Various (rat, cat, rabbit, mouse)
Methylmercury	Central nervous system	Central nervous system, skeletal (rat, hamster, cat)

SOURCE: Nisbet and Karch 1983:97–98.

which gave no evidence of such devastating effects in laboratory animals tested prior to its release in Europe for clinical use.

Thalidomide, despite its profound teratogenic effect in humans, is markedly less potent in laboratory animals. To date, in approximately 10 strains of rats, 15 strains of mice, 11 breeds of rabbits, 2 breeds of dogs, 3 strains of hamsters, 8 species of primates, and in other varied species as cats, armadillos, guinea pigs, swine, and ferrets in which thalidomide has been tested, teratogenic effects have been induced only occasionally. Effects similar to the phocomelic-type limb deformities observed in man have been produced

consistently in only a few breeds of rabbits and in seven species of
primates.   (Schardein 1976:5)

Negative findings in several animal species, therefore, do not in
any way guarantee that a particular agent poses no substantial
risk for humans. Proving both concordance of effect (similarity
in response regarding the effects of the same or similar agents
across species) and concordance of dose (whether humans and
animals are affected at the same or similar doses) is difficult,
although not impossible provided the appropriate species can be
selected in each case.

In an extensive review of the literature the U.S. Food and
Drug Administration (1980) concluded that positive animal studies are at least suggestive of potential human response and that
positive results in multiple species increase their predictive value.
The FDA review analyzed animal data on thirty-eight compounds
for which there are reports of birth defects in humans associated
with intake during pregnancy. Of these compounds all except one
had a positive study in at least one animal test species. Moreover,
80 percent of the compounds were positive in multiple species.
Positive responses were observed 85 percent of the time in rats,
60 percent in rabbits, 45 percent in hamsters, and only 30 percent
in monkeys. Of the less common species that were used to test
only a small number of the substances there was greater than 80
percent correlation with positive human data for the dog, pig,
cow, and cat (at 69823).

On the other hand the FDA review of 165 compounds not
known to be teratogens in humans found 41 percent to be positive
in more than one species. No positive effects were found for
these compounds 80 percent of the time in monkeys, 70 percent
in rabbits, 50 percent in rats, and 35 percent in mice and hamsters
(at 69824). This raises the critical question of whether the dis-
cordance reflected here is the result of nonpredictive animal studies that reflect species variation where animals but not humans
are affected by these compounds or if some of these agents
assumed not to be human teratogens in fact are. According to
Barlow and Sullivan (1982:21), the important reservation on the
FDA review is that human data is likely to be even less reliable
than animal data, i.e., very few of the thirty-eight reported

positive compounds have been adequately studied to be classed as definite human teratogens. Probably even fewer of those not reported as human teratogens have been adequately so confirmed by large epidemiological studies. Despite this critical problem experimental animal data remain a critical and valuable source of information on potential human teratogens. Any agent that consistently shows teratogenic effects across a range of tested animal species must be carefully scrutinized as a potential teratogenic agent for humans as well.

One agent that has been identified as a dangerous cause of birth defects by animal and epidemiological studies is Accutane, a very effective treatment for patients with severe cystic acne. At least sixty-two deformed babies have been born to women undergoing Accutane therapy since the drug went on the market in 1982 (Sun 1988:714). Fetuses exposed to this drug develop major malformations at about twenty-five times the normal rate. The defects are catastrophic. Most commonly affected are the head and face, with small or absent ears, small jaw, and abnormal shape of the skull. Hydrocephalus and abnormalities in brain formation as well as life-threatening deformations of the heart and large blood vessels are also prevalent. The thymus gland, needed for normal immunity, is often underdeveloped ("Accutane Alert," 1986:1). A fetus exposed to Accutane for even a brief period is at very high risk. If the woman discontinues taking this drug at least a month before conception there appears to be no hazard. Because of Accutane's therapeutic use on acne patients unfortunately many young women who are unaware of their pregnancy might be exposed to this potent teratogen.

Although epidemiological studies and animal research have failed to reveal large numbers of agents that, like Accutane, have clear teratogenic effects, certain associations have been confirmed. For instance, the drug danazol, which is the treatment choice for endometriosis, like all androgens, crosses the placenta and causes pseudohermaphroditism when taken in the first trimester of pregnancy. At least twenty-nine cases of danazol use in pregnancy have been documented (Wentz 1982). Of these seven were aborted, five spontaneously and two for medical reasons. Although ten of the sixteen female babies were normal, six had abnormalities of the genital organs. Niebyl (1982) reviews in detail the evidence of teratogenic effects of many prescriptive drugs, Briggs et al. (1986) establish a risk factor for more than five hundred of the most commonly used drugs that have been directly associated with human fetal death. Anticonvulsants, for instance, commonly used to control epilepsy, are associated with fetal growth retardation, head and face abnormalities, and mental retardation. High doses of aspirin may be related to increased perinatal death, intrauterine growth retardation, and teratogenic defects (Briggs, Freeman, and Yaffe 1986:28).

Despite the lack of hard data indicating severe teratogenic effects from commonly used drugs, most observers urge caution in the use of any drugs during pregnancy. Spielberg (1982:116) recommends maximum use of epidemiological studies and the choice of a drug with the "widest human exposure and with data suggesting no increase in risk for birth defects" in situations where a drug is necessary. In contrast Friedman, Little, and Brent et al. (1990:594) argue that while prescriptive drugs are a recognized cause of less than 1 per cent of congenital anomalies, many patients fear fetal damage from any medication taken during pregnancy. This fear, they contend, may complicate necessary treatment of pregnant women and causes undue anxiety. Davis (1976:57), however, advises caution, "It is argued that until more is known about fetal pharmacology the administration of untried drugs to pregnant women should be carefully monitored as a public health exercise and that the onus of proof should be on those who assume that a drug is harmless rather than vice versa."

Scientific Evidence of Workplace Hazards for Women

Although there are many problems in positively identifying workplace hazards that are teratogenic, a growing body of evidence, both animal and human, confirms the hypothesis that many workplace environments can give rise to fetal harm. According to Eula Bingham, then director of OSHA,

> The more we learn about the effects of environmental toxic exposures on reproduction, the more we suspect that it is a substantial

TABLE 3.5
Suspected Human Teratogenic Chemical Agents

Chemical Agent	Effects
Anesthetic gases	Increased spontaneous abortions, stillbirths, decreased birth rate
Beryllium	Increased risk of fatal beryllium poisoning
Cadmium	Impairs implantation, decreased birth rates
Carbon disulfide	Increased frequency of spontaneous abortions and premature births
Carbon monoxide	Increased frequency of spontaneous abortions and stillbirths, low birth weight; brain damage (microcephaly, spasticity, retarded psychomotor development)
Dichloro-diphenyl-tricholoroethane (DDT)	Increased frequency of premature deliveries
Formaldehyde	Toxemia and anemia in pregnancy, increased spontaneous abortions, reduced birth weight
Laboratory solvents	Increased frequency of rare birth defects, chromosomal alternations, spontaneous abortions, stillbirths
Lead	Increased frequency of spontaneous abortions and stillbirths, neurologic defects, intrauterine growth retardation, postnatal failure to thrive
Methyl mercury	Cerebral palsy, chorea, ataxia, tremors, seizures, mental retardation, polyneuritis, blindness
Polychlorinated biphenyls (PCBS)	Dark ("cola" colored) skin, eye defects, premature tooth eruption, gingival hypertrophy, hypotonia, severe acne
Vinyl chloride	Increased frequency of spontaneous abortions, central nervous system defects, craniofacial anomalies, genital organ defects

burden. The list of chemicals and other toxic substances such as radio frequency/microwaves grows almost daily as our research efforts expand. NIOSH now lists 56 substances which are mutagenic in animal tests and 471 teratogens.   (1980)

An increasing number of research studies have evaluated and found ties between selected chemical and physical agents in the workplace and fetal injury or death (Valentine and Plough 1982:147).

Although the precise manner in which may chemicals affect the fetus is unknown, evidence of the devastating impact of a number of substances on the fetus is accumulating (see table 3.5). The NIOSH registry on toxic effects of chemical substances contains entries for over seventy-nine thousand chemicals. Although only thirty to forty of these agents are proven human teratogens, over one thousand exhibit some teratogenic potential in animal studies (NIOSH 1988:2). In 1985 the Council on Scientific Affairs' Advisory Panel on Reproductive Hazards in the Workplace issued its report on a review of one hundred and twenty chemicals that were considered based on an estimation of their imminent hazard (Council on Scientific Affairs 1985). In 1985 the U.S. Congress Office of Technology Assessment also released a report on reproductive hazards in the workplace, which reviewed current data on numerous agents that were suspected teratogens or mutagens.

Out of the tens of thousands of chemicals and substances commonly present in workplaces the one with the most well-documented links to fetal damage is lead (U.S. Environmental Protection Agency 1986). In pregnant women lead rapidly crosses the placental barrier early in gestation, when the fetus is most vulnerable to its effects (Crocetti, Mushak, and Schwartz 1990). Female workers exposed to high lead levels are at abnormally high risk for spontaneous abortion and stillbirths. Maternal exposure to elevated levels of lead during pregnancy has been correlated with mental retardation, intrauterine growth retardation, and neurological disorders in their offspring, and the children of such women are susceptible to convulsions after birth (Rom 1980). A recent study has found that the fetus may be adversely affected at blood lead concentrations well below the 25 mg. per deciliter currently defined by the Centers for Disease Control as the highest acceptable level for young children (Bellinger et al. 1987:1042).

Inorganic and organic mercury, too, have been found to cross the placenta in animals and humans and cause damage to the central nervous system of the fetus, resulting in mental retardation, cerebral palsy, seizures, blindness, as well as heightened rates of stillbirths (Smith 1977). All forms of mercury appear to be teratogenic, capable of altering fetal growth and increasing the incidence of congenital malformations, chromosomal abnormalities, and biochemical changes in the human placenta.

Many other substances widely used in industry are known or suspected to have adverse effects on the reproductive systems of exposed workers. Chromosomal damage has been reported in workers exposed to the solvent benezene, an element in paint strippers, rubber cement, nylon, and detergents. Anesthetic gases (Cohen 1980) produce miscarriages and birth defects in the progeny of both male and female operating room and dental personnel. Exposure to pesticides and chlorinated hydrocarbons used to manufacture drycleaning fluid and other general solvents causes serious fetal damage (Howard 1981). Workers exposed to vinyl chloride risk severe impairment to their reproductive system and exposure has been tied to abnormal rates of miscarriage and chromosomal damage of fetuses. Moreover,

> Among pregnant women working in a biological media preparation laboratory, a high abortion rate and the birth of a child with clubfeet have been related to high selenium levels. Industrial exposure of pregnant women to fat solvents such as xylene, trichloroethylene, methylechloroethylene, and acetone has been related to the birth of children with vertebral defects.
>
> (Furnish 1980:127)

Unidentified Agents by Occupation

In addition to the growing evidence about specific chemical hazards a number of studies have examined the effects of particular workplace settings on reproduction, several of which are critical to working women. One study found that women involved in metal, chemical, wood, textile, and farm industries and medical technicians are at increased risk of a fetal death (Vaughan, Daling, and Starzyk 1984:677). Peters, Adelstein, Golding, and Butler (1984:99) found the highest rates of stillbirth and neonatal deaths correlated with women working in glass and pottery, hospitals, laundry/dry cleaning, the chemical industry, and woodworking and furniture manufacturing. Similarly, a study of pregnancy outcome among women working in a Swedish hospital laboratory found an increase in spontaneous abortion (Strandberg et al. 1978). Another study found an increase in chromosomal abnormalities in women who worked in laboratories and the printing industry (Funes-Cravioto et al. 1977). Two other Swedish studies found that laboratory workers were at heightened risk to have children with congenital malformations of the gastrointestinal tract (Ericson et al. 1982; Meirik et al. 1979). Furthermore, there is an increase in spontaneous abortion among women involved in sterilizing instruments in hospitals, most likely due to exposure to ethylene oxide (Hemminki et al. 1982). The large number of young women working in hospitals and laboratories raises critical questions of fetal risk. Women make up over 80 percent of the total workforce in health services but less than 25 percent in the health-diagnosing occupations (Quinn and Woskie 1988:490).

Another industry heavily dependent on female workers is the textile/clothing industry. In a major Finnish study the highest rate of spontaneous abortion was found among women textile workers (Hemminki et al. 1983). Similarly, a Swedish study found an increased rate of spontaneous abortion among both women and wives of men working in rayon textile jobs (Hemminki and Niemi 1982). Although there was no statistically significant increase in congenital malformations among the progeny of textile workers, in a related study Hemminki, Mutanen, Saloniemi, and Luoma found significant associations between central nervous system malformations and oral clefts and women working in industry, transport, and communication work (Hemminki et al. 1981).

Today more than 75 percent of the workers making semiconductors and printed wiring circuit boards are women. These workers are among the most poorly paid industrial workers in the United States and experience occupational illnesses attributable to toxicant exposure at more than double the rate of the manufacturing industry in general (47 percent to 21 percent respectively) (Quinn and Woskie 1988:489, 490). These women are exposed on a daily basis, often under conditions of inadequate ventilation, to an extensive array of hazardous agents including solvents, acids, resins, adhesives, sealants, rubber, and plastics (Ross 1972). Furthermore, soldering and welding operations result in the formation of toxic gases and may involve solders of diverse metal content including cadmium and lead (Hunt 1979:135). Toluene, polychlorinated biphenyls, and other known teratogens are present in a variety of combinations. A major study of California women found that work in electronics assembly was significantly

TABLE 3.6
Potential Health Hazards to Fetus in Selected Occupations

Occupation	Female Employment (est. 1988)	Potential Risk Factors
Health care (nurses, aids, dental assistants, laboratory technicians)	3,500,000	Ionizing radiation Infection Mercury vapor Anesthetic gases Disinfectants and sterilizing agents Phenolic compounds
Clothing and textile/ laundry and drycleaning	1,350,000	Benzidene-type dyes Formaldehyde Solvents Carbon disulfide
Office workers	14,500,000	Benzene in rubber cement, cleaning compounds, and solvents Ozone or methanol and ammonia from duplicating machines Air contaminants
Hairdressers and cosmetologists	750,000	Bleaches Hair dyes Nail varnishes (acetone, toluene, xylene, plasticizers)
Cleaning, janitorial, household jobs	1,750,000	Cleaning substances Disinfectants Bleach/ammonia Organic solvents
Childcare	1,185,000	Infections

SOURCE: U.S. Bureau of Labor Statistics, *Employment and Earnings,* January 1989.

associated with the delivery of low birth-weight infants but not with spontaneous abortion (Lipscomb et al. 1991).

Table 3.6 shows that these data raise serious questions concerning the high-risk environment of female-dominated occupations. In addition to laboratory and textile workers, office workers and hairdressers (cosmetologists) are exposed to many toxins and potential teratogens. Ironically, one of the most hazardous occupations for a pregnant woman is in health care (Coleman and Dickinson 1984). Not only is there the presence of known chemical teratogens but there is also a heightened risk to a fetus from maternal infections and ionizing radiation. Some recent data also suggest a slight increased risk of miscarriage, preterm birth, and low birthweight babies among women who work the rotating shifts or irregular hours that are common in a hospital setting. (Axelsson, Rylander, and Molin 1989; Armstrong Nolan, and McDonald 1989).

Maternal Infections

Rubella (German measles) is the most striking reminder of the potential effect of maternal disease on the fetus. During the last major epidemic in the United States (1963–1965) approximately fifty thousand fetuses were affected. About 60 percent of these died before birth and the remainder were born with serious birth defects, including microcephaly, heart malformations, deafness, and cataracts.

As with many maternal situations the most deleterious effects of rubella occur upon exposure during the first trimester, especially the first four weeks of pregnancy. Although widespread use of effective vaccines have reduced the occurrence of congenital rubella dramatically in the United States, it remains a major threat in many countries. Because the vaccine contains live viruses, it should not be given to pregnant women nor to a woman within sixty days of conception, otherwise the effect will be the same as if the woman had rubella. As a result immunization programs are targeted at young children on the assumption that exposure to women of childbearing age will thus be diminished.

Congenital toxoplasmosis is thought to occur only after primary maternal infection. Most affected infants do not exhibit symptoms of the disease at birth, but regardless of the initial presentation of the infection, prognosis is very poor. Of those infected 10 to 15 percent die, 85 percent of the survivors display severe psychomotor retardation by age two to four and 50 percent develop visual problems detectable by age one. Although the progression of the disease can be controlled medically, neurological damage cannot be reversed (Devore, Jackson, and Piening 1983).

Another infection that can be transmitted from mother to child is viral hepatitis, particularly hepatitis B virus. Most frequently the infant becomes infested during delivery or soon after birth.

The transfer rate is highest when the mother contracts the virus in the third trimester. When viral hepatitis is transmitted to the fetus the risk of prematurity, stillbirth, and perinatal mortality heighten. Although infants who develop hepatitis B virus often become chronic antigen carriers, very few infants develop acute hepatitis or chronic liver disease. For the few who do, however, the effect is calamitous.

An infection with devastating effects on the fetus is syphilis. Although the incidence of congenital syphilis declined in the 1950s after the introduction of penicillin therapy and prenatal serologic testing, a steady increase has occurred in the past decade. In 1986 more cases of congenital syphilis were reported to the CDC than in any of the preceding fifteen years (Ricci, Fojaco, and O'Sullivan 1989:687). Approximately two hundred and fifty to four hundred infants are born annually in the United States with congenital syphilis. According to a Center for Disease Control study (Journal of the American Medical Association, *JAMA* hereafter 1984), 80 percent of women with primary and secondary syphilis are in their reproductive years. Transmittal of the disease to the fetus if conclusively associated with brain damage, cardiovascular system abnormalities, blindness, and increased rates of spontaneous abortion and perinatal deaths. Evidence indicates that the fetus is at high risk for damage throughout the gestation period and that nearly every organ in the body can be affected. Prevention of fetal damage depends on early diagnosis of syphilis and treatment with high doses of penicillin for mother and child. Mascola and associates (1984) argue that congenital syphilis can be reduced primarily through improving prenatal care for high-risk populations.

The frequency of genital herpes infections has increased markedly in the last decade, leading some observers to term it an epidemic. There is now evidence suggesting that infection in the first trimester may lead to increased risk of spontaneous abortion, although more research is necessary for confirmation. In one study of 184 cases of herpes simplex infection of newborns, 41 percent were of low birth weight. By one week after birth, 59 percent of infected babies had experienced seizures or developed a fever, conjunctivitis, or lesions of the skin (Stone et al. 1989).

Herpes infections at term are also clearly associated with heightened risk of microcephaly, retinal dysplasia, mental retardation, and perinatal death. Neonatal herpes is a relatively devastating disease with a fairly high morbidity and mortality. The major risk is the acquisition of the disease from exposure to infection in the birth canal in a woman who develops herpes for the first time during pregnancy (Corey 1982).

Whether or not the mother has visible lesions 30 to 50 percent of newborns delivered through the birth canal contaminated with herpes virus are infected, and of these half will die or be severely damaged. Approximately 70 percent of all neonatal herpes infections are disseminated, affecting the internal organs, especially the liver, adrenals, and central nervous system. Of those infants who contact the disseminated form 60 to 90 percent die (Devore, Jackson, Piening 1983:1661).

Although disseminated herpes simplex virus (HSV) infection during pregnancy is uncommon, at present it is accompanied by high maternal and fetal morality and morbidity (Peacock and Sarubbi 1983). Jacob et al. (1984), in a study of 215 middle-income, white, suburban women revealed that 4.6 percent had positive herpes cultures near term, though none bore a child with neonatal herpes. However, Sever (1980:174) contends that herpes infections will require "considerable" emphasis in the 1980s because of the explosive increase in the rate of infection among women of reproductive age, the recurrence of infections after dormant periods, and the current lack of satisfactory treatment. Corey (1982) recommends virologic surveillance in pregnant women. He advocates that women with a history of genital herpes or whose current or past sexual partners have had herpes be monitored to identify those with clinical or asymptomatic viral shedding at or very near term. Those who test positive are candidates for a cesarean section, although Lagrew and associates (1984) argue that treatment with the antiviral agent for HSV, acyclovis, presents fewer risks than an emergency cesarean section and has produced encouraging results.

One of the most troubling trends in the incidence of AIDS is the vertical transmission of the virus from mother to fetus, which is reported to range from 20 to 60 percent (Hoff et al. 1988).

Approximately one-third of the infants born to women testing positive for the human immunodeficiency virus antibody will die or show evidence of infection within one year of birth (Witwer 1989:282). Many of these infants will become "boarder babies" who will spend their entire short life in a hospital setting. Although the prevalence of babies infected with the AIDS virus varies depending on the specific population and geographical location, average figures for the United States are two per one thousand pregnant women or approximately two thousand infants per year. In New York City and other urban areas the prevalence is considerably higher—as high as 20 percent in some hospitals. Rates of HIV are significantly higher among black and Hispanic infants than white infants.

Furthermore, infants born to mothers with AIDS related conditions are at high risk for other infections including hepatitis B and congenital toxoplasmosis (Scott et al. 1985). Although Scott and associates (1985:363) conclude that their observations do not clarify the source of infection in the mother (twelve of the sixteen mothers were Haitian, three reported using intravenous drugs, and one was an acknowledged prostitute), they do support the argument that infant cases likely result from transmittal from the mother rather than other household members. Also, because the infants developed symptoms of AIDS at a mean age of four months, the data suggest that transmission occurs either in utero or during the perinatal period.

Ionizing Radiation

In addition to these chemical substances other agents have been linked to fetal damage. Mammal studies clearly demonstrate that high energy radiation leads to congenital malformations, growth retardation, and embryonic death. Exposure of pregnant women to levels of greater than 20 rads leads to birth defects, while lower levels of exposure are associated with microcephaly and mental retardation, especially with exposure in the first three weeks of pregnancy (MacMahon 1985). "It has been estimated that low doses of approximately 0.2 rads can increase the chance of a child developing cancer by fifty percent. Nurses, physicians, and technicians involved in radium treatments and nuclear medicine have been found to be exposed to double or triple this dose" (Hunt 1978).

There is evidence that radiation exhibits a cumulative dosage effect and that fetal tissue may be as much as twenty-five times more sensitive to radiation than adult tissue. Furthermore, unlike adult, fetal irradiation is essentially a whole body exposure, thereby exposing all organs including the gonads. Finally, there is a small but increased risk of childhood leukemia and other malignancies in children who have been exposed to X rays early in pregnancy (MacMahon 1985). Despite these potential deleterious effects Brent (1980:180) concludes that while it is advisable to limit diagnostic X-ray procedures on women of reproductive age it is also crucial that "the exaggeration of low dose diagnostic radiation risks do not interfere with appropriate medical care to create unnecessary anxiety in exposed women of reproductive age."

In addition to exposure to chemicals, radiation, and biological agents, concern has been raised over reports of heightened rates of spontaneous abortions, miscarriages, and birth defects among operators of video display terminals (VDTs). Also magnetic fields, ultrasound, and radiofrequency/microwave radiation have come under scrutiny as possible teratogens. To date, however, more extensive ecologic studies and an ongoing study by the National Institute for Occupational Safety and Health have not confirmed these case reports. Similarly, preliminary studies of the effects of hot and cold environments, noise and vibration, and psychological stress have failed to find significant threats to fetal health (see OTA 1985:98–106).

Return to the Issue of the Paternal Contribution to Fetal Damage

Although it is generally accepted that the most direct harm to the developing fetus comes through exposure of the pregnant woman to toxic workplace agents, there is growing evidence that fertile males also may contribute to fetal damage. For instance, there is evidence that exposure to lead in males leads, among other things, to a decreased ability to produce normal sperm, a condition that might produce abnormal pregnancies in their mates (Howard 1981). Moreover, wives of males exposed to vinyl chloride experience a significantly higher than normal rate of fetal loss (Infante et al. 1976). Heightened rates of chromosomal aberrations in males who work with vinyl chloride have led medical experts to conclude that occupational exposure causes germ cell damage in the father. Children of male vinyl chloride workers and even children born in communities near vinyl chloride processing facilities have an increased incidence of congenital birth defects. Similarly, there is evidence that males occupationally exposed to chloroprene suffer decreased motility of sperm. Other studies report that wives of workers exposed to chloroprene suffered three times the expected number of miscarriages (Infante 1980). Furthermore, herbicides DBCP; Kepone; 2, 4, 5-T; DDT; 2, 4-D; and Agent Orange have been linked to possible teratogenic impacts on the progeny of exposed males, although findings are not conclusive at this time (OTA 1985:74–78).

Recent epidimeological studies have also found a higher incidence of brain cancer in children of automechanics and electronic workers; heart defects in children of male firefighters, metalworkers, sawmill workers, and janitors; and spina bifida in children of males in logging, painting, pumping gas, and millwork ("Paternal-Fetal Conflict" 1992:3). Moreover, exposure of males to cocaine has been linked to abnormal development in their offspring. A study of Yazigi, Odem, and Polakoski (1991) demonstrates that cocaine can bind directly onto sperm without affecting its motility or viability, thus supporting the hypothesis that sperm may act as a vector to transmit cocaine into the ovum and damage the embryo (at 1956). An unanswered question is how many other toxins can reach the embryo through this same mechanism.

As a result of this evidence of a paternal role to birth defects the March of Dimes launched a campaign in 1991 to increase public awareness of the father's contribution to the health of their progeny (*New York Times*, December 25, 1991). It has also funded at least eight projects to seek further evidence of what substances damage sperm and how such damaged sperm in turn damages the child ("Paternal-Fetal Conflict" 1992:3).

In one case involving parental actions against an employer (*Coley v. Commonwealth Edison Co.* 1989) a U.S. district court granted Commonwealth Edison summary judgment. The two male employees whose work included cleaning up chemical and nuclear spillage alleged that the conditions of their job caused their two children to be born with severe and permanent injuries—one of the children subsequently died. Although the *Coley* ruling was based on the grounds that a wrongful birth tort had nothing to do with the facts of the case, it illustrates potential novel suits of preconception injury from male exposure to workplace hazards.

Despite the evidence in these areas most research continues to focus on the pregnant worker. According to the Council on Environmental Quality, there is at best limited scientific basis for treating men and women differently because of potential adverse effects on the fetus. It is crucial that more research be done on the potential contribution to fetal damage caused by male worker exposure to teratogens or mutagens if we are to analyze the justness of employer policy (Williams 1981). When an employer excludes women of childbearing age from employment because of possible effects of toxicants on the fetus, the employer's policy will in part be judged by factual evidence of harm. It is clear that if a substance harms both men and women and their offspring any policy that excludes only women discriminates on the basis of sex. According to Clement et al. (1987:522), when a workplace toxicant puts both female and male employees at risk and only women are excluded, the men are also discriminated against because they are allowed to work in jobs that endanger their reproductive capacity. Although attention is bound to continue to be directed at women, especially concerning teratogenic agents, the issue over workplace hazards necessitates considerably more research on males as well as females.

Fetal Hazards: A Summary of Evidence

A wide range of maternal and extramaternal factors have been found to be associated with deleterious effects on the fetus. In most cases it appears that the critical period of development occurs between the third and twelfth weeks of human gestation. However, each organ has its own critical period and for some, such as the brain, where cell proliferation does not cease until at least six to eight months after birth, sensitivity to environmental teratogenic agents extends throughout the pregnancy. Although the exposure to potential teratogens later in gestation might not result in gross organ system abnormalities, it might still be associated with other serious dysfunctions.

Furthermore, research on teratogens indicates that it is probable that most teratogensis is caused by the combined effects of a number of more subtle teratogens acting in consort rather than a "single-hit massive teratogenic action." The problem is vastly more complex than often assumed and the solution depends on unraveling the unique contribution of each of a multitude of intimately related factors. Despite the complex nature of the fetal environment and the variation of effects any single stimulus might have on a specific fetus, the evidence demonstrates that there are many ways in which maternal and paternal exposures and health status can impair the proper development of the fetus and in some cases cause irreparable harm. Although data remains inconclusive there is growing evidence of the importance of providing as risk-free a fetal environment as possible.

Within the context of the growing knowledge of workplace hazards the question reemerges as to whether a child has a right to a safe fetal environment and as normal as possible start in life. This growing concern demonstrates the potential conflict of interests between the developing fetus and the pregnant woman's employment choices. Awareness of potential hazards to the fetus has led to the establishment of oversimplistic policies that exclude women of childbearing age from workplaces deemed hazardous or potentially hazardous to developing fetuses. This has produced the policy controversy to which attention is now directed.

4 | Fetal Protection Policies: Protection Through Exclusion

The demise of state sponsored "protection" laws through invalidation by the courts under Title VII did not eliminate the practice of excluding women from certain workplaces but instead shifted the source of such policies from the states to private employers. Although this new employer-initiated protectionism did not alter the ultimate effect of excluding women from many jobs, it did reflect a major change in the alignment for and against such policies. The major proponents of early protectionist policies were government lawmakers, social reformers, and, most important, labor unions. During this period many employers vigorously opposed such policies because they restricted the employer's ability to contract freely with and often exploit women workers (see Baer 1978). In contrast, organized labor was a strong force behind early protective legislation designed primarily to protect their members (mostly male) from female competition and the depression of wages they feared would accompany an infusion of women into their male-dominated workplaces (Maschke 1991:3).

Although supporters of protectionist policies in both periods have used humanitarian arguments to defend their stands, frequently the interests they are protecting are economic ones, and depending on how specific policies are framed the exclusion of women is viewed as a means to that end. This chapter examines the establishment of fetal vulnerability policies in the United States over the past two decades, since state laws were invalidated. As with the early protectionist legislation that was in part based on a genuine need to "protect" women from extremely unsafe and unhealthy work places, these new initiatives do reflect a legitimate concern over the potential hazards to the health of potential children. Similarly, in both instances the policies, no matter how well intentioned, fail to achieve their stated objectives and in reality create more problems than they resolve. Arguments of proponents and opponents and an analysis of the impact of fetal vulnerability policies are presented here before turning to the government response in chapter 5.

The Emergence of Fetal Vulnerability Policies

The elimination of state protective policies was followed by an accelerated movement of women into formerly male-dominated industries in the late 1970s. In part this resulted from considerable pressures exerted by the Equal Employment Opportunity Commission (EEOC) and the Office of Federal Contract Compliance under the Carter administration on employers to hire women into unionized, blue-collar jobs they had been traditionally denied. During this same period there were reports of growing scientific evidence that occupational exposure to certain toxicants could affect a worker's capacity to produce normal children. Although as early as 1942 the U.S. Department of Labor recommended that pregnant women should avoid workplace exposure to a few known toxic substances, the issue came to public prominence with the publication of a U.S. Department of Health, Education, and Welfare report on occupational health problems of pregnant women (Hunt 1975). The large number of women entering these industries along with a rising concern over the health of pregnant women in the workplace and a fear by employers of liability torts led to the establishment of fetal protection policies (FPPs).

According to an Office of Technology Assessment (OTA) study, there is a tremendous diversity in company exclusionary policies (1985:261). Some of the policies are grounded in epidemiological and toxicological research findings regarding specific substances, while others are more speculative about potential health hazards and offer little scientific support. Moreover, while some FPPs are carefully written and documented, others are unwritten and ambiguous. OTA found that in large manufacturing companies policies are generally announced to employees and their unions prior to implementation. Smaller companies, on the other hand, appear to formulate and apply policies as perceived problems arise (OTA 1985:261). Finally, while many FPPs apply only to women a few recognize that a fetal hazard may be mediated through either male or female workers.

Although FPPs vary both in scope and substance, in most cases they generally target women for exclusion from particular jobs deemed to have high risk, not necessarily for the health of the woman but rather for her potential unborn. Often they exclude any woman of childbearing age who cannot prove she is infertile from holding jobs, although in some cases they have targeted only pregnant women. Estimates on the number of women affected or potentially affected by these exclusionary policies vary considerably but all indicate that the numbers are large. In 1985 the Centers for Disease Control stated that each year fourteen million workers are potentially exposed to known or suspected reproductive hazards. Other estimates have ranged as high as twenty million (Committee on Education and Labor 1990:11). Of these positions, however, many would be filled by males or represent traditionally female-dominated workplaces where, it is interesting to note, there has been little motivation to exclude fertile women.

In 1979 the number of jobs from which fertile women were excluded by FPPs was estimated to be one hundred thousand. More recently the House Committee on Education and Labor stated that "hundreds of thousands of jobs are closed to women" as a result of these policies, "and the situation may get much worse" (1990:11). If these estimates are close to the actual number of positions formally restricted, the number of jobs from which women are effectively barred is significantly higher, because often the jobs from which women are formally excluded are part of a line of progression under union contract (Becker 1986:1226). Without experience in the restricted job a woman is unable to advance to higher jobs, even though they might not formally be closed to her. Also, in some instances the effect of an exclusionary policy limiting exposure to certain toxicants is to deny any employment to any fertile women in a particular plant (Becker 1986:1226). Randall (1987:89) estimates that as many as two-thirds of all working women could be affected by FPPs. Any estimates on the actual impact of FPPs on the employment of women, therefore, are problematic.

One of the reasons it is difficult to get accurate projections on the number of jobs actually excluded to fertile women is that there are no accurate figures on the number of FPPs in effect nor data on how those in existence are enforced. The evidence we have, however, suggests that FPPs were numerous but not widespread during the 1980s. Even though an early survey of spokespersons of chemical companies found that every respondent agreed that no woman biologically capable of bearing children should be exposed to substances that pose a direct risk to the health and viability of the unborn child, no figures were given on actual implementation of exclusionary policies (Rawls 1980). OTA (1985:235) reported that at least fifteen of the Fortune 500 companies as well as numerous hospitals excluded fertile and/or pregnant women from some jobs.

A more extensive survey conducted for OTA in 1989 concluded that 8 percent of the health officers in the 178 companies that responded precluded employment of individuals for certain positions on the basis of pregnancy. In the overall ranking of various factors for exclusion from the workplace pregnancy came third, after back problems and vision impairment and ahead of diabetes and hearing problems (OTA 1991:13). Of the twenty-four mentions by companies the specific positions, jobs, or sites barred to pregnant women include exposure to:

Lead or heavy metals (4)

Chemicals or chemical toxins (5)

Radiation or radioactive materials (3)

Materials harmful during pregnancy (8)

Jobs requiring heavy lifting or physical labor (2)

Other, or all positions (3)

The most detailed survey data on exclusionary practices comes from a study of 198 chemical and electronics manufacturing industries in Massachusetts. Paul and associates (1989:272) found that thirty-seven companies, or almost 20 percent, excluded certain categories of workers from substances, work areas, or occupations on the basis of reproductive health concerns. Collectively, these companies had a total of fifty-eight restrictions. All but one of these restrictions applied solely to female employees. Furthermore, by far the greatest number of restrictions (thirty-nine) applied specifically to pregnant women. "In fact, every company with exclusions restricted the work of pregnant women, with seven of these companies restricting the work of all women or women of childbearing age" (Paul, Daniels, and Rosofsky 1989:273). Seven restrictions applied to women who were trying to conceive and only one restriction applied to men whose partners were trying to conceive.

Of the twenty-eight companies that excluded pregnant women 93 percent offered female workers the option to transfer to another job, reportedly with full wage retention. In addition, 59 percent of the companies offered restricted pregnant workers the option of a leave of absence. Of these, 88 percent continued health benefits, 71 percent retained some proportion of wages, and 82 percent retained seniority during pregnancy leave. The five companies that restricted women trying to conceive also offered the option of temporary job transfer with retention of the same rate of pay during the transfer period (Paul, Daniels, and Rosofsky 1989:273). Researchers also found that restrictive policies were significantly more frequent in companies with over five-hundred employees (57 percent) than firms with less than five-hundred employees (13 percent). Of the companies that did not have restrictive policies, 16 percent granted transfers to workers who had concerns about reproductive hazards, and in all cases only women were permitted to transfer voluntarily out of jobs

TABLE 4.1
Corporations That Instituted Fetal Protection Policies

Allied Chemical	Firestone Tire and Rubber
American Cyanamid	General Motors
ASARCO	Globe Union (Johnson Controls)
BASF Wyandotte	Gulf Oil
B. F. Goodrich	Monsanto
Delco-Remy	Olin Corporation
Dow Chemical	Shell Oil
Dupont	Sun Oil
Eastman Kodak	St. Joseph Minerals
Exxon	Union Carbide

SOURCE: Committee on Education and Labor (1990:6) and Randall (1987:89).

because of reproductive concerns (Paul, Daniels, and Rosofsky 1989:274).

Given the lack of systematic national data this study is informative in that nearly one in five companies were found to have exclusionary policies. Furthermore, because these policies are more common among the larger corporate size groups, the actual number of women potentially affected is of greater significance. Although this study was limited to Massachusetts, there is no reason to believe that this state is unique in implementing these industrial policies, particularly since many of the firms surveyed are nationally based. If anything, the authors of the report suggest (at 277) a "cautious underreporting" by firms is understandable because the survey was conducted during a time when there was a vocal public outcry from legal, women's, and worker advocacy groups concerning exclusionary policies in high-tech industry following the release of a highly criticized University of Massachusetts study commissioned by Digital Equipment Corporation that found increased spontaneous abortion rates among women computer chip fabrication workers at the corporation's Hudson, Massachusetts facility (Pastides et al. 1988).

A more extensive description of selected companies's FPPs is detailed below and in the discussion of government response in chapter 5. Table 4.1, however, lists those companies that have been identified by various sources as having instituted FPPs during the 1970s and 1980s. In addition, in January 1987 American

Telephone and Telegraph banned all pregnant women from its semiconductor production lines in response to the aforementioned University of Massachusetts study commissioned by Digital Equipment Corporation (Pastides et al. 1988).

One of the first companies to adopt an FPP was the Bunker Hill Mining Company in Kellogg, Idaho. In 1975 the company instituted a policy that prohibited women from working in areas exposed to lead unless they could provide proof that they had been sterilized. At least three female employees underwent sterilization within several months after the policy was enacted solely to be allowed by the company to return to their former jobs (Randall 1987:89). Although an administrative investigation by the EEOC led to a number of concessions by Bunker Hill over wage and job provisions for women, the women were basically told to accept exclusion from jobs that exposed them to lead. Similarly, OSHA dropped a citation against Bunker Hill after the Occupational Safety and Health Review Commission in a ruling on a similar FPP (American Cyanamid) determined that OSHA did not have statutory authority to investigate exclusionary policies (Maschke 1991:9).

Although the Bunker Hill FPP raised concern among many advocacy groups, it was the policy instituted by American Cyanamid in 1978 that raised broader media attention and public consciousness. After more than a year of deliberation American Cyanamid put into effect a fetal protection policy for employees working with lead in its Willow Island, West Virginia plant. The policy excluded all women between the ages of sixteen and fifty from jobs requiring exposure to lead unless they had proof of sterilization. The company claimed that these women could become pregnant, that fetuses were more susceptible to harm from lead than adults, and that fetal harm could be caused by maternal exposure prior to or after conception before they knew they were pregnant.

American Cyanamid's FPP gained national prominence after five women employees who were sterilized in order to retain their jobs in the lead pigment department went public. The case was made more poignant in that the lead pigment department at

Willow Island was shut down one year later. Despite the heightened concern over FPPs raised by the disclosure of this case, however, similar policies continued until the Supreme Court ruled in 1991 that FPPs were illegal under Title VII of the 1964 Civil Rights Act and the Pregnancy Discrimination Amendments of 1978. Before examining the legal and regulatory response to these policies in chapter 5, the rationale for FPPs and the arguments against them are presented here.

Rationale for Fetal Protection Policies

Employers have generally justified FPPs on two grounds. First, they argue that they have a societal and moral obligation to protect future generations from damage imposed through a pregnant woman's exposure to toxicants in the workplace. On humanitarian grounds they do not want to assume a moral responsibility for children born with workplace-related injuries. They often point out that the exclusionary policies are but a part of a more complete package of features including orientation and information sessions to alert employees to potential reproductive hazards, elimination of hazards where feasible, monitoring exposure levels when practical, job rotation to minimize exposure levels, and counseling of pregnant employees.

DuPont, for instance, used a four-step procedure for management of female employees of childbearing capability in order to protect the fetus:

1. Employees who may be affected are informed of the possible consequences of exposure to such substances and appropriate safe handling procedures are established and communicated.

2. Engineering controls are used to the extent practical to reduce and maintain exposure to embryotoxins to and at acceptable levels. Such controls are augmented by appropriate administrative controls.

3. Whenever engineering and administrative controls are not practical to keep exposure at or below acceptable levels, personal

protective equipment and training for its proper use are provided and required to be used by employees who may be affected by such compounds.

4. Females of childbearing capability are to be excluded from work areas where: (a) there is potential for exposure to an embryotoxin for which an acceptable exposure level cannot be set or (b) whenever engineering and administrative controls augmented as appropriate by personal protective equipment are determined to be inadequate to ensure acceptable levels of exposure.

In accordance with known scientific criteria, DuPont scientists designated seven substances that required special controls because of their potential teratogenic effects (OTA 1985: 265). Boxes A and B illustrate somewhat different approaches to fetal protection by Shell Oil Company and Exxon.

BOX A

Fetal Protection Policy of Shell Oil Company

Shell has an explicit policy for protection of the embryo/fetus in the workplace. Its purpose is to address and/or manage the risk when existing standards, if any, may not be adequate; when releases may occur despite controls that could lead to excessive exposure; or when the employee may not know that she is pregnant. The focus of the policy is to provide as much information as is available on the risk to an embryo/fetus through individual counseling of female employees. In hiring women there is no distinction made on the basis of age, reproductive, or marital status. A woman is informed of the company's assessment of risk and is also urged to consult her own physician for additional advice if she becomes pregnant or is planning a pregnancy.

First, attempts are made to reduce exposure through the use of engineering or other controls; jobs in which a fetotoxic or teratogenic agent is present are classified according to the potential for exposure to such agents. For example, a class A job is deemed to present no significant risk; class B jobs may have levels of exposure that pose a potential threat through the mechanism of fetotoxicity; class C jobs may have levels of exposure that pose a risk through the mechanism of teratogenicity.

The specific criteria for job categorization are as follows:

○ Category A. Job assignments involving substances that have been suggested to have embryo-fetotoxicity but for which the company believes the pattern of evidence does not indicate that the health of an embryo/fetus would be endangered.

○ Category B. Job assignments determined by the company as posing a potential threat to the embryo/fetus as a result of cumulative exposure or possible exposure above normal operating conditions, but where the company believes the threat to the embryo/fetus prior to detection of pregnancy is not significant.

○ Category C. Job assignments determined by the company as posing a clearly defined risk to an embryo/fetus because of the possibility of early embryo/fetotoxic and/or teratogenic effects occurring before a pregnancy is detected.

Categorization is to be based on both qualitative and, where possible, quantitative assessment of the likelihood that a given substance could produce adverse effects on the embryo/fetus. This is accomplished through a thorough review of the available scientific literature relative to the substance under consideration. Reported effects, if any, are assessed with due consideration for the levels that produced those effects and the comparable levels of exposure in the workplace.

The effectiveness of engineering (or other) controls is factored into the categorization process when we examine existing air-monitoring data as a part of risk assessment.

The risk to the woman who is unaware of her pregnancy is explained in the definition of category C above. A job may be categorized as C irrespective of the level of exposure should we identify a possibility of an accidental release, spill, or other event that might result in high levels of exposure for a short period.

Although local union contracts and policies may vary as to eligibility for medical transfer, a woman in any job category may ask to be transferred to another job if she is planning to be pregnant or is pregnant. There is no mandatory rule that a woman inform the company when planning a pregnancy.

In general, the company's experience to date in assessing risks has been that controls instituted to protect against carcinogenic risk more than adequately protect against adverse effects on the embryo/fetus.

SOURCE: OTA 1985: 264–265.

BOX B

Exxon Guidelines for Handling
Reproductive Risks in the Workplace

A developing body of scientific evidence indicates that some exposures of humans to such environmental factors as personal lifestyle choices, drugs, certain chemicals, and physical agents such as ionizing radiation can lead to reproductive effects in both males and females. These effects may result in infertility, miscarriages, embryotoxicity, birth defects, and changes in genetic material capable of being inherited. There is particular concern about exposures to the fetus, since it may be especially susceptible to the effects of external agents at exposures that have no effect on an adult. Moreover, an embryo often is most vulnerable to the effects of toxic substances during its earliest development, perhaps even before the mother-to-be is aware of her pregnancy.

Currently, no well-defined or generally accepted approach to the prevention of reproductive risks to employees exists, because of scientific uncertainties and differing public opinion. However, the company has a moral obligation to concern itself with the potential reproductive effects of substances or agents used or produced in its operations.

In accordance with the policy on toxic and hazardous substances and in recognition of the company's obligation to provide healthful working conditions, the company's guidelines to reduce the potential for reproductive hazards in their workplaces are outlined below:

A. Review operational and associated biological, chemical, and physical workplace exposures in light of the best presently available information to identify those that might have the potential to be a reproductive hazard.

B. Inform all exposed employees of any potential hazards to the reproductive system from toxic substances to which they are exposed and educate them in the use of personal protective equipment and safe work practices.

C. Control the exposure to such potential hazards to acceptable levels for all employees through the best combination of:
   1. process or equipment engineering designs
   2. work practice arrangements (such as shortened exposure times where necessary), and
   3. personal protective equipment.

When there is insufficient basis for the scientific definition of an exposure level with an acceptable reproductive risk, the medical department will designate an interim standard that incorporates an appreciable safety factor, and will seek the development of information required for a "permanent" standard.

D. In cases where certain employees are particularly susceptible to the known toxicity of a specific agent, and where exposure cannot be controlled to acceptable levels, implement the indicated protective work assignment practices, including, if necessary, total restriction from potential exposure.

E. Seek on a continuing basis new information on the potential reproductive toxicity associated with manufacturing processes and materials produced, used, transported, and sold by the corporation.

F. Terminate the manufacture or use of such toxic substances where it is not possible to prevent unacceptable risks to reproductive functions.

SOURCE: OTA 1985:266–267.

Exclusionary policies are viewed by some industries as a necessary action because less extreme precautions are infeasible or unworkable. Industry representatives maintain that the elimination of hazards is not technically feasible to make many workplaces—such as lead smelters—completely safe for the fetus (Randall 1987:89). Furthermore, economic constraints and scientific uncertainty often make a fully safe workplace environment impossible. The director of Health and Environmental Services at Dow Chemical, Perry J. Gehring, on defending his corporation's perspective stated, "The difficulty and cost of implementing good industrial hygiene shouldn't be used as a blanket excuse to exclude women. But if the cost is going to rise exponentially to reach a level for uniquely fetal toxins, it's justified to take women out of the workplace" (Bayer 1982:636).

Similarly, it is argued that the monitoring of exposure levels may pose numerous difficulties (e.g., monitoring might be technically infeasible, financially burdensome, or intrusive). Also, scientific uncertainty may remain regarding the degree of hazard and the threshold exposure levels of specific agents (OTA 1985:264). For these reasons employer representatives defend the conservative policy of excluding pregnant women to avoid even the remote chance that they would receive close to the permissible level of exposure to the fetus. In the terms of the Synthetic Organic Chemical Manufacturers Association, "Since the fetus derives no primary benefit from its unknown or known presence in the workplace, it should not be exposed to excessive risks . . . this is a small price for mothers, potential mothers, and society to pay" (Bayer 1982:644).

There is some evidence to suggest that pregnant women are especially vulnerable to workplace toxicants. Many physiological functions operate at peak efficiency during pregnancy. Blood volume increases by about 50 percent and there is increased overall metabolic activity as the body ensures its full access to oxygen and nutrients. Ironically, according to Chavkin (1984:198), this physiologic efficiency in an environment full of toxins probably magnifies their effects. Also, because of marked changes in respiration during pregnancy the pregnant woman achieves a higher concentration of inspired gas in her lungs, thus increasing the amount of potential toxicants absorbed. The increased flow of blood further heightens this effect. Finally, particularly during the first half of pregnancy there is an extensive storage of fat, which expands the depot where fat-soluble toxins such as pesticides and organic solvents can be stored. "The peak physiological efficiency that characterizes pregnancy may be a double-edged sword, magnifying a pregnant woman's effective exposure to environmental hazards" (Chavkin 1984:199). Although these facts might not justify exclusionary policies, they do warrant concern over the health of pregnant workers.

Several arguments are used by employers to extend exclusionary policies from pregnant women to all fertile women. First, although the risk of fetal damage (other than spontaneous abortion, which is likely to go unnoticed) is low at the very beginning of gestation, beyond that early stage but before the woman knows she is pregnant major structural injury to the fetus may occur. Policies of temporary job rotation based on notification of pregnancy to the employer, therefore, would be ineffective, because major damage might have already occurred. A second reason given for excluding all fertile women is that some toxicants such as lead are retained in the body long after exposure. Thus, even if the woman is not exposed after she becomes pregnant, the fetus could be harmed by the woman's preconception exposure.

The second rationale used to defend implementation of fetal protection policies centers on employer concern over the economic costs of possible liability suits from children who are exposed to toxicants through their mother during gestation. It is not surprising in our litigious society that employers are fearful of liability stemming from workplace hazards. Even though no lawsuit has been won on behalf of a child born with occupationally related birth defects, concern of employers over the economic ramifications of huge damage claims and the resulting negative publicity is an understandable one. Unlike the claims of injuries to workers themselves, claims by the children of exposed workers are not covered by workman's compensation laws, which strictly limit the economic stakes even where injury is clearly work-related. Furthermore, the courts have generally agreed that workers' compensation is an exclusive remedy, effectively precluding all other remedies including tort action (see the discussion of these statutes later).

Because workers' compensation coverage has not been extended to children who suffer prenatal injuries resulting from reproductive hazards in the workplace, Katz (1989:213) argues that employers' fear of future tort liability is a legitimate one. Children who suffer prenatal (or preconception) injuries therefore might sue the employer in tort for limitless money. "Moreover, even if a female employee risked the exposure to a reproductive hazard and sought workers' compensation, she could not forfeit the tort cause of action that accrues to the child. Employers are therefore exposed to a potentially tremendous financial burden" (Katz 1989:213)).

Interestingly, employers have tended not to justify FPPs based on a risk of early spontaneous abortion. Becker suggests this is because employer liability for such incidents would be limited; the female employer would usually be able to seek, at most, medical expenses and disability benefits for any period of temporary disability under the applicable workers' compensation system (1986:1228–1229). Because there is no born child to sue in such a case and because the combination of Title VII and *Roe v. Wade* (1973) would make it difficult to justify FPPs on such a basis, spontaneous abortion has not been accorded attention as a reproductive risk warranting exclusion by most employers.

Some employers have maintained that they have been put into a legal bind because of incompatibility between requirements of the Occupational Safety and Health Act (OSH Act) of 1970 and Title VII. They contend that under the OSH Act they are charged with the responsibility of providing a safe and healthy workplace, and that the only way to guarantee a safe workplace for the fetus is through the exclusion of the female worker from the hazardous workplace setting. On the other hand under Title VII they are responsible for ensuring equal employment opportunities for women. Employers adopting FPPs have opted for fetal health (even though the OSH Act does not include mention of the fetus) and have argued that a good faith belief that a policy promotes fetal health should insulate them from liability for sex discrimination under Title VII.

In part because of the need to defend FPPs on the basis of fetal health responsibilities and because courts have held that the avoidance of tort liability in itself is not an adequate defense of discriminatory policies, most employers have emphasized the humanitarian arguments in their defense of FPPs. Furthermore, because Title VII does not allow differential treatment of women for economic reasons, most public statements in support of exclusionary policies cite the moral duty to avoid injuring future generations as the prime rationale in instituting FPPs.

Despite the obvious constraints that concern for fetal vulnerability to workplace hazards puts on women's advances and its conflict with trends toward equality in the workplace, concern for fetal welfare is growing. "The fetal protection programs that exist today are evidence that the balance between women's privacy rights and fetal health is moving toward the interest in preserving fetal health" (Clement et al. 1987:524). Supporters of fetal protection policies emphasize state interest in protecting the health of the fetus. Attorneys Nothstein and Ayres (1981:316), for instance, assert that the state "probably has the right to promulgate safety standards in order to preclude women with reproductive capacity from exposing themselves to workplace hazards that significantly increase the risk of birth defects, even before a child is conceived." Another observer concludes:

> But when fetal health is implicated, sex-based discrimination may well be excusable. Given the social and economic costs of producing and caring for defective children and the substantial likelihood that the employment of workers in unhealthful environments will result in the birth of such children, it is justifiable to exclude some members of one sex from a very narrow class of industries in order to prevent this outcome—as long as the exclusion is in fact narrowly tailored, objectively applied, and based upon credible scientific evidence.   (Howard 1981:836).

What constitutes "credible scientific evidence" and "objectively applied" exclusion? And most important, who decides: the woman, the employer, the government?

Criticisms of Fetal Protection Policies

Opponents of FPPs hold that the arguments of supporters used to justify exclusionary policies are fallacious on many grounds. First, the fear of employer liability is greatly exaggerated. In the only reported case involving a child's exposure to lead through maternal employment (*Security National Bank v. Chloride Inc.* 1985) the child lost, even though it argued that the employer had violated the OSHA lead standard. Although Becker argues that it is impossible to state with certainty the standard for employer liability in tort for injuries to workers' children, under general tort principles there "would seem to be no basis for holding an employer liable for fetal harm if Title VII bans sex-specific fetal vulnerability policies, the employer fully informs the woman of the risks, and the employer has not acted in a negligent manner"

(1986:1244). Under these circumstances the employer has done only what it was legally obligated to do under Title VII. Furthermore, even if the child could prove negligence on the part of the employer, physical causation for fetal torts would be difficult to prove because of the lack of firm evidence linking maternal workplace exposure to fetal injury (Becker 1986:1245). At best, then, employers' concern over potential liability in the absence of FPPs is based on a misguided interpretation of tort law, according to some legal analysts.

Employers are also open to criticism for a consistency in setting risk levels for exclusion. Although some companies defend FPPs on the ground that any risk of harm to the fetus no matter how remote is unacceptable and therefore ground for exclusion of all fertile women, they do not set the same stringent standards to protect the workers themselves. Of course, if they did exclude all workers from hazardous workplaces using the same conservative criteria, many industries would have to close. Similarly, while some company managers have argued that they should establish FPPs on the basis of a good faith belief that the policy protects the fetus without conclusive scientific evidence of a risk to the unborn, they have argued for a considerably different standard of evidence when OSHA has attempted to impose the costs of worker health on employers. For instance in *Industrial Union Department v. American Petrol Institute* (1980), employers successfully argued that the costs of worker safety could be imposed on them only when there was scientifically proven evidence of health risks, not simply when OSHA in good faith believes a risk exists (Becker 1986:1228).

In targeting women of childbearing age, employers assume that the female reproductive system is at greater risk from workplace hazards than that of the male and that fetal health risks are greater through pre- and postconception maternal exposure than preconception paternal exposure. They further assume that every woman of childbearing age will get pregnant and that women are not capable of planning pregnancies (Chavkin et al. 1983). According to the majority staff of the House Committee on Education and Labor, these assumptions are seldom supported by medical or scientific evidence, either because such evidence does not exist or because it contradicts the assumptions. As a result FPPs often "constitute a pretext for a new form of arbitrary gender stereotyping in which employers incorrectly assert that fetal health risks are primarily or exclusively traceable to women (1990:7).

Fetal protection policies are criticized as being both over- and underinclusive. Critics claim that policies that exclude all fertile women are overinclusive because not all women of childbearing age are going to become pregnant. Such policies assume that the probability that any given fertile woman will become pregnant is sufficiently high to justify excluding her from a job for which she is otherwise qualified. This assumption ignores the fact that most women choose to control their reproductive lives. In addition, by age thirty-four at least 89 percent of all women have borne all the children they expect to bear (Scott 1984:181). Moreover, only one out of five thousand women aged forty-five to fifty-nine has a child in a given year, and for blue-collar women over age thirty the birth rate may be less than 2 percent (Becker 1986:1233). FPPs that exclude all fertile women therefore are overinclusive and ignore the fact that many of these women will not have children.

On the other hand FPPs are criticized as being underinclusive because they assume that exposure of only the fertile female employee puts a child at risk. As discussed in chapter 3, at this time gender-based exclusion is not warranted on the basis of available medical and scientific evidence. As the 1985 OTA study concluded, "There is no biological basis for assuming that either the embryofetus or the female is more susceptible [to reproductive toxicants] than the male" (1985:68). By excluding only fertile females, therefore, FPPs are neither protecting potential children nor the reproductive health of fertile males.

In some cases employers have implemented FPPs without any scientific evidence to support their sex-based distinctions. Others have investigated a suspected hazard only to find that the necessary research does not exist or that there is evidence of risk through the female but no comparative research regarding risks to the male reproductive system. In their study of Massachusetts' industries, Paul, Daniels, and Rosofsky found that the criteria used for exclusion of female employees "bore little relationship to current scientific knowledge about the effects of particular substances or about the categories of workers truly at risk" (1989:277). For instance, only women were excluded from working with lead and radiation, even though exposures may present reproductive risks to both male and female employees.

Despite OSHA's assumption that a health hazard affects both men and women unless proven otherwise as a matter of general policy, FPPs seldom address the risks posed by workplace hazards in a comprehensive manner. Whether employers have actually disregarded hard evidence of male-related fetal health risks or have chosen to avoid finding out if such risks exist, they have generally adopted underinclusive policies that serve neither the interests of workplace health nor the employment rights of women (Committee on Education and Labor 1990:8).

FPPs are especially hard on women because the years of childbearing roughly correspond to those years for advancement in most occupations. Many women who are going to achieve success in their preferred professions lay career foundations between ages twenty and thirty-five, the same years when they are likely to have children (Chamberlain 1984:4). FPPs, therefore, threaten to undermine the attempts of women to choose a career at the very point in their lives when work is most critical to achieve that goal.

Fetal Protection Policies: Old Protectionism Under a New Guise?

Many observers see the FPPs established in the 1970s and 1980s as a return to the protectionist policies applied to women early in the century, which were supposedly eliminated by Congress and the Court (Becker 1986; Accurso 1985; Hubbard 1990). Rosalind Petchesky contends that this focus on fetal rights brings us back "to the Victorian notion that a woman's childbearing capacity—in short her biology—should determine where and whether she may work" (1979:233). For Petchesky and other feminists the real goal of these exclusionary policies is not to protect the women employee or even her potential child but rather to reverse the gains made because of Title VII and the PDA.

By viewing women as a class in terms of their reproductive function FPPs, it is argued, fail to treat women as individuals with a capacity to make decisions (Accurso 1985). Similarly, Linda Howard (1981:836) rejects the "romantic paternalism" of industry's attempts to protect women by not allowing them to work in high-risk positions. Karen Maschke rejects the term "protection" as applied to these policies and contends that its "application to women workers has been inconsistent, its meaning has been distorted, and its extension to male workers has been free of the restrictive aspect that applies to women" (1991:2). While Judith Baer does not suggest that these policies result from some "secret conspiracy among corporations," she concludes that fetal protection policies have an "eerie similarity to the old protective labor laws" (1991:9).

Some of the similarities between recent FPPs and old protective laws are, indeed, striking. Although FPPs are often less explicit than state protective laws and do not depend on direct state action for implementation, many of their basic assumptions and their ultimate impact on women are identical. According to Mary Becker (1986) there are at least five problems that are common to both types of protective policies. First, in each case exclusionary policies have been adopted without adequate scientific grounding. Although the data concerning the reproductive health risks of a few toxicants are more conclusive than they were in the past, what "is known about reproductive health hazards is far outweighed by what is unknown. . . . There are consequently no reliable estimates as yet of the basic measures of reproductive risk in the workplace" (OTA 1985:3).

Second, supporters of state protective laws, no matter how well intentioned, did not consider the alternatives women who were excluded from jobs faced. They saw women uniformly dependent on men and assumed that women's financial contributions to their families were less important than their biological functions. If anything, today women's economic role is even more critical. Families with children often need two incomes to make ends meet (Chamberlain 1984:4). Furthermore, with an ever greater proportion of households headed by women and with an increasing proportion of those households in poverty, entry into tradition-

ally male, high-paying positions is important both to women and
their dependents (Becker 1986:1229–1230). When a woman worker
is fired or not hired under an FPP, she might very well end up
unemployed and almost certainly lower paid, with fewer fringe
benefits. As with the proponents of state protective laws, supporters of FPPs do not consider the negative effects both on the
woman and her family of being excluded from a high paying
position. Finding alternative employment will be especially difficult for a pregnant woman and loss of health coverage at this
critical time might in fact cause more risk to the fetus than the
workplace hazard.

The third problem present in both types of exclusionary policies is that women are not regarded as individuals who have
autonomous interests and potential apart from their families.
Women are viewed primarily in terms of their reproductive functions and any independent interests in employment or career
they have must yield to the interest of their potential children.
Their interests are viewed as so weak that they are "easily trumped
by the interests of beings who may never exist" (Becker
1986:1232). FPPs that exclude all fertile women assume they
have domestic responsibilities for others that take precedence
over any economic role.

The fourth problem similar in both early protectionist policies
and FPPs is that women are excluded only when they are viewed
as marginal workers, that is, where male workers traditionally
have filled the positions. No state laws or FPPs protect women
from hazards in those industries that depend heavily on a female
work force. Despite known reproductive hazards in the clothing/
textile industry, in laundry/drycleaning establishments, for mi-
grant workers, and for hospital workers, FPPs are uncommon in
these work areas. In fact, FPPs have been adopted almost exclusively in unionized industries with rigid pay scales where the
increased costs of hiring women cannot be offset by paying women
less. The conspicuous absence of FPPs in occupations that are
highly dependent on women to supply relatively low-cost labor
raises serious questions concerning the motivation for such policies and for the genuineness of society's concern for the fetus.
The argument that fetal protection is but another pretext for

exclusion of women from high-paying jobs in industry is difficult to refute under these circumstances.

Finally, as in the earlier debate over protectionist laws, proponents of FPPs have dismissed the possibility that women are in a better position than employers to make reproductive decisions. Women continue to be viewed by many employers as incompetent to make choices that affect their potential offspring. As pointed out by Becker, however, unlike the employer, the individual woman is able to consider the advantages and the disadvantages of a particular job for herself and her dependents (1986:1241). Moreover, because a pregnant woman is especially concerned with the health of her progeny, if she decides to continue working in a hazardous job after being fully informed of the risk by the employer, then it is likely that the alternatives to the hazardous job are less advantageous to the unborn child in which she has the most interest.

Fetal protection policies although not widespread or uniform throughout industry have engendered considerable controversy because they exclude women from selected workplaces, not out of concern for women's reproductive health but in the interests of fetal health. Although the focus of protection differed from past state protective laws the result was identical; the exclusion of women from high-paying, male-dominated occupations. At the same time there were virtually no corresponding attempts to implement FPPs in hazardous workplaces such as hospitals, dry-cleaners, and the textile industries, all of which are heavily dependent on a female work force. It is not surprising that the establishment of FPPs led to calls for government action to invalidate them on grounds of society's commitment to equal employment opportunity for women. Chapter 5 analyzes the response of the courts and regulatory agencies to FPPs.

5 | Government Response to Fetal Protection Policies After Title VII

As discussed in chapter 2 the passage of Title VII of the Pregnancy Discrimination Act in 1978 made it clear that the intent of Congress was to include discrimination on the basis of pregnancy as a clear case of sex discrimination. Although this amendment put pregnancy discrimination on a par with other forms of sex discrimination, Title VII provided exceptions to the prohibition of discrimination. The stringent BFOQ defense against facially discriminatory treatment of women is available to employers who can prove that pregnancy or pregnancy-related conditions are a hindrance to the performance of a particular job. Alternately, in cases of disparate impact the less stringent business necessity defense is allowable if the employer can prove that there is a "sufficiently compelling" business interest that overrides the discriminatory impact of an otherwise sex neutral policy.

Court Response to Fetal Protection Policies

Court action in pregnancy discrimination cases in the 1980s largely turned on the application of these defenses. Questions focused on whether discriminatory policies of employers could stand on a business necessity defense or required the more narrow BFOQ defense. The varied and contradictory responses of both trial and appellate courts to the application of fetal protection policies under Title VII led the way to clarification in 1991 by the Supreme Court in one of the few unanimous decisions of that term.

Wright v. Olin Corporation

The first appellate court to hear a Title VII sex discrimination suit grounded on the pregnancy-based distinction was the Fourth Circuit Court in *Wright v. Olin Corp.* (1982). In this case a class of affected workers and the EEOC brought suit against Olin Corporation charging that certain practices and policies of the employer were in violation of Title VII. Prominent among these alleged violations was the defendant's "female employment and fetal vulnerability program" that excluded women from some jobs and restricted access to others based solely on fertility or pregnancy.

Olin's "fetal vulnerability" program created three job classifications. "Restricted jobs" were those that require contact with or exposure to chemicals known or suspected to be harmful to fetuses. Only women over sixty-three years of age or medically diagnosed as infertile could be placed in restricted jobs. "Controlled jobs" were those that may require very limited contact with harmful chemicals. Pregnant women could work in controlled jobs only after case-by-case evaluation. Nonpregnant women could work in controlled jobs after signing a form stating that they recognized the existence of risk. Finally, "unrestricted jobs" were those that present no known hazard to a pregnant woman or her fetus. These jobs were open to all women. The trial court concluded that the program did not violate Title VII. The central finding was that the policy was instituted for "sound medical and humane reasons," not with the intent or purpose to discriminate against females because of their sex but with the goal to protect the unborn fetus. The plaintiffs appealed the decision to the Fourth Circuit U.S. Court of Appeals.

The appellate court clearly made an effort to reconcile Title VII and fetal vulnerability to workplace hazards. It addressed the critical question, Under what circumstances and on what basis

can employment practices avowedly designed to protect the unborn fetuses of women from workplace dangers be justified despite their "disproportionate adverse impact upon women's employment opportunities?" Reversing the district court the appellate court conceded that the fact situation before them did not "fit
with absolute precision" into any of the developed theories of
Title VII claims and defenses. The court agreed that the plaintiffs
had established a prima facie case of Title VII violation and
summarily rejected Olin's contention that the facts presented a
facially neutral disparate impact case. However, the court also
rejected Olin's contention that the facts required a facial discrim-
ination-BFOQ analysis because, the court noted, the extreme
narrowness of the job performance BFOQ defense "would prevent the employer from asserting a justification defense [i.e.,
business necessity] which under developed Title VII doctrine it is
entitled to present" (at 1185, n. 21). The court concluded that
disparate impact-business necessity theory was more suited for
application to fetal vulnerability policy cases than the discriminatory treatment analysis applied by the trial court.

Using the disparate impact model the *Olin* court determined
that Olin's fetal vulnerability policy did have a disparate impact
on women and therefore constituted a prima facie violation of
Title VII that could only be rebutted by a business necessity
defense. The court rejected the argument, however, that all classifications based on pregnancy constitute disparate treatment for
women and went about setting specific principles and evidential
requirements necessary to establish a business necessity defense.

According to *Olin*, the employer must prove by the "best
available scientific evidence" that: (1) significant risks of harm to
the unborn children would result from exposure of pregnant
women to toxic hazards in the workplace; (2) the risk is substantially confined to female and not male workers; and (3) the fetal
protection policy is effective in significantly reducing the risk (at
1190). Moreover, the burden may not be carried by proof that
the employer subjectively and in good faith believed its program
to be necessary and effective for that purpose. The essentially
scientific nature of these issues requires opinion evidence of qualified experts in the relevant scientific fields. To establish the

requisite degree of risk the employer need not prove the existence of a general consensus within the qualified scientific community. The employer must show, however, that within the community there is a considerable body of opinion that significant risk exists and that the risk is substantially confined to women workers, so that an employer could not responsibly fail to act on the assumption that this opinion might be the accurate one (at 1191). Once the employer has established the business necessity defense, the plaintiff may nevertheless prevail by proving that there are "acceptable alternative policies or practices" that would better accomplish the business purpose or accomplish it equally with less disparate impact.

In establishing a case for the possible protection of the unborn by limiting maternal employment opportunities, the *Olin* court placed fetuses in a larger classification of business licensees and invitees, whose safety as a proper matter of business concern lies somewhere between the two established classes of workers and customers. Unwilling to believe that Congress intended to strip all protection from licensees and invitees, the court concluded that this class of individuals—including unborn children—qualifies as a class whose safety might be the subject of business necessity (at 1189).

Noting that the trial court had not applied the appropriate analysis as laid down by *Olin*, the court remanded the claim to the trial court to allow Olin Corporation an opportunity to assert the affirmative defense of business necessity in a manner consistent with the court's guidelines. After the case was remanded, plaintiff Wright moved for voluntary dismissal on the grounds that her own claim was moot and that she no longer was a proper class representative. The trial judge refused to dismiss the case and a trial was held in which only Olin participated. The judge rendered another judgment favorable to Olin and on appeal from that remand, the Fourth Circuit vacated the trial court's opinion.

Although one observer conceded that the *Olin* opinion "strikes a needed balance between the employment rights of women and the moral responsibility of self-interest of employees," he concluded:

Unfortunately, because of the complexity and novelty of the cases presented and the absence of clear congressional intent concerning the tension between employment rights and the social and economic concerns surrounding fetal health, the Fourth Circuit's decision in *Wright* v. *Olin Corp.* may prove no sturdier than a house of cards. The court's opinion rests on three conclusions: (1) that the Pregnancy Discrimination Act did not transform all pregnancy-based distinctions into instances of disparate treatment; (2) that each established Title VII defense is not limited to one corresponding type of Title VII claim; and (3) that the defense of business necessity is sufficiently elastic to include concern for fetal vulnerability within its scope. Should the Supreme Court reject any of these findings, *Wright's* effect would be seriously undermined.   (Phillips 1983:337)

Hayes v. Shelby Memorial Hospital

The Eleventh Circuit (*Hayes v. Shelby Memorial Hospital* 1984) applied its own interpretation of how fetal protection policies should be treated under Title VII. In this case a certified X-ray technician was fired upon informing her supervisor she was pregnant. In light of scientific evidence on the risk of the fetus from nonionizing radiation the radiology department recommended that Hayes be removed from all areas where radiation was used. The hospital claimed that it fired Hayes because it was unable to find alternative employment for her. Following her dismissal the technician filed a sex discrimination suit against the hospital. The hospital defended its action on grounds of BFOQ and business necessity. The trial court concluded that the hospital had violated Title VII and awarded the technician damages. The hospital appealed the decision to the Eleventh Circuit.

The *Hayes* court examined the case under both facial discrimination and disparate impact theories and found the hospital's policy in violation of Title VII. The court began by establishing a presumption that if an employment policy applies only to women or pregnant women the policy is facially discriminatory. That presumption can be rebutted only if the employer can demonstrate that although its policy applies only to women it is both necessary and neutral in the sense that it effectively and equally protects all employees. In a fetal protection case the employer must show that there is an unreasonable risk of harm to fetuses of pregnant women employees from exposure to specific workplace hazards and that the hazards and that the hazard applies to pregnant women but not to men. Furthermore, in order to "avoid Title VII liability for a fetal protection policy, an employer must adopt the most effective policy available, with the least discriminatory impact possible" (at 1553). If the employer is unable to produce sufficient evidence to rebut the presumption of facial discrimination, the only defense the employer may raise is the more stringent BFOQ. Such a defense requires the employer to prove the excluded class is unable to perform the duties constituting the "essence" of the job. The court noted, however, that potential for fetal harm is irrelevant to the BFOQ issue unless it adversely affects the mother's job performance. But since that potential will seldom affect job performance, a successful BFOQ defense in a fetal protection case "should be rare," according to the *Hayes* court (Simon 1990:497).

In applying its analysis to the facts of the plaintiff's termination the *Hayes* court concluded that the hospital had failed to prove that its policy was necessary, neither had it established a BFOQ. It therefore affirmed the trial court's judgment in the plaintiff's favor. Like *Olin*, however, the *Hayes* court intimated that more exhaustive consideration of scientific information and more carefully crafted language could make exclusionary policies legally acceptable (Buss 1986:583). According to *Hayes*, a fetal vulnerability policy that applies to only one sex is in violation of Title VII unless the employer demonstrates "(1) that a substantial risk of harm exists; (2) that the risk is borne only by members of one sex; and (3) the employee fails to show that there are acceptable alternative policies that would have a lesser impact on the affected sex" (at 1554).

Related Pregnancy Discrimination Cases

During the same period that *Olin* and *Hayes* were decided several other pregnancy discrimination cases gave contradictory interpretations of Title VII. In *Harriss v. Pan American World Airways*

(1980), the Ninth Circuit Court read Title VII to transform all pregnancy distinctions into disparate treatment violations. It also allowed only the more difficult BFOQ defense for disparate treatment. Because fetal injuries do not ordinarily hamper the employee's job performance, however, employers would have a very difficult time using the BFOQ defense of discrimination against pregnant women to protect the fetus.

Although on the surface the facts surrounding *Zuniga v. Kleberg County Hospital* (1982) were almost identical to *Hayes* (the firing of a pregnant X-ray technician), because the events in *Zuniga* occurred prior to the effective date of Title VII a pregnancy-based distinction could not be characterized as facial discrimination. Nevertheless, the Fifth Circuit found the hospital policy to be discriminatory because of its impact on women and rejected the business necessity defense because the hospital failed to employ an "available, alternative, less discriminatory means of achieving its business purpose" (at 992). The plaintiff had explicitly requested a leave of absence in accordance with the hospital's own leave policies, but the request was denied. Moreover, the court suggested that the health of the fetus is more the concern of the mother than the employer, and unlike *Hayes*, cited conflicting authority as to whether the economic consequences of tort liability might ever constitute a business necessity for a fetal protection policy (at 992 n. 10).

Contradictory opinions were also rendered by two U.S. circuit courts in very similar cases involving women flight attendants. In *Levin v. Delta Air Lines, Inc.* (1984), the Fifth Circuit held that the airline's policy of removing pregnant flight attendants from flight duty was not in violation of Title VII. The court ruled that the discriminatory policy was justified by business necessity and was a reasonable response to the airline's safety concerns.

In contrast, the Fourth Circuit (*Burwell v. Eastern Air Lines, Inc.* 1980) refused to consider Eastern's concern for the health of the employee or her fetus a valid business necessity and held that its policy, which grounded pregnant flight attendants out of concern for the health of the fetus, was in violation of Title VII.

Eastern's contention that an element of business necessity is its consideration for the safety of the pregnant flight attendant and her unborn child is not persuasive. If this personal compassion can be attributed to corporate policy it is commendable, but in the area of civil rights, personal risk decisions not affecting business operations are best left to individuals who are the targets of discrimination.   (at 371)

Interestingly, unlike the *Hayes* or *Olin* courts, the *Burwell* court refused to limit its rejection of protective exclusionary policies to those that could not be objectively justified. Regardless of how commendable the employer's motives or evidence presented, excluding women from the workplace denies them their civil right to equal opportunity in employment (Buss 1986:587).

Johnson Controls

The key court decisions that led to the 1991 ruling of the Supreme Court centered on the fetal protection policy of Johnson Controls, a manufacturer of automotive batteries. Before the Civil Rights Act of 1964 Johnson Controls (previously Globe Union) did not employ women in its battery manufacturing jobs. In June 1977, however, it announced its first official policy regarding employment of women in lead exposure work. Although the policy stopped short of excluding women of childbearing age from lead exposure, it emphasized that a woman who expected to have a child should not choose a job with such exposure. The company also required a woman who wished to be considered for employment to sign a statement that she had been advised of the risk of having a child while she was exposed to lead.

Five years later, in 1982, Johnson Controls shifted from a policy of warning to a policy of exclusion. Between 1979 and 1983 eight employees became pregnant while maintaining blood levels in excess of 30 micrograms per deciliter, the critical level noted by OSHA for a worker planning to have a family. The company responded by announcing a broad exclusion of women from jobs that exposed them to lead. The policy stated that "women who are pregnant or who are capable of bearing children will not be placed into jobs involving lead exposure or which could expose them to lead through the exercise of job bidding, bumping, transfer or promotion rights." The policy defined women capable of bearing children as all women except those whose "inability to bear children is medically documented." Two separate and conflicting rulings involving this policy, one state and one federal, were given in response to Johnson Controls' fetal protection policy.

In April 1984 petitioners filed in the U.S. District Court for the Eastern District of Wisconsin a class action challenging the policy as sex discrimination in violation of Title VII. Among the plaintiffs were Mary Craig who had chosen to be sterilized in order to avoid losing her job, Elsie Nelson, a fifty-year-old divorcee, who had suffered a loss in compensation when she was transferred out of a job where she was exposed to lead, and Donald Penney, who had been denied a request for a leave of absence for the purpose of lowering his lead level because he intended to become a father. Upon stipulation of the parties the district court certified a class consisting of "all past, present and future production and maintenance workers" in United Auto Workers bargaining units at nine of Johnson Controls plants who have been and continue to be affected by the fetal protection policy. In 1988 (680 F. Supp.309) the district court granted the employer's motion for a summary judgment. Applying the three-part business necessity defense established in *Hayes* and *Olin*, the court concluded that while "there is disagreement among the experts regarding the effect of lead on the fetus," the hazard was established, by a "considerable body of opinion," that "a great body of experts are of the opinion that the fetus is more vulnerable to levels of lead that would not affect adults" and that the petitioners had "failed to establish that there is an acceptable alternative policy which would protect the fetus" (at 315–316). The court concluded that in view of the disposition of the business necessity defense it did not have to undertake a BFOQ analysis (at 316, n. 5).

In 1989 the Court of Appeals for the Seventh Circuit affirmed the summary judgment by a seven to four vote (886 F.2d 871). After citing a long history of concern for employee health by Johnson Controls, the majority held that the fetal protection policy was reasonably necessary to industrial safety. They noted that the proper standard for evaluating fetal protection policy was the defense of business necessity, but that even if the proper standard was BFOQ Johnson Controls was still entitled to summary judgment. According to the court, available scientific data indicates that the risk of transmission of harm to the fetus as a result of lead is confined to fertile female employees (at 889). Therefore, the employer's fetal protection policy was based upon real physical differences between men and women relating to childbearing capacity and was consistent with Title VII. The court also held that the union failed to show that less discriminatory alternatives would be equally effective to achieve Johnson Controls' purpose of protecting fetuses from substantial risk of harm created by lead exposure (at 901).

Dissents by several justices would have reversed the judgment and remanded the case for trial. Judge Posner, whose dissent was later cited extensively by the Supreme Court, argued that under Title VII a fetal protection policy that explicitly applied only to women could be defended only as BFOQ. His primary problem with the majority opinion was that whether Johnsons' policy is reasonably necessary to the normal operation of its business is a matter of degree that cannot be assessed "once and for all on so meager a record" (at 902). It would be a rare case where the lawfulness of such a policy could be decided on the defendant's motion for summary judgment. Judge Easterbrook went further and held that a fetal protection policy should never qualify as a BFOQ. Johnson Controls' stated objective of concern for the next generation is unrelated either to the company's ability to make batteries or to any women's ability or inability to work. "Concerns about a tiny minority of women (those who might become pregnant and whose exposure to lead might cause fetal harm) cannot set the standard by which all are judged" (at 913).

In a conflicting state ruling the California Court of Appeals, Fourth District (*Johnson Controls, Inc. v. California Fair Employment and Housing Commission* 1990), reversed a superior court decision finding that Johnson Controls' fetal protection policy did not violate the California Fair Employment and Housing Commission. The appellate court held that the fetal protec-

tion program "unquestionably discriminates against women" because only women are affected by its terms (at 160). Although
the court admitted that the dispute is "fraught with public policy
considerations" and pits state interests in protecting the health of
employees and their families against state interests in safeguard-
ing equal employment opportunities for women, it concluded that
categorical discrimination against a subclass of women such as all
women of childbearing capacity except those proven to be sterile
violates the California statute prohibiting discrimination on the
basis of sex. "However laudable the concern by businesses such
as the Company [Johnson Controls] for the safety of the unborn,
they may not effectuate their goals in that regard at the expense
of a woman's ability to obtain work for which she is otherwise
qualified" (at 178). Moreover, even though Johnson Controls
counseled against sterilization the fetal protection program that
precluded hiring women capable of childbearing in certain high-
paying jobs was an invitation to women to have themselves
sterilized if they had a great enough need for the job. The
program thus violated the statute precluding employers from
requiring employees to become sterilized as a condition of employment (at 165). Contrary to the U.S. Court of Appeals in
International Union the California court held that Johnson Controls could not defend its fetal protection program as a BFOQ.

On March 20, 1991 the U.S. Supreme Court issued its ruling
on *International Union, UAW v. Johnson Controls, Inc.* on an
appeal from the Seventh Circuit. In a unanimous nine to zero
decision (with two concurring opinions) the Court reversed and
remanded the Seventh Circuit. The Court stated that the "bias in
Johnson Controls' policy is obvious" because fertile men, but not
fertile women, are given a choice as to whether they want to risk
their reproductive health by holding a particular job (at 7). They
noted that since their grant of certiorari the Sixth Circuit had
reversed a district court's summary judgment for an employer
that had excluded fertile female employers from foundry jobs
involving exposure to specific concentrations of air-borne lead. In
Grant v. General Motors Corp. (1990) the Sixth Circuit stated:
"We agree with the view of the dissenters in *Johnson Controls*
that fetal protection policies perforce amount to sex discrimina-

tion, which cannot logically be recast as disparate impact and cannot be countenanced without proof that infertility is a BFOQ" (at 1310). The majority opinion, authored by Justice Blackmun, agreed that Johnson Controls' fetal protection policy creates a facial classification and requires a BFOQ defense.

The Johnson Controls' policy classifies on the basis of gender and childbearing capacity rather than fertility alone, because it does not seek to protect the unconceived children of its male employees, despite "evidence in the record about the debilitating effect of lead exposure on the male reproductive system" (at 9). Johnson Controls chose to treat all its female employees as potentially pregnant; that choice "evinces discrimination on the basis of sex" in clear violation of Title VII (at 10). Furthermore, the absence of a malevolent motive does not convert a facially discriminatory policy into a neutral policy with a disparate impact.

After establishing the need for a BFOQ defense the Court turned to the question of whether Johnson Controls' policy is one of those "certain instances" that come within a BFOQ exception. In citing its previous holding in *Dothard v. Rawlinson* (1977), where danger to the woman herself does not justify discrimination, the Court reiterated that to qualify as a BFOQ a job qualification must relate to the "essence" or "central mission" of the employer's business (at 14).

> The unconceived fetuses of Johnson Controls' female employees, however, are neither customers nor third parties whose safety is essential to the business of battery manufacturing. No one can disregard the possibility of injury to future children; the BFOQ, however, is not so broad that it transforms this deep social concern into an essential aspect of battery-making.   (at 14)

Furthermore, within the Pregnancy Discrimination Act, Congress made clear that the decision to become pregnant or to work while being either pregnant or capable of becoming pregnant was reserved for each individual woman to make for herself. The Court concluded that the language of both the BFOQ provisions and the PDA that amended it as well as the legislative history and case law prohibit an employer from discriminating against a woman because of her capacity to become pregnant unless her reproductive potential prevents her from performing the duties of her job. The Court, therefore, had "no difficulty concluding that Johnson Controls cannot establish a BFOQ" (at 17).

Although the Court was divided on whether any fetal protection policies could ever conceivably be justified under the BFOQ defense (in concurring opinions White, Rehnquist, Kennedy, and Scalia did not rule this out), all nine justices agreed that Johnson Controls' policy did not. No matter how sincere Johnson Controls' fear of prenatal injury, it does not "begin to show that substantially all of its fertile women employees are incapable of doing their jobs" (at 18).

Finally, regarding the issue of liability Justice Blackmun concluded that the prospect of legal liability for employers in the absence of fetal protection policies seems "remote at best." Although more than forty states currently recognize a right to recover from prenatal injury based on either negligence or wrongdoing, and the concurring opinion of White states that "it is far from clear that compliance with Title VII will pre-empt state tort liability" (at 3), according to the majority,

> Without negligence, it would be difficult for a court to find liability on the part of the employer. If, under general tort principles, Title VII bans sex specific fetal-protection policies, the employer fully informs the woman of the risk, and the employer has not acted negligently, the basis for holding an employer liable seems remote at best.   (at 19)

Moreover, when it is impossible for an employer to conform with both state and federal requirements the Court had previously held that federal law preempts that of the states (see, e.g., *Florida Lime and Avocado Growers, Inc. v. Paul* (1963). If state tort law furthers discrimination in the workplace and prevents employers from hiring women who are capable of manufacturing the product as efficiently as men, then it will impede that accomplishment of Congress's goals in enacting Title VII (at 21).

According to the Court, the tort liability argument reduces to two "equally unpersuasive propositions": that Johnson Controls can solve the problem by resorting to exclusionary policy in violation of Title VII and the fear that hiring women will cost more because of law-suit damages. "The extra cost of employing members of one sex, however, does not provide an affirmative Title VII defense for a discriminatory refusal to hire members of that gender" (at 21). Congress specifically addressed the second proposition, according to the Court, and made the decision in the Pregnancy Discrimination Amendment to forbid special treatment of pregnancy despite the social costs associated with it. The Court concluded by reiterating its prior decisions that the incremental cost of hiring women cannot justify discriminating against them (at 21).

The impact of *Johnson Controls* on the status of prenatal injury torts will be discussed later. Suffice it to say, however, that the Court's implication that compliance with federal civil rights laws would shelter employers from damage suits if they met or exceeded OSHA standards of compliance raises serious concerns over women's tort alternatives. In the end, what was perceived by many women's rights groups as a decisive legal victory might be a bittersweet one. Judith Baer (1991:16), for instance, is troubled by Justice Blackmun's statement that "decisions about the welfare of future children must be left to the parents who conceive, bear, support, and raise them," because it is justification for the absence of childcare, parental leaves, and other programs that would make the lives of employed mothers less burdensome. Furthermore, "The reader [of Blackmun's opinion] searches in vain for any suggestion that employers have a duty not to expose their workers to harmful substances, or that women as childbearers have any rights to assistance from society" (Baer 1991:16). The ultimate impact of *Johnson Controls* will depend on how employers respond in the absence of fetal protection policies and how the courts deal with future workplace liability cases. This ruling also shifts emphasis back to the regulatory context of workplace hazards.

Regulatory Context of Fetal Vulnerability Policies

Another area of activity regarding fetal protection policy centers on state and federal regulatory action. Because of the varying and often confusing standards that have come through case law, some observers have argued that a more fruitful solution is to be found in government regulation of workplace hazards.

> As workplace pollutants, fetal hazards are more appropriately controlled through regulation than through judicial action. Courts, confined by the particular facts of a case and lacking administrative powers and scientific expertise, provide inadequate protection against environmental hazards.   (Buss 1986:591)

Ashford and Caldart (1983:562) agree that industrial control of reproductive hazards will come about not by court applications but rather by industry response to economic constraints or compliance with government regulations. In contrast, however, other observers doubt that regulation itself is capable of reconciling the conflicting interests through political mechanisms (Furnish 1980).

Reproductive hazards can potentially be regulated by a variety of federal agencies. Part of the regulatory confusion today results from jurisdictional conflict among these agencies. There are three appropriate sources of regulation: the Occupational Safety and Health Act (OSH Act), the Toxic Substances Control Act (TSCA), and Title VII of the Civil Rights Act.

The OSH Act was passed in 1970 in response to the Black Lung disease movement and pressure from labor unions for protection from workplace hazards. The purpose of the OSH Act is "to assure so far as possible every working man and woman in the Nation safe and healthful working conditions" (29 U.S.C. Sec. 6516, 970). The OSH Act gives the secretary of labor various mechanisms for regulating workplace safety and health, including a broad general duty clause, which provides that each employer "shall furnish to each of his employees employment and a place of employment which are free from recognized hazards that are causing or are likely to cause death or serious physical harm to his employees" (29 U.S.C. Sec. 654 (1)).

In 1978 OSHA promulgated the lead standard that, among other things, called for periodic blood tests of all workers exposed to lead, required medical removal of workers found to have blood lead levels exceeding standard acceptable levels, and mandated job protection with full pay and benefits upon removal for up to eighteen months (29 C.F.R.1910.1025 1984). Importantly, OSHA expressly rejected the notion that its lead standard should be different for men and women. According to OSHA, "The record in this rulemaking is clear that male workers may be adversely affected by lead as well as women. . . . Genetic damage in the egg or sperm cells . . . which can be passed on to the developing fetus . . . occurs prior to conception in either father or mother" (43 *Federal Register*, 52966, November 14, 1978). Despite this clear statement the Lead Industries Association, which represented all industries affected by the lead standard, continued to support only the exclusion of fertile women. Furthermore, it filed a lawsuit against OSHA challenging its rulemaking procedures, the substantive provisions of the standard, and the evidence used to frame the standard. It charged that the lead standard was set too low and that OSHA had exceeded its statutory authority in adopting the medical removal requirement (Maschke 1991:10).

In 1980 OSHA reiterated its view that all exclusionary policies like those imposed against pregnant women undermine the principle that the workplace should be a safe environment for all persons. Instead of discriminating against women of childbearing age or coercing them into ending their fertility exposure standards should be set that recognize such vulnerability. In other words, OSHA argued that high-risk industries should not be able to reduce their liability for damage awards by excluding classes of workers. Moreover, no worker should be forced to sacrifice her reproductive right to privacy in order to hold her job. OSHA became embroiled in the case involving American Cyanamid's exclusionary policy, which resulted in five women being sterilized at the Willow Island, West Virginia plant to keep their jobs. After considerable administrative litigation, in April 1981 the Occupational Safety and Health Review Commission dismissed OSHA's citation against American Cyanamid's Fetus Protection Policy, concluding that as a matter of law the hazard alleged by the secretary was not intended by Congress to be included under OSHA. Furthermore, the commission declared that the choice of sterilization is not the product of corporate policy but rather "grows out of economic and social factors which operate primarily outside the workplace."

The case eventually ended up in federal court (*Oil, Chemical and Atomic Workers v. American Cyanamid Co.* 1984) and was heard by the Circuit Court for the District of Columbia. Although the court admitted that the women who were sterilized in order to keep their jobs at the Willow Island plant "were put to a most unhappy choice" (at 450), it held that the "language of [OSHA] cannot be stretched so far as to hold that the sterilization option of the fetus protection policy is a 'hazard' of 'employment' under the general duty clause" (at 445). Furthermore, it stated that "the general duty clause does not apply to a policy as contrasted with a physical condition of the workplace" (at 448). In light of this decision it is questionable whether fetal protection policies would fall within the regulatory powers of the secretary of labor under OSHA.

Perhaps anticipating this response by the courts, late in the Carter administration guidelines were drawn up by OSHA, the EEOC, and the Office of Federal Contract Compliance Programs to specifically regulate these corporate policies. These guidelines, which focused on the rights of the woman to control her reproductive capacity and employment, would have tolerated exclusionary policies for pregnant women only as a last resort. Also, such protective actions would be temporary, pending full examination of systematic research as to the contribution of the male to fetal harm. Due to opposition from a broad variety of business groups concerned with governmental intrusion and feminist and trade union groups arguing that the guidelines were not strong enough, the proposed regulations were politically vulnerable. The decision on the part of the Reagan administration to withdraw the proposed guidelines was no surprise (Bayer 1982:650).

Although OSHA has authority under the OSH Act to set and enforce standards, perform inspections, and monitor industry compliance, court-imposed restrictions along with political interference and perennial staffing and funding shortfalls have limited its effectiveness. For instance, it has been stripped of its power to make surprise inspections and must obtain a court order to investigate a complaint. Moreover, OSHA itself has stated that inconclusive scientific evidence and its lack of jurisdiction over protection of the fetus make the agency's limited role in that area appropriate (OSHA 1987). As a result OSHA has virtually no involvement in regulating workplace hazards to the fetus. Consistent with the authorizing statute, whatever standards are established will be specifically designated to protect today's workers, not future generations (Sor 1986–87:171).

The EEOC was created as the administrative agency to enforce the provisions of Title VII, the primary basis for federal court actions on sex discrimination in the workplace. The EEOC has ninety days to act on any complaint of discrimination. It can investigate and either dismiss the complaint or find cause for the complaint and then attempt to conciliate between the parties. If the employer cannot or will not settle the case, the claimant has a right to sue in federal court. In theory then the OSH Act and the EEOC acting under Title VII together should be able to mandate a safe and healthy workplace for all employees without discrimination. Like OSHA, however, the EEOC has not taken a vigorous role in the debate over FPPs.

As noted earlier, according to a majority staff report released by the House Committee on Education and Labor (1990), the EEOC abdicated its enforcement responsibilities during the 1980s both in terms of individual case handling and interpretive guidance. The EEOC's decision under Chairman Clarence Thomas not to make a determination for complaints of discrimination resulting from FPPs represented an "entombment" of charges and helped keep exclusionary policies off the public agenda for a decade (Committee 1990:10). Although the commission made attempts to resolve these charges in 1989, most of the cases closed were "resolved" for administrative reasons such as a failure to locate the claimant rather than on the merits. Over one hundred charges were filed with the EEOC, and most challenged employer practices and policies that were facially discriminatory.

> The Commission nevertheless directed its investigative staff to forward all such charged to the agency's Office of Legal Counsel, which was instructed to do nothing. The EEOC never offered these charging parties any explanation as to why it refused to resolve their charges or enforce their civil rights.
>
> (Committee 1990:16).

The rationale given by EEOC was that it was unable to resolve these complex charges on a case-by-case basis because it lacked a comprehensive policy directive. According to the majority staff report, however, the failure to establish a comprehensive policy directive was the EEOC's own doing (Committee 1990:17).

In 1988 the EEOC finally issued its first policy guidance on reproductive and fetal hazards. The policy guidance declared that any practice that denies employment opportunities to one sex because of reproductive or fetal hazard, without similarly barring the other sex, is unlawful under Title VII. The EEOC, however, recognized the application of the less stringent business necessity defense in fetal liability cases, although it stated that employers invoking the defense must demonstrate that there is a substantial risk of harm to the fetus, that the risk is transmitted only through women, and that there are no less restrictive alternatives to excluding women from the workplace. Any such denial of employment must be justified by objective, scientific evidence, which the EEOC recognized as difficult given the inconclusiveness of much of the research on fetal hazards. Although the 1988 policy guidance did not attempt to declare unlawful every fetal protection policy, it was designed to prevent unnecessary restrictions on women's employment opportunities.

In January 1990 the EEOC published additional policy guidance in reaction to the Seventh Circuit Court's decision in *Johnson Controls*. The EEOC rejected the court's finding for placing the burden of proof on the employee. Because fetal protection cases involve facially discriminatory policies, the burden of proof must be on the employer to prove that its policy is a business necessity rather than on the plaintiff to prove that it is not. Moreover, the commission found that the significantly more narrow BFOQ is a better approach than business necessity to fetal protection policies. Therefore, in cases it handled after 1990 the EEOC required employers to prove that protection of fetuses from risk is reasonably necessary to the normal operation of their businesses and that the exclusionary policy is reasonably necessary to implement protections. Again, the emphasis is on objective evidence of substantial harm in order to restrict access to jobs. A subjective or good faith belief that an exclusionary policy is necessary to protect employees or to minimize liability is not a valid defense of exclusionary policies.

A third regulatory strategy would be to use Environmental

Protection Agency (EPA) powers under TSCA to regulate fetal hazards in the workplace. TSCA is a comprehensive statute that deals exclusively with toxicants. It provides a mechanism for the systematic testing of potential toxicants to determine whether they present a risk of injury to human health or the environment and it provides a means to control the production or use of those substances that present an unreasonable risk of injury. TSCA requires chemical producers, processors, and distributors to report to the EPA all information indicating that a substance presents a substantial risk. Moreover, the statutory threshold for triggering EPA action is low in that the information need only indicate there "may be a reasonable basis" to conclude the toxin is hazardous (15 U.S.C. Sec. 2603 (f2)). Despite the clear intention of Congress that TSCA be used to regulate reproductive hazards, the EPA has not generally exercised its authority to control suspected teratogens or mutagens (Ashford 1984:229).

It seems reasonable, as Emily Buss (1986:595) suggests, that any employer who concludes on the basis of scientific evidence that its workplace is not safe for the developing fetus should be considered in possession of information required under TSCA to be reported immediately to the EPA. Any evidence of workplace toxins deemed hazardous enough to women employees and their fetuses to justify an exclusionary employment policy should trigger a regulatory response. As logical as this approach seems, however, there appears to have been little initiative in this direction by the EPA under either the Reagan or Bush administrations despite their stated concern for protecting the health of the unborn. Also, the economic ramifications of this strategy could be significant and are likely instead to increase pressures for fetal protection policies implemented at the expense of women's employment rights.

Conclusions: The Government Response to FPPs

Although there are at least three regulatory strategies and enforcement agencies for dealing with policy issues surrounding reproductive hazards in the workplace and for dealing with fetal health, none have been effective in resolving the problems. For a combination of scientific, legal, and political reasons, OSHA, EEOC, and the EPA have been unable or unwilling to marshal their collective regulatory authority and act aggressively to deal with the difficult issue of reproductive hazards in the workplace, particularly as they relate to fetal health. Furthermore, until the Supreme Court invalidated FPPs in 1991, the judicial landscape was confusing and offered little guidance for employers or employees.

Despite the Court's prohibition of FPPs in *Johnson Controls*, the issues of what to do about reproductive and fetal health remain. Although the Court clarified the legal status of FPPs and restated the preeminence of women's rights to employment in these industries, it did not address the broader policy problems of how best to minimize occupational hazards to reproduction and maximize the health of our future children. Other than Justice Blackmun's opinion on the inapplicability of torts for fetal injury in the workplace, the Court did not address how those individual adults and children suffering injury due to workplace exposures ought to be compensated. Chapter 6 analyzes the current two-pronged compensation system and finds it lacking on all counts.

6 | Compensation for Reproductive Damage in the Workplace

There are currently two separate and largely exclusive systems for compensating victims of reproductive injury or disease resulting from workplace hazards. The differences in applicability and operation between the two systems help explain why employers seem to be less concerned with reproductive damage to the male or female workers, themselves, than they are with the potential economic loss resulting from those considerably less frequent situations where a fetus might be harmed through the exposure of its mother to workplace hazards during gestation. Whether the fears of the employers of liability in fetal harm are fully justified or not, the contrast between the two compensation systems is significant. The two approaches of compensating victims of occupational-related injury or disease are workers' compensation and civil torts.

Workers' Compensation

Each state requires that employers be covered by a form of insurance termed "workers' compensation." Under workers' compensation laws in all states workers are entitled to receive monetary compensation for medical expenses, lost wages, and other costs incurred as a result of job-related injury, disability, or death. Under workers' compensation the claimant does not have to prove employer fault or negligence nor even show that the worker was without fault or negligence. Monetary payments may be in the form of scheduled or formula benefits, depending on the state statute and the form of disability. In each case, the employer or its insurer may either accept the claim, settle it, or contest it. In the latter eventuality the claim can be appealed by either party to an appeals board or taken to the courts.

Although the details vary by state for most injured employees workers' compensation is the only official source of compensation. Because payments tend to be low, whether scheduled or formula, workers' compensation is often criticized as providing insufficient compensation and little incentive for providing a safe workplace (OTA 1985:179). This low level of compensation induces a liberal construction of the workers' compensation law, since huge sums of money are not at stake in any individual claim. On the other hand because it constitutes the exclusive remedy for the injured worker and abrogates the workers' rights to sue under common law, workers' compensation severely limits the possibility of large damage claims and thus protects the employer from the kinds of costs that can result if a case goes to court. In fact, employers are willing to liberally construe the laws in order to avoid the alternative of forcing failed workers' compensation claims into the tort system and exposing themselves to much higher economic risks.

Despite the general tendency of workers' compensation systems to be liberally interpreted, according to OTA (1985:289), reproductive harms will not generally satisfy the criteria for compensation because of three major requirements that are common across the state systems. First, workers' compensation requires evidence of diagnosis of personal injury or disease to the employee. It, therefore, generally precludes compensation for harm suffered to third parties as a result of the worker's exposure. Second-hand injury to the worker's spouse, fetus, child, or descendents is unlikely to be compensable (See table 6.1). The harm would have to be to the worker, such as injury resulting in infertility. As a result of this requirement cases involving damage

TABLE 6.1
Eligibility for Compensation for Reproductive Harms:
Personal Injury Criterion

	Victim		
Circumstances of Harm	Worker	Spouse	Embryo/Fetus or Offspring
1. Accidental injury to worker reproductive system or fetus	Eligible	Not eligible	Not eligible
2. Physical stress on worker	Eligible	Not eligible	Not eligible
3. Acute or chronic exposure of reproductive system or of fetus, spouse, or offspring	Eligible	Not eligible	Not eligible
4. "Side effect" cases (worker reproductive function impaired due to other injuries or diseases	Eligible but "other" injury or disease will be primary personal injury for compensation purposes—not reproductive injury	Not eligible	Not eligible

NOTE: "Personal" injuries include: sexual dysfunction (libido, potency), sperm and ovum abnormalities, infertility, illness during pregnancy and parturition, early and late fetal loss, and worker's age at menopause. Personal injuries do not include any injury to any person other than the worker (e.g., spouse, fetus that results in offspring, or offspring).
SOURCE: Office of Technology Assessment (1985:289).

to a fetus under present laws would go to the courts, thereby heightening the risk of a significantly larger employer payout if the claim is successful.

Even if a claim survives the personal injury requirement and satisfies the many procedural requirements, the claimant must show that he or she is disabled or otherwise qualified for some type of benefit. The most common types of benefit are those for job disability or loss of earnings, medical costs, and death and burial. This requirement of disability generally prevents the award of benefits for most claims of reproductive harm, because such harms do not usually disable the worker or prevent him or her from resuming work at the same job. If a reproductive injury or disease is sufficiently disabling to prevent the employee from performing the job for a temporary period, as in cases of injury to reproductive organs or job-induced miscarriage, the worker is entitled to collect disability benefits.

However even when workers are able to make a connection between a workplace exposure and their disability, the short duration of the disability period makes such workers much more likely to take advantage of employer-provided sick leave and health insurance benefits than face the expense, risk of the claim being denied, loss of medical privacy, and low benefits endemic to workers' compensation claims.   (OTA 1985:290)

In most cases, therefore, even though they theoretically are amenable to workers' compensation coverage, reproductive harm to workers is not in practice claimed.

The third requirement that must be met in most states is that compensation coverage applies only to claims "arising out of and in the course of employment." The burden of proof is on the claimant to convince the compensation board that the harm is a result of a workplace-induced injury or exposure. Again, even with relatively low requisites of evidence, because causation is so difficult in cases involving harm to the reproductive system it is often not possible to prove that it has resulted from a workplace hazard. Proof is especially difficult for those workers who have a type of reproductive problem that can result from nonoccupational causes such as sexual dysfunction, infertility, or spontaneous abortion. Because of the inherent problems in isolating causation, often due to the multiple etiologic factors involved, few workers' compensation cases involve reproductive harms (OTA 1985:294).

Despite the fact that state workers' compensation statutes are designed to be the exclusive remedy for workplace-induced injuries or diseases, most workers who are reproductively harmed do not qualify. To make matters worse, because this "exclusivity of remedy" doctrine has generally been construed by state courts as barring tort actions by the workers against the employer even if the worker does not file a workers' compensation claim, these victims of hazardous occupational exposure will by default bear the burden of their exposures to workplace health hazards (OTA 1985:13).

Although exceptions to the exclusivity rule have been explicitly rejected in approximately half the states, a few states have accepted causes of action from workers under narrow circumstances. For instance, a few states accept the "dual capacity" argument when the employer is also a manufacturer of the prod-

TABLE 6.2
Summary of Harms, Victims, Benefits Criteria and Causation Problems

Circumstances of Harm	Victim		
	Worker	Spouse	Fetus and Offspring
1. Accidental injury to worker reproductive system or fetus	Personal injury: eligible for compensation for medical benefits in all states and loss of function and disfigurement in a few states; no disability benefits unless earnings loss; no special causation problems.	No personal injury therefore no compensation	No personal injury therefore no compensation
2. Physical stress on worker	Personal injury: eligible for compensation for medical benefits in all states and loss of function in a few states; no disability benefits unless earnings loss; no special causation problems.	No personal injury therefore no compensation	No personal injury therefore no compensation
3. Acute or chronic exposure of worker, spouse, or fetus	If personal injury, will be for compensation for medical benefits in all states and loss of function benefits in a few states; no disability benefits unless earnings loss; special causation problems	No personal injury therefore no compensation	No personal injury therefore no compensation
4. "Side effect" cases where reproductive function impaired due to other injuries or diseases	Probably not applicable since other injury or disease will be primary personal injury for disability compensation, not the reproductive injury	Not applicable	Not applicable

SOURCE: Office of Technology Assessment (1985:293).

uct that causes the worker's injury (*Bell v. Industrial Vangas, Inc.* 1981, *Mercer v. Uniroyal, Inc.* 1977) or when a hospital employer provides negligent medical services to a hospital worker (*D'Angona v. Los Angeles County* 1980). Similarly, employer tort liability has been granted when an employer with knowledge of medical information as to an employee's risk of ill health fails to inform said worker (*Union Carbide Co. v. Stapleton* 1956) or when the employer acts negligently (*Reed Tool Co. v. Copelin* 1981).

A final exception available in a significant minority of states applies when an employer acts in a willful, deliberate, or intentional manner to cause injury. Under this exception employers have been sued for failing to warn workers of a known workplace hazard and not reporting that hazard as required by law (*Blankenship v. Cincinnati Milacron Chemicals, Inc.* 1982) or for deliberately failing to install safeguards at the workplace that are required to comply with OSHA standards (*Mandolidis v. Elkins Industries, Inc.* 1978). One employer was found negligent for fraudulently concealing the nature and extent of an employee's workplace-related injuries when this action aggravated the worker's condition (*Johns-Manville Corp. v. Contra Costa Superior Court* 1980).

For the most part, however, the courts have set very high standards of proof of deliberate intent, making it difficult for an injured worker to win. For instance, in *Phifer v. Union Carbide Corp.* (1980) failure of the employer to warn an employee of a hazard or provide protective clothing was held not to rise to the level of deliberate intent needed to invoke an exception to the exclusivity rule by a federal district court. Similarly, a Delaware court rejected an employee's claim against an employer for deception regarding the hazards of asbestos under the exclusivity rule (*Kofren v. Amoco Chemicals Co.* 1982).

> Thus in most States, recklessly endangering an employee is not enough to create tort liability for an employer . . . an employer who has knowledge of an occupational disease hazard but fails to warn the employees at risk, or who in fact fraudulently misrepresents the safety of the workplace . . . is still protected by the exclusivity rule and escapes tort liability.   (OTA 1985:318)

It is particularly difficult to obtain court exceptions to the exclusivity rule for reproductive harm even when the disability does not qualify for workers' compensation. The Michigan Court of Appeals (*Cole v. Dow Chemical Co.* 1982), for example, rejected a suit by a couple seeking damages for sterility alleged to be caused by workplace exposure to the nematocide Dibromochloropropane (DBCP)—even though the worker's sterility was not compensable under Michigan's workers' compensation statute. Also, a tort action brought by five workers against Dow Chemical claiming that their exposure to DBCP caused carcinogenesis, mutagenesis, and sterility was dismissed on the grounds that claims were subject to the exclusive jurisdiction of workers' compensation (*Vann v. Dow Chemical Co.* 1983).

Even in those jurisdictions where exemptions from the exclusivity rule are allowed, however, if the companies comply with OSHA or other regulatory requirements and disclose known risk information to the workers it is unlikely that torts for reproductive harm to workers will be successful. To some extent this explains why industry seems less concerned about reproductive hazards for their employees than about harm to potential unborn. Because those unborn so harmed are unlikely to be covered by conventional workers' compensation schemes and the strict limits for monetary payments they contain, employers are faced with the possibility of unlimited liability claims from children injured prenatally or even preconceptionally through the presence of their mother in a hazardous workplace. Attention is now turned to the current status of prenatal injury torts to determine whether they in fact represent the threat that employers feel they are.

Framing a Cause of Action for Prenatal Injury

In the past several decades major changes have occurred in the body of case law surrounding the processes of birth and pregnancy. Preconception, conception, and prenatal legal actions are commonplace, in part due to alterations in social values regarding birth and pregnancy. Major causes of the growing legal attention to these subjects are the recent advances in medical science discussed earlier, which have brought about significant changes to the physiological aspects of the birth process and altered perceptions of it. "In short, the advances in medical science have reshaped the way American society thinks about birth" (Winborne 1983:4).

Along with the altered values and the advances in medical science many legal controversies have arisen regarding prenatal and preconception injuries as well as the birth process. The growing number of these birth and pregnancy cases are forcing judicial consideration of many new and novel causes of action. This cluster of topics surrounding prenatal injury "presents a series of anguished questions, inevitably enmeshing the torts watcher in what Darwin called 'the web of life' " (Lambert 1983:65). Terms like "wrongful pregnancy", "wrongful life," and "wrongful birth" are quickly emerging, and they result in a critical questioning of previous legal and policy assumptions. It is not surprising that there is wide divergence in the reaction of the courts to these novel cases, both in recognizing a cause of action and in determining the appropriate amount of damages if any to be awarded.

The child's right to recover from a third party for prenatal injuries, although largely unquestioned today is a very recent judicial development. Prior to 1946 the courts largely accepted the precedent of *Dietrich v. Inhabitants of Northampton* (1884) where the Massachusetts' Supreme Court disallowed recovery for negligently inflicted prenatal injuries in a wrongful death action of a child that did not survive its premature birth. In that case a women four to five months pregnant slipped and fell because of a defect in the highway and subsequently had a miscarriage. The plaintiff was alive when delivered, but was too premature to survive. In arriving at its decision the *Dietrich* court relied on the lack of precedent and upon the concept that the fetus was part of the mother and not a separate entity.

Similarly, in *Walker v. Railroad Co.* (1891) after an accident on a train whereby the mother and her unborn fetus were seriously injured, so that the child was born crippled and deformed, all of the judges agreed that the suit could not be maintained because "when the act of negligence occurred the plaintiff was not a person, or a passenger, or a human being. Her age and her existence are reckoned from her birth, and no precedent has been found for this action" (at 71).

In *Allaire v. St. Luke's Hospital* (1900) the Illinois Supreme Court, following *Dietrich*, held that an action for injuries could not be maintained by a plaintiff who at the time of injury was a prenatal infant with no separate legal existence. In this case the infant plaintiff's claim came from injuries sustained while in the womb when his mother was severely injured in an elevator accident. As a result of the accident the child's left side and limbs were "wasted, withered, and atrophied" and he was "sadly crippled for life." Interestingly, the court rejected the cause of action of the child against the owners of the elevator because it might set a precedent for a child to sue its mother.

Despite the growing realization that the *Dietrich* reasoning was faulty, it was relied upon as controlling until the U.S. District Court of D.C. dismissed it in *Bonbrest v. Kotz* (1946). In the case infant Bette Gay Bonbrest attempted by her father to recover for injuries sustained when she was negligently removed by a physician, a clear instance of injury to a viable child. To distinguish itself from *Dietrich* the court emphasized that the plaintiff was viable and capable of surviving outside the womb.

> As to a viable child being 'part' of its mother—this argument seems to me to be a contradiction in terms. True, it is in the womb, but it is capable now of extrauterine life—and while dependent for its continued development on sustenance derived from its peculiar relationship to its mother, it is not a 'part' of the mother in the sense of a constituent element. . . . Modern medicine is replete with cases of living children being taken from dead mothers. Indeed, apart from viability, a non-viable foetus is not a part of its mother. (at 140)

The *Bonbrest* court, therefore, reasoned that once the child demonstrated it was capable of survival outside its mother's womb the argument that the fetus had no independent existence was inexplicable. If a child after birth is denied right of action for prenatal injuries there is a wrong inflicted for which there is no remedy (at 141).

After *Bonbrest* the right to recover for injuries sustained in utero gained rapid and widespread acceptance. For instance, in *Woods v. Lancet* (1951) a New York appellate court concluded that "to hold, as a matter of law, that no viable fetus has any separate existence which the law will recognize is for the law to deny a simple and easily demonstrable fact. This child, when injured, was in fact, alive and capable of being delivered and of remaining alive, separate from its mother." In *Williams v. Marion Rapid Transit, Inc.* (1949) the Supreme Court of Ohio held that a viable fetus was a "person" within the mean of the Ohio constitution, and thus after birth could maintain an action for tortious prenatal injuries. Shortly thereafter the Supreme Court of Minnesota (*Verkennes v. Corniea* 1949) held that the representative of a stillborn child could maintain an action for wrongful death because it was viable at the time of the injury. Likewise, the Supreme Court of New Jersey (*Smith v. Brennan* 1960), in a case where the infant plaintiff sustained injuries during an automobile collision while in his mother's womb, stated:

> Regardless of analogies to other areas of the law, justice requires that the *principle be recognized that a child has a legal right to begin life with a sound mind and body* [italics mine]. If the wrongful conduct of another interferes with that right, and it can be established by competent proof that there is a causal connection between the wrongful interference and the harm suffered by the child when born, damages for such harm should be recoverable by the child.   (at 503)

The *Smith* court concluded that the semantic argument of whether an unborn child is a "person in being" is irrelevant to recovery for prenatal injury. Furthermore, the difficulty of proving fact of prenatal injury to the infant in the mother's womb is not sufficient reason for blocking all attempts to prove it (at 503).

Although there is a clear case law trend in favor of allowing a claim for prenatal injury regardless of the stage of gestation during which the injury occurred, the courts are far from unanimous on the question of viability. The viability rule developed originally as a means of distinguishing cases from *Dietrich*, which assumed that the fetus was part of the mother. In *Bonbrest* the court refuted *Dietrich* by concluding that a viable fetus could sustain life independent of the mother and was, therefore, a distinct legal entity. Courts relying on *Bonbrest* thus often limited the authority of their decisions to suits involving injuries incurred after viability. For instance, in *Albala v. City of New York* (1981) the Supreme Court Appellate Division of New York upheld the viability requirement when it refused recovery for injuries suffered by a previable fetus (also see *Evans v. Olson* 1976). The court held that a cause of action did not lie in favor of the child, whose injuries allegedly resulted from the perforated uterus suffered by its mother during an abortion performed prior to the child's conception. A primary rationale used by many courts sustaining the viability rule is that proving causation is difficult when the injury occurs in the previable stages of fetal development.

Increasing numbers of courts, however, have either expressly renounced the viability rule or ignored it. The Georgia Supreme Court (*Hornbuckle v. Plantation Pipe Line Co.* 1956) held that viability was not the deciding factor in a prenatal personal injuries action and that recovery for any injury suffered after the point of conception should be permitted. In another case arising out of an automobile collision the Supreme Court of New Hampshire (*Bennett v. Hymers* 1958), held that the fetus from the time of conception becomes a separate organism and remains so.

> It is not our intention to engage in an abstruse and technical discussion of the exact moment when conception occurs and the life of a new being starts. However, it seems to us that if an infant is born alive and survives bearing physical or mental injuries medically provable to have been incurred by it while en ventre sa mere it is being oblivious to reality to say that the mother alone was injured by the tortious act and not the child.   (at 109)

According to the court in *Smith v. Brennan* (1960 at 504), "Whether viable or not at the time of injury, the child sustains the same harm after birth, and therefore should be given the same opportunity for redress." In *Sylvia v. Gobeille* (1966) a Rhode Island appellate court stated: "We are unable logically to conclude that a claim for injury inflicted prior to viability is any less meritorious than one sustained after."

The trend toward abolition of the viability rule is a just one because the harm sustained by the child may be the same whether the injury occurred before or after viability.

> Once the child is born alive, it is a separate human being deserving of compensation, regardless of whether it was a separate legal entity at the time the injury was originally inflicted. At birth, and throughout its life, the child exhibits the injury which was caused by the prior negligent act.   (Simon 1978:55)

In *Wilson v. Kaiser Foundation Hospital* (1983) the California Court of Appeals, Third District, agreed with this reasoning and concluded that birth is the condition precedent that establishes the beginning of the child's rights. A tort action may be maintained if the child is born alive—whether the injury occurred before viability or after is immaterial once birth takes place. However, if the injured child is not born alive a cause of action for prenatal injuries does not arise on its behalf, because a still-born fetus is not a person within the wrongful death statute of California (at 650). In fact, as pointed out in chapter 3 injuries inflicted in the first trimester are likely to produce the most severe congenital deformities. Thus, the viability rule precludes many of the most meritorius claims. The presumption here is that the fetus from the time of conception becomes a separate organism and remains so throughout its existence.

In a further extension of this logic some courts recently have recognized a cause of action for personal injuries that occurred prior to conception. In *Renslow v. Mennonite Hospital* (1977) a physician was held liable for injuries suffered by an infant girl as a result of a blood transfusion to the mother that occurred nine years before the child's birth. These "preconception torts" arise when a negligent act has been committed against a person not yet conceived but whose eventual existence is foreseeable (also see *Turpin v. Sortini* 1982 and *Harbeson v. Parke-Davis* 1983).

Although inconsistencies exist in case law as to viability, proof of causation and so forth, a consensus now exists in all fifty states that there is a right of a child to bring common law action for injuries suffered before birth. This unanimity has been achieved in a short span in part because new medical knowledge of the deleterious effects of particular action on the unborn permitted causation susceptible to legal proof. As in all tort action the plaintiff must prove existence of a legal duty on the part of the defendant to conform to a specific standard of conduct for the protection of the plaintiff against unreasonable risk of injury as well as a breach of that duty by the defendant. For the breach to occur there must be actual misfeasance—the defendant must be found to have been affirmatively negligent. Moreover, it must be proven that damage was suffered by the plaintiff and that the proximate cause of the damage was the negligence of the defendant. Legal causation may be established even though the biological processes that bring about the injury are not precisely understood. Legal cause does not need be the sole or even predominant cause of the injury. It is only required that the defendant's conduct must be a substantial or material factor in bringing about the injury—but for the defendant's negligent conduct the injury would not have occurred.

To date, tort actions predicated on prenatal injury have arisen from various factual settings including automobile accidents and medical malpractice. Most prenatal injury suits have been brought against third parties, particularly physicians and other health providers who allegedly failed to exercise the proper standard of care and through their negligence caused damage. Once the fetus was recognized as a legal entity separate from the mother, torts for prenatal injury became identical in principle to other malpractice suits.

One case, however, demonstrates the unique nature of many emerging causes of action in this area. *Payton v. Abbott Labs* (1981) was a class action suit brought by approximately four thousand women exposed to the drug diethylstilbestrol (DES). These women sued because their mothers ingested DES while pregnant and transmitted the drug to them in utero. As a result they are at increased risk for a rare type of genital cancer as well as abnormalities of the reproductive organs. The defendants were pharmaceutical companies, including Abbott, Eli Lilly, Merck, Rexall, Squibb and Sons, and Upjohn, all of which manufactured and marketed DES as a miscarriage preventive between 1945 and 1976. The plaintiffs contended that the defendants were negligent in marketing DES and that they should be compensated for the higher risk of cancer and other abnormalities they incurred. To complicate the situation even more, most of the plaintiffs were unable to identify the specific manufacturer of DES ingested by their mothers.

Based on precedents treating in utero injury resulting from ingestion of a drug by the mother, the court held that the plaintiffs could maintain a cause of action. The *Payton* court rejected the defendants' arguments that recovery should be denied because of the difficulty of proving causation and because of the risk of fictitious claims. The difficulties of proof or the possibility of false claims could not bar action by plaintiffs with medically demonstratable injuries. Of course, they would have to satisfy the normal requirements of any tort action.

Although *Payton* was rendered in response to a certified question by the federal court as to whether there is a cause of action in Massachusetts for those injured by a drug prior to birth, the precedental force was expected to be substantial. According to Seksay (1983:266), the prenatal injury holding in *Payton* results in a potential increase in liability for anyone who negligently supplies a pregnant woman with drugs or medication. Under *Payton* Massachusetts' courts, in accord with the courts and legislatures of other jurisdictions, are gradually extending legal rights to the unborn.

Torts for Wrongful Life

A related but more recent variety of prenatal torts is the tort for wrongful life. A tort for wrongful life is a suit brought on behalf of an affected infant, most commonly against a physician or other health professional who, it is alleged, negligently failed to inform the parents of the possibility of their producing a severely ill child, thereby preventing a parental choice in avoiding conception or birth of the child. The unique aspect of such suits is the assumption that a life has evolved that should not have. If not for the negligence of the defendant the child plaintiff would never have been born. Although the term "wrongful life" has been applied to a variety of situations including those where parents are suing for damages to the child, it is more precise to limit wrongful life action to that brought solely by the affected *child*. Most recent suits for wrongful life have been brought on behalf of children with severe mental or physical defects, asking for monetary damages to be awarded on the basis of their very existence as compared to a state of nonexistence. Wrongful life suits differ from traditional negligence actions in that the harm acknowledged is being born, even though compensation ultimately is asked in the form of monetary damages.

Legal questions surrounding wrongful life action, therefore, center on whether the defendant has a legally cognizable duty to the infant plaintiff even though the plaintiff was not born or even conceived in some cases at the time of the defendant's allegedly negligent act. There is considerable disagreement, however, over whether the plaintiff is harmed by the defendant's negligence and if so, how such damages can be measured. A question that the courts traditionally have been unwilling to face is whether or not the infant plaintiff is damaged by being born with defects when the only alternative is nonexistence. The plaintiff here must successfully argue that he or she would have been better off had he or she never been born. On public policy grounds, which have been interpreted by many legal observers as always favoring life over nonexistence, most courts have asserted that the plaintiff cannot be harmed by his birth.

Despite continued debate over the concepts of duty, harm, and proximate cause, recent court decisions indicate that some courts are now willing to accept such causes of action. Additionally, many legal observers have come out in support of such action. Rogers (1982:757) argues that recognition of wrongful life claims would promote societal interest in genetic counseling and prenatal testing, deter medical malpractice, and at least partially redress a clear and undeniable wrong. Kashi (1977:1432) argues that while the child's life is not "wrongful," neither is it as it should be. He states that the rejection of causes of action for wrongful life represent "a clear case of meritorious case of action being denied because of its ill-chosen label."

Prior to the late 1970s the courts unanimously refused to recognize the possibility of a cause of action for wrongful life. In *Gleitman v. Cosgrove* (1967) the New Jersey Supreme Court declared that the preciousness of human life, no matter how burdened, outweighs the need for recovery by the infant. To award damages to the affected child would be counter to public policy, which views the right to life as inalienable in our society. In 1975 the Wisconsin Supreme Court *(Dumer v. St. Michael's Hospital)* dismissed a suit filed for wrongful life but found that the parents had a cause, thus producing a clear legal distinction between torts for wrongful life and torts for wrongful birth and giving legal cognizance to the latter.

During the late 1970s the courts while continuing to reject a wrongful life cause of action began to make subtle distinctions that shifted toward recognition of legally cognizable harm to the child. Moreover, a number of trial courts ruled in favor of the plaintiffs and increasingly strong dissents on the higher courts acknowledged causes of action for wrongful life. According to Cohen (1978:217), *Park v. Chessin* (1977) "marked the first step toward judicial acceptance of the theory of 'wrongful life.' " The suit was brought, on the child's behalf, for conscious pain and suffering resulting from a specialist's advice to the parents to have another child although they already had one child die from polycystic kidney disease, "a fatal hereditary disease of such nature that there exists a substantial probability that any future baby of the same parents will be born with it" (Perkoff 1970:443). Although later overruled an intermediate appellate court held that both the parents and the child had a cause of action and declared that "decisional law must keep pace with expanding technological, economic and social change" (at 112). For the first time a cause of action was stated for the child, because "once having been born alive . . . said child comes within the 'orbit of the danger' for which the defendants could be liable."

This recognition of a legally cognizable action for wrongful life, however, was short-lived, or at least sidetracked. The *Park* decision was reviewed by the New York Court of Appeals as a companion case in *Becker v. Schwartz* (1978) and overruled. Although the parents in both cases were allowed to recover their pecuniary loss, the court refused to permit recovery for emotional or psychiatric damages, arguing that this would "inevitably lead to drawing of artificial and arbitrary boundaries" as well as offend public policy. The infant plaintiffs in both *Park* and *Becker* were barred from recovery of any damages because of the inability of the law to make a comparison between life with handicaps and no life at all. The court specifically refused to accept the idea that a child may legally expect a life free from deformity, and direct reference to the lower court decision stated: "There is no precedent for recognition . . . of 'the fundamental right of a child to be born as a whole, functional human being.' "

Although it is yet too early to predict that future wrongful life decisions will recognize a cause of action for the affected child, a distinct trend continues in that direction. *Curlender v. Bio-Science Laboratories* (1980), in which a California appeals court agreed that a Tay-Sachs infant was entitled to seek recovery for alleged wrongful life, represents a step toward that end. The court concluded that the breach of duty of the laboratory was the proximate cause of an injury cognizable at law—the birth of the plaintiff with such defects. The court dismissed without discussion the central rationale for barring recovery in previous wrongful life cases since *Gleitman*—the value of nonexistence versus life with handicap—and focused attention instead on the resulting condition of the child.

> The reality of the "wrongful-life" concept is that such plaintiff both exists and suffers, due to the negligence of others. It is neither necessary nor just to retreat into meditation on the mysteries of life. We need not be concerned with the fact that had defendants not been negligent, the plaintiff might not have come into existence at all. The certainty of genetic impairment is no longer a mystery. In addition a reverent appreciation of life compels recognition that plaintiff, however impaired she may be, has come into existence as a living person with certain rights.
>
> (at 488)

In *Curlender* the court argued that perceptive analysis of the wrongful life concept requires recognition of the great distinctions in the conditions of the particular plaintiffs as well as the changing policy context. The court noted the "progression in our law" toward allowing recovery in such cases as well as the "gradual retreat" from use of "impossibility of measuring damages" as the sole ground for barring recovery by infants. The dramatic increase in genetic knowledge and skills needed to avoid genetic disease were also introduced as mitigating factors. Finally, the court cited the persistence of wrongful life litigation despite the "cool reception" from the courts as evidence of the "serious nature of the wrong" and an "understanding that the law reflects, perhaps later than sooner, basic changes in the way society views such matters." In reversing the superior court's dismissal of this tort the appeals court stated: "We see no reason in public policy or legal analysis for exempting from liability for punitive damages a defendant who is sued for committing a 'wrongful life' tort (at 490).

In *Schroeder v. Perkel* (1981) the New Jersey Supreme Court agreed with *Curlender* and allowed an infant plaintiff born with cystic fibrosis to collect for his "wrongful," "diminished" life. In *Procanik v. Cillo* (1984) the New Jersey Supreme Court ruled that a congenitally defective child may maintain an action to recover at least the extraordinary medical expenses he will incur over a lifetime, although it refused to allow recovery of general damages for emotional distress or "diminished childhood." Moreover, in January 1983 a unanimous decision of the supreme court of Washington State in *Harbeson v. Park-Davis* strongly approved the principle of wrongful life as well as wrongful birth. The court found that the parents have a right to prevent the birth of a defective child and that health care providers have a duty to impart to the parents material information about the likelihood of birth defects in their future children. The child born with such defects has a right to bring a wrongful life action against a health provider. According to the court, it would be illogical to permit only parents, not the child, to recover for the cost of the child's own medical care. The child's need for medical care and other special costs related to his or her defect will not disappear when the child attains majority. The burden of these costs should fall not on the parents or the state, but on the party whose negligence was the proximate cause of the child's need for extraordinary care. The child should be able to collect a lifetime of medical and educational costs or any other costs of the deformity, according to the court. However, following the reasoning of the California Supreme Court in *Turpin v. Sortini* (1982), the Washington Supreme Court denied the child recovery for general damages such as pain and suffering.

Although these cases might demonstrate a trend in tort law, many courts continue to refuse to recognize wrongful life actions. In *Siemieniec v. Lutheran General Hospital* (1987) the supreme court of Illinois held that a child has no cause of action on his behalf for extraordinary medical expenses he expected to incur during his majority. It ruled that a child born with hemophilia could not maintain a wrongful life action against physicians who allegedly were negligent in failing to advise, counsel, or test his parents during his mother's pregnancy concerning the risk that fetus would have hemophilia. According to the court, recognition of a legal right not to be born rather than to live with hemophilia was contradictory to public policy.

Similarly, in *Ellis v. Sherman* (1984) the superior court of Pennsylvania affirmed a lower court's refusal to recognize an infant's cause of action for wrongful life. This case involved the failure of an obstetrician to diagnose the manifestations of neurofibromatosis, a hereditary disorder exhibited by the father. Likewise, in *Alquijay v. St. Luke's-Roosevelt Hospital Center* the New York County Supreme Court Appellate Division held that there is no cause of action on behalf of an infant to enable her to recover extraordinary expenses that would result from a disease after she reached her majority. In this case an infant girl afflicted with Down Syndrome was suing the hospital whose personnel conducted amniocentesis that erroneously indicated the mother would give birth to a normal male child. The court reiterated its opposition on public policy grounds and concluded that recognition of such a cause of action would require legislation. Moreover, in *DiNatale v. Lieberman* (1982) the Michigan Appellate Court denied a cause of action for wrongful life because of the difficulty in assessing damages for being born, while in *Dorlin v. Providence Hospital* (1982) and *Nelson v. Krusen* (1982) the child's claim for wrongful life was rejected because the assessment of damages would be too speculative. The judicial landscape, then, continues to be eccentric and confusing.

Civil Rights of the Fetus

In *Douglas v. Town of Hartford* (1982) a federal district court held that a five-and-a-half-month-old fetus is a person capable of maintaining an action under 42 U.S.C. 1983. Section 1983 provides a civil cause of action for violation of constitutional or federal statutory rights. According to the court, the viable fetus, who was born with severe head injuries allegedly the result of an attack by a policeman on the mother, was a person within the parameters of the Civil Rights Act of 1871, despite other federal court rulings to the contrary. Although *Douglas* conflicts with other federal court interpretations (for instance, *Harman v. Daniels* 1981) that section 1983 does not protect the unborn, according to Rice (1983), this decision does reflect the trend of courts to recognize an array of fetal rights in all areas. It must be noted that section 1983 creates no rights but only provides a remedy for violations of protected rights. This decision has little practical significance for the fetus unless fetuses are granted substantive rights. If Congress or the courts should grant constitutional or federal statutory rights, section 1983 would provide a remedy for deprivations of those rights, according to *Douglas*.

Although the *Douglas* court's ruling is very limited it is further evidence of the trend both in common law and statutory law to grant the fetus some protectable rights. While *Roe v. Wade* (1973) would seem to deny a previable fetus entitlement to constitutional rights or protection, and human life bills seem at this time not to have sufficient support to become law, after viability even the *Roe* Court implicitly recognizes that the fetus may have some entitlements if the states recognize a compelling interest in the potentiality of life.

It seems logical that the federal government's interest in protecting life would be equal to that of the states, but this recognition would have to come from Congress. Although any statutory action by Congress along this line would presumably fail on constitutional grounds as long as the *Roe* precedent persists, this does not eliminate the possibility of granting substantive federal civil rights to viable fetuses. The state law trend might encourage Congress or the federal courts to give legal protection to the unborn by expanding federal statutory rights at least for the viable fetus. Such action might be necessary to overcome current inconsistencies among the various jurisdictions. To date, however, Congress has not passed a law specifically protecting fetal rights, and as long as the battle lines are drawn around the point of conception little movement to this end appears forthcoming. Furthermore, although some state courts have interpreted state statutes as establishing protection for the unborn, federal courts have thus far refrained from interpreting any federal statutes that broadly.

According to Rice (1983), the courts should define the fetus as a "person" with protectable rights at least in those cases where the fetus's rights will not conflict with the Constitutional rights of other persons. In cases where the mother and fetus are both victims—for instance, if someone commits a violent act on a pregnant woman—the rational underlying abortion considerations no longer apply, because the rights of the mother and the fetus are parallel, not conflicting. It is logical that in such cases fetuses should be given protectable civil rights under section 1983. The *Douglas* decision represents a clear, although limited, break with the tradition of denying a civil cause of action and further evidence of a changing attitude among courts toward according legal rights to fetuses.

Child Claims Against Employers

Despite considerable disparity in detail it is general court policy that a child born alive can bring a tort action for prenatal injuries. Even the viability criterion has been weakened significantly with a number of jurisdictions refusing to accept that distinction. In a few cases preconception injury has been accepted as cause for action, although the judicial landscape there is more clouded. The question then is whether the courts will find employer liability for injuries during gestation resulting from either maternal or paternal exposure to workplace toxicants. To date there has been no clear guidance in this regard.

One unanswered question is whether the exclusivity rule will be used to bar suits by the child harmed by parental workplace exposure. As noted earlier it is generally agreed that the unborn child is not covered by workers' compensation. Despite this, in *Bell v. Macy's California* (1989) the California Court of Appeals held that the child injured in utero was barred from bringing a separate tort action against the employer. The court argued that because the injuries to the child were the direct result of the employer's negligence to the mother, these injuries were compensable under workers' compensation and thus effectively barred from tort action. Allowing a separate court action would expose the employer to "serious risk" and would encourage employers to exclude women from the workplace out of fear of heightened liability. According to the court's view, the mother and fetus are inseparable during gestation and, therefore, only the mother can sustain a cause of action against the employer. To complete the circular argument, the exclusivity rule bars the worker from claiming tort liability.

The *Bell* ruling seems to hold that fetal injury resulting from workplace exposure might represent a separate category of tort law in jurisdictions that do not allow exemption to the exclusivity rule for fetuses. This interpretation is supported by the court's acknowledgment that an injured child would have a cause of action if the injury to its mother had not occurred in the workplace. The determination of whether a child injured through workplace exposure of its mother (or father) has a cause of action will have to await further action by many additional courts. *Bell* demonstrates, however, that employers' fears of widespread liability for fetal damage is at best highly premature.

The second issue concerning tort liability for prenatal injury centers on potential action against parents who knowingly expose themselves to workplace hazards. Is there a parental responsibility to provide the fetus with a safe as possible environment that precludes their taking employment in a known high-risk workplace? If a woman has clear warning by the employer as to the risks and she chooses to work despite this knowledge during pregnancy, will she bear legal responsibility for any harm the fetus suffers? A review of current trends in the courts suggests that such suits might stand under certain circumstances.

Parental Liability for Prenatal Injury

The high incidence of congenital defects caused by the fetal environment has given rise to increased concern for the rights of the unborn child to be born free from avoidable prenatal injury. It is clear from the discussion of trends in tort law that despite considerable variation among jurisdictions the fetus is being accorded an expanding protection of civil law against injury caused by third parties. Although these trends appear to conflict with some aspects of the *Roe* decision, ironically, the legalization of abortion aroused concern for the unborn child and has facilitated this pattern. As noted earlier new technical innovations and knowledge of fetal development have helped clarify the deleterious effects of certain environmental influences and reinforced the acceptance of prenatal torts. It is not surprising that there is a clear trend toward recognition of causes of action against parents by children injured prenatally. This trend produces a conflict between the child's right to be born free of parentally induced prenatal injury and the parental right of autonomy.

Two basic legal developments have been especially critical in this emergence of parental responsibility. The first is simply the expanding sphere of liability for prenatal injury, which logically leads to those individuals most likely to cause injury, the parents. The second legal development is the abrogation of the intrafamily immunity doctrine, which traditionally protected the parents from liability. The former trend was discussed above—the latter is briefly examined here.

Until recently the parent-child (or intrafamily) immunity doctrine barred any tort action brought by a child against his or her parent. This doctrine was first enunciated in *Hewlett v. George*

(1891), where the Mississippi Supreme Court reasoned that an action by a child against his parents would disrupt peace in the family and was against public policy. This precedent held even in cases of intentional and malicious injury to the child by the parents (*McKelvey v. McKelvey* 1903 and *Roller v. Roller* 1905). According to Simon (1978:61), the immunity rule was not predicated upon a lack of duty of reasonable care owed the child by the parent, but solely on the child's procedural disability to sue. "The parent avoids liability on the theory that the child's right to recovery should be sacrificed for the public good." Despite this, for nearly a century this doctrine, itself based on no precedential authority, prevented unemancipated minor children from taking legal action against their parents. As late as 1987 an Illinois appellate court *(Chamness v. Fairtrace)* held that the parental tort immunity doctrine precluded the father, as administrator of the estate of a viable fetus, from bringing wrongful death action against the mother of the fetus whose negligence resulted in an automobile collision that was the proximate cause of the death of the fetus. To do so, the mother could benefit from her own negligence since the mother and father were husband and wife.

In recent decades, however, the immunity rule has come under heavy criticism and its validity has been challenged by many courts. The traditional arguments in favor of denying tort action by children against parents—that it would destroy family harmony (*Dunlap v. Dunlap* 1930), disturb parental discipline and control (*Brennecke v. Brennecke* 1960), undermine the welfare by weakening the family unit (*Tucker v. Tucker* 1964), and result in fraud and collusion against insurance companies (*Hastings v. Hastings* 1960)—have gradually been dismissed by the courts, either through the granting of a widening series of exceptions or by judicial abrogation of the doctrine entirely.

Abandonment of the parental relationship (*Dunlap v. Dunlap* 1930), emancipation of the child (*Logan v. Reeves* 1962), injury in the course of a business activity (*Trevarton v. Trevarton* 1963), and intentional or reckless injury of the child by the parent (*Teramano v. Teramano* 1966) have all been accepted by courts as exceptions to the immunity doctrine. According to Simon

(1978:66), the common denominator underlying these exceptions is that the rule of immunity is applied only where clear reasons for the rule are present. Although the parents should be immune for liability in torts committed in their parental status, courts have allowed action in those cases not arising directly out of the parent-child relationship or where the parent has relinquished his or her status as parent.

Courts in other jurisdictions have gone beyond this reasoning and abrogated the parent-child immunity doctrine entirely. Since 1963 when the Wisconsin Supreme Court (*Goller v. White* 1963) threw out the immunity rule, an increasing number of states have abandoned support of the rule and allowed tort actions of children against parents (*Ard v. Ard* 1982). In *Plumley v. Klein* (1972), for example, the court held that parent tort immunity should be overruled and that a child may maintain a lawsuit against his or her parent for injury suffered as a result of ordinary negligence of the parent. The court noted, however, that exceptions exist if the alleged negligent act involves the exercise of reasonable parental authority over the child.

At this point, over forty states have abrogated the immunity doctrine. In the remainder exceptions to the rule are freely granted such that it seems unlikely prenatal injury torts against parents would be summarily dismissed. The courts generally agree that the child's personal rights are worthier than property or contract rights that are already protected (*Hebel v. Hebel* 1967). Also, it is argued that society's best interests dictate that those individuals who are tortiously injured be compensated for their injury so that they do not become wards of the state (*Streenz v. Streenz* 1970). Finally, the courts see little family tranquility protected in denying a tort action solely on the basis of the immunity rule (*Peterson v. Honolulu* 1969). According to the Massachusetts Supreme Court in *Sorenson v. Sorenson* (1975), it is the injury itself, not the lawsuit, that disrupts harmonious family relations. The child's relationship to the tortfeasor should not result in denial of recovery for a wrong to his person (*Briere v. Briere* 1966).

Some jurisdictions continue to make distinctions between situations directly involving parental discretion over the control of the minor child and other negligent acts by a parent. In *Silesky v. Kelman* (1968), for example, the Minnesota Supreme Court abrogated parental immunity except where the alleged negligent act involves the exercise of reasonable parental authority or discretion with respect to providing necessities for the child. One method that has been viewed favorably by several courts is the use of a "reasonable parent standard" to determine when parental conduct is actionable. According to Atchison (1983:1003), such a standard strikes a balance between the child's right to recover for a tortiously inflicted injury and the parent's need to discipline and to use authority, judgment, and discretion in raising the child.

The clear trend of many state courts to disregard the parent-child immunity rule opens the way logically for expanding prenatal injury causes of action to include suits of children against parents for negligence in the prenatal period. Along with the rapidly advancing state of medical knowledge in fetal development and the growing medical evidence of the deleterious effects of maternal behavior on the fetus, there is a heightened recognition of parental liability for negligent injury to minor children by the courts. This is reinforced by the universally recognized liability of third parties for prenatal injury. Based on these factors an action by a child against its parents for negligent injury suffered prior to birth seems increasingly likely and logically consistent. Although no court has yet awarded damages for such an action, several recent court decisions demonstrate its imminence.

In *Grodin v. Grodin* (1980) the Michigan Court of Appeals recognized the possibility of maternal liability for prenatal conduct. The court upheld the right of a child allegedly injured prenatally to present testimony concerning his mother's negligence in failing to take a pregnancy test when her symptoms suggested pregnancy and her failure to inform the physician who diagnosed the pregnancy that she was taking tetracycline, a drug that might be contraindicated for pregnant women. Noting that the Michigan Supreme Court had determined that a child could bring suit for prenatal injury and that the immunity doctrine had been discarded, the Grodin court ruled that the injured child's mother would "bear the same liability as a third person for injurious, negligent conduct that interferred with the child's 'legal right to begin life with a sound mind and body.' "

The key question in *Grodin* was whether or not parental immunity should insulate the mother (and her homeowners' policy) from liability where the alleged negligent act involved an exercise of "reasonable parental discretion" in medical decision making. According to the court, a woman's decision to continue taking drugs during pregnancy is an exercise of her parental discretion. The crucial point is whether the decision reached by the woman in a particular case is a "reasonable exercise of parental discretion." (Also see *Matter of Danielle Smith* 1985 and *Matter of Gloria C. v. William C.* 1984, where family courts found a cause of action for in utero neglect.)

Similarly, in *Payton v. Abbott Labs* (1981) the court's decision in favor of a cause of action for an infant injured prenatally against anyone who negligently supplies a pregnant woman with drugs leaves the door open for a child to sue family members for injuries resulting from the improper administration of a drug to its mother during gestation. The *Payton* opinion patently approves of recovery for any prenatal injury if the harm can be demonstrated by medical evidence and proven in court. In *Stallman v. Youngquist* (1988), however, the Illinois Supreme Court held that no cause of action exists by or on behalf of a fetus subsequently born alive against its mother for unintentional infliction of prenatal injuries. In this case, in which action was brought by the infant against the mother for prenatal injuries sustained in an automobile accident, the supreme court reversed the appellate court's finding for action.

Wrongful Life Action Against Parents

One extension of the concept of wrongful life that promises a severe impact on social values and on notions of responsibility is a damage claim brought against the parents charging their liability for their own child's birth under handicap. For instance, what liability do parents have if, given accurate advice from the physician regarding the risk of genetic disease, they disregard it and either fail to undergo amniocentesis or refuse to abort the abnormal fetus, resulting in a child with a genetic disorder? If a claim for damages against a physician can stand, cannot a suit against the parents also succeed? Until now in cases of genetic disease, one could argue successfully that the parents should not be held accountable for circumstances beyond their control and that the child's handicap is simply an unfortunate fate. However, there is evidence, given the state of human genetic technology, that the legal climate might be fluctuating toward sympathy for the affected child.

Despite suggestions that torts for wrongful life against parents by affected children are improbable as well as undesirable, the thrust of the progression of the decisions summarized here illustrates that the courts are, indeed, moving in that direction. The majority in *Curlender* (488) argued that fears over the determination infants having rights cognizable at law would open the way for such plaintiffs to bring suit against their own parents for allowing them to be born are "groundless." The majority goes on to note, however, that if the parents make a conscious choice to proceed with the pregnancy despite full knowledge that a seriously impaired infant will be born, "we see no sound public policy which should protect those parents from being answerable for the pain, suffering and misery which they have wrought upon their offspring."

At least partly in response to *Curlender* in 1981 the California legislature passed and the governor signed a bill providing that no cause of action arises against a parent of a child based upon the claim that the child should not have been conceived or, if conceived, should not have been allowed to have been born alive. No such action has been taken in any other state and it is unclear whether courts presented with the appropriate facts would hold parents civilly liable for not aborting their child (Doudera 1982).

Margery Shaw (1980) agrees with the principle implied by *Curlender*. Women who are informed that their fetus is affected should incur a "conditional prospective liability" for negligent acts toward their fetus if they fail to utilize their constitutional right to abort. She (1980:229) would permit children harmed by the behavior of their mother during pregnancy to sue their mothers.

Withholding of necessary prenatal care, improper nutrition, exposure to mutagens and teratogens, or even exposure to the mother's defective intrauterine environment caused by her genotype, as in maternal PKU, could all result in an injured infant who might claim that his right to be born physically and mentally sound had been invaded.

It is unclear how Shaw would view the culpability of a woman who knowingly continues to work in a hazardous workplace while pregnant, but it seems likely she would agree that they too ought to be open to liability.

In contrast George Annas (1981:9) argues that while this position might be a logical extension of permitting the child a cause of action on its own behalf, there are policy objections that focus on protecting the unborn child. Rejecting the notion that there is a "right to be born both physically and mentally sound," he contends that such a "right" could easily turn into a "duty on the part of potential parents . . . to make sure no defective, or 'abnormal' children are born."

Cohen (1978:231) contends that because of strong public policy considerations, the acceptance of wrongful life is not likely to lead to the "acceptance of intrafamily wrongful life actions." Since liability in an intrafamily wrongful life action would turn on the moral question of whether the parents should have had the child, it should be beyond the scope of judicial review. Given the constitutional guarantee of the right of privacy parents have, not only to choose not to have a child *(Roe v. Wade)* but also to be free to choose to give birth to a child *(Eisenstadt v. Baird)*, "A child should not be able to sue his parents for making such a choice" (Cohen 1978:231). This choice represents a moral question on the part of the parents, not a legal one, and should not give rise to a cause of action by a deformed child against his parents.

What are the implications if litigation by an infant plaintiff (most likely initiated by counsel representing his or her rights) is successful and he or she is awarded damages from the parents for birth with specific disabilities because the parents' "irresponsible" action had contributed to the disability? Furthermore, what if that "irresponsible" action was a decision by a women to work in a known hazardous workplace after she had been warned of the possible effects on her child? Although the resulting constraints on women's employment choices would be less explicit than FPPs, the eventual impact would be the same. The women's right to choose her occupation would come into conflict with a perceived legal duty to refrain from having children under a variety of circumstances or to forgo her employment rights. Many observers view this possibility with repugnance, but Margery Shaw envisions beneficial results in this redefinition of parental responsibility:

> If the freedom to choose whether or not to have a child is limited by the threat of civil liability for having a child who is genetically defective, our posterity will be the beneficiaries. We will have decided that there is no "absolute right to reproduce" and that instead it is a "limited privilege" to contribute one's genetic heritage to future generations.   (Shaw, 1978:340)

The patterns in civil law reviewed here demonstrate a growing reluctance by the courts to deny a cause of action for prenatal injury of a fetus. Although there continues to be significant inconsistency across jurisdictions the trend is unmistakenly moving in the direction of recognizing some form of protection for the health of the unborn and of compensation for damages incurred during the prenatal period. Moreover, legal distinctions between viable and nonviable fetuses are becoming less definitive as courts attempt to keep up with rapid changes in medical knowledge and technology.

Although few cases to date have dealt with civil liability of mothers for their actions during pregnancy, the abrogation of intrafamily immunity and the heightened awareness and evidence of the deleterious effects on the fetus of certain maternal behavior make it possible that such suits will proliferate. Furthermore, the logic that increasingly allows causes of action against third parties for prenatal injuries or fetal death is bound to extend to causes for parental negligence, particularly where a parent knowingly chooses to act in a way that places the unborn child at risk.

Compensation for Harm to Fetus from Workplace Hazards: Climate of Uncertainty

The legal framework of compensation for injury to fetuses resulting from workplace exposure to pregnant women or fertile men and women is largely uncharted. Even though there is a clear trend toward finding causes of action for prenatal injuries in general, and *in theory* employers' concern over liability is thus warranted, torts for prenatal injury due to specifically workplace hazards are problematic. What evidence in case law exists is confusing and contradictory but does not indicate such actions will be widespread.

The review of both tort law and workers' compensation statutes here suggests that despite all the stated concern for the health of unborn children neither system provides adequate compensatory mechanisms. Furthermore, the fear of a rash of massive damage suits by harmed children often expressed by employers in defending exclusionary policies is unwarranted in the foreseeable legal climate. If anything, the system is strongly skewed against fair compensation for reproductive damage in general and fetal injury in particular. Chapter 8 offers recommendations for revamping the compensation system to better protect the reproductive health of all workers, especially pregnant women and their unborn children, and to reduce the possibility of tort action against parents for the employment choices they make.

7 | Alternatives to Fetal Protection Policies

Within the context of the debate over exclusionary policies and their discriminatory effect on women it is not surprising that most observers sympathetic with women's rights have been critical of industry's emphasis on protecting fetal health. Because of this focus with a few exceptions (Chavkin 1984) feminist authors have neglected the other dimension, i.e., that women must have the opportunity to carry out their pregnancies free from occupational hazards whenever possible. It is not against the interests of the fertile woman to protect her from exposure to hazardous workplace environments. More than any other person, the pregnant (or potentially pregnant) woman has the highest stake in the health of her progeny. Of greater long-term concern might be the fact that large numbers of women are daily exposed to toxicants in workplaces where no policies have been established to protect either their health or the health of their potential offspring. As discussed in chapter 3, millions of women are employed in laundries, hospitals, textile industries, and so forth, where overall risk might exceed those in industries that have adopted exclusionary policies. What should be done to protect their health?

It is estimated that 85 percent of the female labor force will be pregnant at some point during their working lives. Increasingly U.S. women are likely to be working while they bear and raise young children. In most cases they are either contributing significantly to family income or they are the family's sole means of support (Chavkin 1984:206). It is critical then, if we desire to protect the health of potential children, that we provide their mothers with adequate maternity leaves, prenatal care, on-job protections, temporary reassignment to safer jobs during pregnancy, and other means necessary to eliminate unnecessary risks to pregnancy. At present neither the employee's reproductive ability nor the health of the fetus are well protected. After reviewing the feasibility of less intrusive alternatives to FPPs, this chapter will examine in more detail the option of maternity leaves.

Cleaning up the Workplace

The first option often cited by opponents of FPPs is to clean up the workplace and eliminate all potential risks to the reproductive health of workers and offspring. Although there is no dispute that this option is preferred, it is unlikely to be attainable. Most observers, even critics of FPPs, acknowledge that while reduction of risk is possible, elimination of all risk to workers, much less the fetus, is unrealistic. For Sor, although cleaning up the workplace is "the most attractive resolution of the problem . . . it is the least achievable" (1986–87:222).

However, the fact that this goal cannot be reached in full does not mean that the first priority should not be to develop policies aimed at reducing workplace toxicants to generally safe levels wherever humanly possible. By their very nature some workplaces, such as Johnson Controls' battery division, are high-risk. Another problem in this alternative is that the current level of scientific knowledge of toxicants gives us little conclusive guidance as to what the risks of certain workplace environments are. OSHA standards only exist for a handful of potential toxicants, and even for those few risk levels are not fully known.

Short of eliminating reproductive risks employers could reduce exposure of workers to toxicants. A multifaceted approach to this end would include establishing safe handling procedures, instituting engineering controls designed to reduce exposure (e.g., installation of advanced ventilation systems and closed systems for chemical processing), use of respirators and protective equipment and clothing, and use of detoxification agents where feasible. There is no doubt that expansion of already existing company practices along these lines would increase production costs. It seems likely, however, that industries that gave their best effort to reducing hazards would minimize their risk of liability. Moreover, if these practices were standardized across industry there would be no competitive edge to companies that did not impose these expensive protections on their employees (Logan 1983:622). In some ways, however, the court in Johnson Controls unintentionally discouraged this alternative by indicating that tort liability of employers was improbable if they met only the minimal standards set by OSHA or other regulatory bodies. Still, the removal of toxicants through technological controls and the substitution of less harmful substances where possible would support the contention that industry is in fact concerned about the reproductive health of employees and the health of their children. Ultimately, the costs of these alterations in the workplace would be passed on to consumers anyway, thus spreading the economic burden through the wider population. If need be, tax incentives could be offered to induce cleanup policies.

Education and Full Disclosure

A greater emphasis on education at several levels is needed. First, employers must be educated concerning the risks of reproductive toxicants. Evidence continues that many employers are ignorant of the actual workplace hazard risks. In the Massachusetts study of chemical and electronics manufacturing, for instance, 60 percent of the employers were found to be either unaware or misinformed about reproductive hazards at their work site (Paul, Daniels, and Rosofsky 1989). Furthermore, this lack of awareness cut both ways: some employers had FPPs that bore little relationship to the actual risks while others had no policies to protect workers from exposure to known hazards. According to McGill (1990:20), while there is no simple solution to the problem of workplace hazards, the responsible use of information about reproductive hazards in the workplace is the foundation for informed choices by employees and rational approaches by employers.

> The first goal of education would be to ensure that employers take appropriate, nondiscriminatory action toward employees at risk. The education of all employers in a specific industry would promote recognition of reproductive hazards industry-wide and would allow for a concerted effort and pooling of resources to discover methods for abatement of the hazards apart from the exclusion of pregnant and fertile women.   (Katz 1989:228)

Worker education regarding reproductive risks has also been found to be inadequate. (For a discussion of current disclosure obligations see Susser 1986–87.) Despite regulations in Massachusetts that require employers to provide workers with Maternal Safety Data Sheets and training that pertains to hazardous substances used on the job, among those companies using one or more of the reproductive hazards identified by OSHA 40 percent failed to educate workers about potential reproductive risks (Paul, Daniels, and Rosofsky 1989:276). Not only does this lack of training fail to disclose information necessary for informed worker choice but it also may leave workers unprepared to take proper precautions to protect their health.

Education for employees is essential in order to facilitate each individual worker's ability to make an informed decision concerning employment. The employer has a responsibility to furnish each worker with the most complete information available regarding the reproductive hazards of each particular job. This information should be as accurate and objective as possible and should be presented in an understandable manner. "A thorough and accurate knowledge of all the potential adverse effects associated with one's job, as well as the probability of occurrence, is necessary for employees to make an informed choice whether to remain in that job or to pursue other options" (Katz 1990:229). Although the burden of protection cannot be shifted to the employee simply by full disclosure of the risks of employment, once they have this information they are in the best position to make the decision as to whether they wish to take the risk. Again, as with employer efforts to make the workplace as safe as possible, implementation of well-documented worker education programs on a continuing basis will also protect the employer from tort actions for reproductive harm. In any case, programs designed to assist employees in making their own decisions regarding the reproductive risks they are willing to bear are preferable to exclusionary decisions made for employees by employers.

Job Transfers

Education programs in themselves are of little advantage to workers if there are no attractive employment options available. Another option to FPPs is the provision of alternative employment opportunities. Temporary removal from a hazardous workplace and transfer to a safe area while being protected against loss of income, security, and fringe benefits is a more reasonable alternative in large companies. As long as the option includes comparable pay and benefits there appears to be little opposition from supporters of women's rights. However, the transfer of pregnant employees under such conditions might be costly for large employers and impossible for small companies. Furthermore, if risk is perceived as present throughout childbearing years, it is meaningless to talk about temporary positions. Therefore, although the notion of job transfer to less hazardous positions is intuitively attractive and seemingly simple, it is often impractical.

A combination of the provision of temporary transfer with an education program that encourages employee notification of pregnancy or planned pregnancy would largely overcome the concern of employers to protect fetal health. Moreover, this two-pronged strategy has the advantage of avoiding the necessity for blanket exclusionary policies. As noted above, however, its implementation even in large industries would be difficult and administratively cumbersome. A more reasonable alternative is to permit pregnancy leave with retention of fringe benefits, seniority, and job protection. This option will be discussed in detail later.

Other Alternatives to Exclusionary Policies

There are several additional alternatives to FPPs that have been raised in the literature. One approach is to implement individual screening programs to differentiate among those individuals who are and are not susceptible to specific occupational hazards. This approach would normally utilize genetic tests that identify individuals with heightened susceptibility to potential toxicants (Ashford et tl. 1990 and Brokaw 1989–90). At present approximately fifty human genetic traits have been identified as having the potential to enhance susceptibility to toxic or carcinogenic effects of particular types of environmental agents (OTA 1990b:83). This number is expected to increase substantially as a result of the current initiatives designed to map out the entire human genome in the 1990s (Blank 1992a). Although it is likely that workplace genetic screening and monitoring will become prevalent unless regulatory action is taken to restrict its use, it is difficult to see how this will offer an alternative to exclusionary FPPs. One possibility is that if genetic tests are developed to identify women who are less able to metabolize specific toxicants, policies might be implemented to exclude only those women who test positive from workplaces that contain these substances.

If anything, FPPs might be seen as the leading wedge, followed by similar exclusionary policies for groups of individuals identified as being hypersusceptible to a wide range of workplace hazards (Scott 1984:182). Table 7.1 shows some of the current genetic factors affecting susceptibility to workplace agents. In addition, it is more likely that genetic screening will be used as another component of preemployment medical exams to identify workers at heightened risk for health problems (Blank 1992b:83).

Another alternative to exclusionary policies that although frequently alluded to have severe legal and practical problems combines full disclosure to the employee of known workplace hazards with some type of signed statement by the employee acknowledging the risks she or he accepts in taking the job. Usually this statement takes the form of a waiver of legal rights to sue for reproductive or fetal injury caused by these workplace agents. Although on one hand such a release form is less extreme than

TABLE 7.1
Genetic Factors Affecting Susceptibility to Environmental Agents

High-risk Groups	Environmental Agents to Which Group Is (May Be) at Increased Risk
RBC conditions	
G-6-PD deficiency	Environmental oxidants such as ozone, nitrogen dioxide, and chlorite
Sickle cell trait	Aromatic amino and nitro compounds, carbon monoxide, cyanide
The thalassemias	Lead, benzene
NADH dehydrogenase deficiency (MetHb reductase deficiency)	MetHb-forming substances
Catalase hypocatalasemia	Ozone, radiation
Low SOD activity	Wide variety of environmental oxidants, paraquat, radiation, ozone
ALA dehydratase deficiency	Lead
Hb M	Carbon monoxide
Erythrocyte porphyria	Chloroquine, hexacholorobenzene, lead, various drugs including barbiturates and sulfonamides
GHS-Px deficiency	Environmental oxidants
GSH deficiency	Environmental oxidants
Liver metabolism	
Defect in gluocuronidation	Wide variety of zenobiotics including polychlorinated biphenyls
Gilbert's syndrome	
Crigler Najjar syndrome	
Defect in sulfation	Wide variety of zenobiotics, tyramine-containing foods
Acetylation phenotype, slow v. fast	Aromatic amine-induced cancer, numerous drugs, e.g., isoniazid and hepatitis
Gout	Lead
Oxidation center defects	Numerous zenobiotics requiring oxidative metabolism for detoxification
OCT deficiency	Insect repellant (DET)
Paraxonase variant	Parathion
Rhodanese variant	Cyanide
Sulfite oxidase deficiency heterozygotes	Sulphite, bisulfite, sulfur dioxide
Inadequate carbon disulfide metabolism	Carbon disulfide
Alcohol dehydrogenase variant	Metabolize (e.g., ethanol) more quickly than normal
Wilson's disease	Copper, vanadium
Serum variants	
Albumin variants	Unknown
Pseudocholinesterase variants	Organophosphate and carbamate insecticides, muscle relaxant drugs

SOURCE: Office of Technology Assessment 1990b:84.

outright exclusion, on the other it represents a type of employment blackmail and therefore is more insidious than straightforward exclusion. A waiver policy also "directly conflicts with the established doctrine prohibiting employment contracts from including clauses that limit or waive employer liability for work-related injury" (Logan 1983:624). Moreover, the policy fails to protect either the reproductive health of the employee or the interests of the potential unborn. Such waivers do nothing but attempt to shift possible legal blame from industry to worker. As such, their use would undermine the very moral responsibility for fetal health that many industries have used to defend FPPs in the first place.

Even if such waivers were determined to be binding by the courts for reproductive harm to the worker, which is highly doubtful, under tort law no parent has the ability to waive the legal rights of his or her offspring once born to sue for prenatal damage. It is even questionable whether waivers would be allowed in court as evidence of an employee's willingness to accept the risks of a job. Despite their doubtful legality waivers disguised as consent or acknowledgment documents might dissuade workers so harmed from initiating lawsuits on the assumption that their signed statements in fact do preclude legal action against the employer. As Logan notes, an "informal understanding, based on accurate and complete disclosure and employee consent, might provide a defense under traditional tort law; however, given the constant flux in this area, the outcome of such a case would be difficult to predict" (1983:624).

A final alternative that might have a place—but only where the risk of fetal injury due to a parent's exposure to a workplace toxicant is probable—is a policy requiring employees of reproductive age to consent to practice birth control, secure an abortion upon conception, or be sterilized to secure employment (Logan 1983:625). Although it is possible to imagine such a powerful toxicant, it is preferable that any hazard with such certainty of harm be prohibited from all workplaces. At present there is no known toxicant in any workplace that warrants this policy. The risk of fetal injury from even a proven teratogen such as lead is unlikely to justify the establishment of an industrial policy that

imposes severe restrictions on reproductive autonomy of its employees. Furthermore, if such a substance is identified and it
cannot reasonably be removed from a workplace, it is likely that
it would put both men and women at risk, thus requiring similar
restraints on workers of both sexes.

In the future, as more safe and effective long-term contraceptives become available (perhaps like NORPLANT or other sub-
dermal implants developed for women and men) these might be
offered to employees for their use on a voluntary but not mandatory basis. The combination of full disclosure, the availability
of reversible means of fertility control for workers, and adequate
counseling and education programs might give maximum protection for the health of potential children as well as protect the
reproductive choice and employment opportunities of workers.

Maternity Leave Policies in Other Countries

For Lise Vogel, "it is always a shock to find out how little
substantive support for pregnancy and parenting is available in
the United States" (1990:11). This failure to guarantee adequate
pregnancy and maternal leave is all the more shocking when
compared to policies in other countries, which provide comprehensive benefits to eligible workers for childbirth and childrearing. There are currently 119 countries around the world including highly industrialized and developing nations where medical
costs are covered and paid job- and benefit-protected leaves for
maternity and parenting are provided as a matter of national
policy. Of the industrialized countries, only South Africa and the
United States have no national maternity leave policy (Bookman
1991:68). According to Sheila Kamerman,

> Almost all industrialized countries provide maternity and/or par-
> enting leaves and related cash benefits as statutory social insur-
> ance benefits, wherein pregnancy and maternity are defined as
> societal as well as individual risks that result in a temporary loss
> of income and, therefore, are subject to protection by social
> insurance.   (1988:243)

In Europe maternity leave averages around five months paid
leave with additional unpaid leave. Usually about six weeks of

TABLE 7.2
Paid Maternity and Parenting Leave Provisions

Country	Benefits Level	Length of Leave	Supplementary Paid or Unpaid Leave	Available to Father
Austria	100%	16 weeks plus 10 months at lower level	2 years for low income single women w/o daycare	
Belgium	80%	14 weeks		
Canada	60%	15 weeks		
Denmark	90%	24 weeks	Up to 2 years maternity leave	Yes
Finland	80%	10.5 months	2 years at flat rate	Yes
France	90%	16 weeks	Up to 2 years maternity leave	
Germany	100%	14 weeks	15 months at flat rate	Yes
Greece	50%	12 weeks		
Ireland	80%	14 weeks		
Israel	75%	12 weeks		
Italy	80%	5 months		
Netherlands	100%	12 weeks		
Norway	100%	18 weeks	Yes	Yes
Portugal	100%	3 months	Yes	
Spain	75%	14 weeks		
Sweden	100%	9 months plus 3 months at flat rate	Up to 3 more months 6 hour workday until child is 8	Yes
United Kingdom	90%	6 weeks plus 12 weeks at flat rate	Up to 2 years maternity leave	

SOURCE: Kamerman 1991:18.

the leave is taken before the expected birth, with prenatal and postnatal medical and hospital coverage for delivery included. Often job modification without penalty and the right to nurse at work are standard (Chavkin 1984:206). As seen in table 7.2 benefit levels range from 50 percent in Greece to 100 percent (up to the maximum covered by social security) in Austria, Germany, Netherlands, Norway, Portugal, and Sweden. Some countries provide additional leave to single mothers, for second and subsequent children, for difficult deliveries, or for multiple births. Many permit mothers, and in some cases fathers, to take additional leave time paid at a lower rate or with job protection.

The United Kingdom, for instance, has three different types of maternity pay: statutory maternity pay, maternity allowance, and pay received under contractual maternity pay (McRae 1991: 86–87). The specific benefits vary according to the length of time

the woman has been in the paid labor force. A woman who has
worked continuously for six months prior to delivery receives
under statutory maternity pay a maximum of eighteen weeks of
leave based on a flat rate weekly payment (in 1988 the rate was
fifty-two dollars for married women and ninety-six dollars for
single women). If a woman has worked two years full-time (at
least sixteen hours per week) or five years part-time (eight to
sixteen hours per week) prior to pregnancy, she receives 90
percent of her earnings for six weeks and the flat rate for the
remaining twelve weeks. Furthermore, a maternity allowance is
paid to self-employed women and lump-sum payments are made
to poor families to help them obtain necessities for baby care
(Stoiber 1989:14). Also, since 1981 a pregnant woman is entitled
to paid time off to receive prenatal care (McKechnie 1984:191).
Despite these generous maternity benefits relative to the United
States, when compared to other European countries maternity
benefits in the United Kingdom are paid on a "niggardly scale"
(Chamberlain 1984:12).

Sweden provides more comprehensive maternity and prenatal
leave at higher reimbursement levels than Britain. Five types of
paid leaves are available including a twelve-week maternity leave
(six weeks before and six weeks after birth); an extended pregnancy leave if medically required; a paternity leave giving fathers
ten days off after the birth; a nine-month parental leave; and an
extended parental leave of up to nine months. Sweden has actually expanded its benefits over the last decade, despite budget-
ary problems (Kamerman 1991:17). Leaves are funded through a
combination of payroll taxes (85 percent) and general revenues
(15 percent), while medical costs related to pregnancy are paid
through a sickness insurance system. According to Bookman,
mothers and fathers in Sweden "experience almost no loss of
income in fulfilling their parental responsibilities to newborn,
adopted, or sick children" (1991:69).

Germany also has a generous leave policy, although it has not
been extended to fathers. In Germany employed birth mothers
have an eight-week paid maternity leave that is funded partly
through an insurance fund and partly by the employer. A childrearing leave program permits one parent to stay home full time

for up to three years. During that time the parent is paid three hundred and sixty dollars a month and may work up to eighteen hours per week. Finally, Germany provides paid leaves to care for sick children—up to ten days per child annually for each child under eight (Bookman 1991:69).

As illustrated in table 7.2 most other European countries offer paid leave to pregnant women and new parents. In addition some countries such as Finland and Holland provide domiciliary help to pregnant and recently delivered women (Chamberlain 1984:8). Although all of these countries' policies include job protection during the paid leaves, some countries, such as France and Austria, have instituted supplementary childrearing policies that allow the parent after exhaustion of paid leave to take off a still longer period of job-protected time with more modest financial support (Kamerman 1991:18). Although Canada's maternity leave program is less generous than its European counterparts, women are usually eligible to receive around seventeen weeks' leave at 60 percent pay with job, pension, and security preserved (Vogel 1990:11).

It is important to note that maternity leave programs are not limited to more affluent Western democracies. Currently, eighty-one developing countries have established policies that give women a period of paid leave both before and after birth of each child. Despite the severe economic burdens many of these Third World countries face, they have committed significant resources to paid maternity leaves, usually funded by some combination of employer and social security system (Bookman 1991:70). Cuba and Chile, for instance, have mandated eighteen-week paid leaves, while even Tunisia provides thirty-day maternity leaves (Pizzo 1988:277). Clearly, the data demonstrate that the United States stands virtually alone in lacking a national maternity and parental paid leave policy.

While the debate in the United States continues to center on whether *unpaid* leave with return job guarantees is feasible, most other countries have established *paid* maternity leave. The argument that paid leaves would threaten to bankrupt small and medium-sized firms and substantially burden the large ones seems not to be supported in the experience of every other industrialized nation—and many developing nations. Most damaging to the opposition of paid maternity leave is the fact that Canada, a country whose economy has been linked heavily with that of its southern neighbour, gives women almost four months of leave. The major difference between the United States and other nations is that childbearing elsewhere is viewed as a social contribution with attendant social responsibilities. The costs of this enterprise, therefore, have been placed on the state and are seen as a normal factor of conducting business. Although this premise of societal responsibility is explicitly accepted by social welfare states, it runs counter to the individualistic culture of the United States where parental choice entails significant personal financial investment. Despite all the concern postulated over the state and corporate interest in protecting the health and safety of the unborn, there is little evidence of a shift toward this perspective in the United States.

Although there is some incongruity with policies that encourage and heavily subsidize childbearing in an era of world overpopulation, because the production of children with sound minds and bodies is touted as a high society priority, access to prenatal care and social support of pregnant women and new parents are essential elements toward achieving that goal. Moreover, although unpaid leave with job security and benefits might be an adequate means of assuring women financial resources to cover the costs of the time off work, many single women—particularly those working in the lowest paying jobs—are unlikely to maximize their or their offspring's health without some remuneration. For these women unpaid leaves, although preferable to none at all, do little to achieve the objective of fetal health.

Guaranteed Access to Prenatal Care

U.S. society in general ought to place a considerably higher priority on preventive programs (see Blank 1988). Nowhere is this strategy more essential than in the protection of fetal health. Health promotion activities, including education starting in the early grade, counseling, particularly of women in high-risk populations, and the provision of preemptive treatment programs, are critical societal responsibilities for reducing the occurrence of ill babies. Until society makes a concerted effort to carry out these responsibilities efforts to protect fetal health by constraining women are premature and counterproductive. As Martha Field concludes, if the real goal is not control of women but "protection of the child-to-be and creation of as healthy a newborn population as possible, then appropriate means are education and persuasion, free prenatal care, and good substance abuse rehabilitation programs, available free of charge to pregnant women" (1989:125).

A growing realization of these facts was reflected in the report of many panels in the late 1980s. The Institute of Medicine (1985, 1988), the U.S. Public Health Service Expert Panel on the Content of Prenatal Care (1989) and OTA (1988) all called for universal access to prenatal care for pregnant women as the critical strategy to improve the health of infants. For instance, the Institute of Medicine concluded that the nation should adopt as a new social norm the principal that all pregnant women should be provided access to prenatal, labor and delivery, and postpartum services appropriate to their need. It admits that this will require considerable resources to reorganize the entire maternity care system, including removal of all barriers (including personal and cultural) to such care, a vigorous education effort in schools, media, family planning clinics, social service networks, and places of employment, and research on how to motivate women to seek this care.

The most comprehensive discussion of how to implement prenatal care to deal with these problems is found in the report of the Public Health Service Expert Panel on the Content of Prenatal Care (1989). This report demonstrates that the objectives of prenatal care, instead of pitting mother against fetus, are designed to serve the interests of the woman, the fetus/infant, and the family. The panel places considerable emphasis on the need for preconception care to prepare for pregnancy because often it is too late to ensure a healthy pregnancy once it has begun. In fact, the preconception visit "may be the single most important health care visit when viewed in the context of its effect on the pregnancy" (1989:26). The birth of a healthy baby, then, depends in part on the general health and well-being of the woman (and her mate) before conception as well as on the amount and quality of prenatal care. Health care before pregnancy can ameliorate disease, improve risk status, and help prepare the woman for childbearing (Jack and Culpepper 1990:1147). In addition to the risk assessment component, preconception care emphasizes health promotion. Promotion of healthy lifestyle choices, counseling about the availability of services, and education on the importance of ongoing prenatal care are critical to the success of this component.

The moral responsibility to protect the health of unborn children that industries claim would seem to be more effectively directed toward the provision of preconception and prenatal education and care than the establishment of FPPs. Although there are costs involved in this strategy they are not substantial and in the long run are likely to pay off economically as well as through reduced health care costs. Data from those countries that employ the European approach discussed earlier appear to substantiate this, particularly since all rank below the United States in infant mortality and morbidity.

Preliminary data from U.S. companies that have initiated comprehensive prenatal health programs have shown positive results (Swerdlin 1989). For instance, in 1982 the First National Bank of Chicago found that over 40 percent of all short-term disability absences and 15 percent of all health care costs paid by the medical plan were due to pregnancy-related problems. In response, First Chicago implemented a comprehensive women's health program that included prenatal education and on-site gynecological examinations (Burton, Erickson, and Briones 1991). First Chicago offers prenatal classes to women who normally received insufficient care due to economic, time, or convenience barriers. In addition to prenatal education and no-charge general gynecologic care provided on-site by a part-time consulting gynecologist, the bank runs a series of lunchtime seminars on topics such as "Early Prenatal Care," "Healthy Lifestyles," and "Nutrition and Exercise During Pregnancy." To encourage participation employees and spouses who complete the classes by the fourth month of pregnancy are eligible to have the $225 deductible waived for the newborn. Furthermore, First National is considering on-site prenatal care for employees (Burton, Erickson, and Briones 1991:349).

Sunbeam-Oster Company has taken a further step by mandating participation by pregnant women in prenatal classes conducted on company time for one hour every other week. The program is offered on a voluntary basis to spouses of male employees as well. There is also a continuing individual assessment of each pregnant woman's condition and follow-up provided by an on-site company nurse. Although the mandatory aspect of Sunbeam's policy is problematic, the program appears to be successful in reducing the incidence of prenatal and neonatal health problems—since the plan was implemented in 1986 no employee has given birth to a premature infant (Breese 1987:41). In comparison, prior to implementation in 1984 Sunbeam paid out over $1 million for medical care for four premature babies born to workers. Moreover, in the first year of the program the average cost per maternity case decreased by almost 90 percent from the cost incurred two years previously, dropping from $27,243 in 1984 to $2,893 in 1986 (Breese 1987). As in the case of First National Bank of Chicago, the costs of the program were minimal as compared to the economic savings alone.

Although the goals and results of Sunbeam's prenatal education program are worthy, the mandatory nature is troublesome, particularly since there are less restrictive alternatives that are likely to be as successful without this degree of coercion. Data from similar contexts show that voluntary programs achieve the same goals (Swerdlin 1989) without violating the employee's autonomy or creating problems of medical data confidentiality that might occur when the course of pregnancy is monitored by medical personnel who are in effect agents of the company. Less intrusive alternatives include offering employees incentives for participation in the program (e.g., First National's waiving of the deductible) or requirements making insurance coverage dependent on certification of prenatal education, care, and compliance without mandating participation in the company's own program.

Maternity and Parental Leave

Another area where the United States could learn from the experiences of other Western nations centers on the applicability of pregnancy and parental leave. Again, if the goal of industry is to protect the health of the potential children of employees, the establishment of realistic pregnancy leave policies is preferable to FPPs. Unfortunately, while other countries were implementing paid leave plans, the debate in the United States focused on the legality and affordability of unpaid pregnancy leaves. Even many feminists were hesitant to draw attention to pregnancy-related needs of women out of fear that the emphasis would imperil newly gained jobs (Chavkin 1984:202). With the invalidation of FPPs by the Supreme Court the climate is more amenable to debate over the special needs of women during pregnancy and immediately after childbirth. "In the absence of a comprehensive and natural maternal leave policy, mothers in the United States who need to take time off are frequently compelled to exit the labor market" (Garrett, Lubeck, and Weak 1991:30). This situation does nothing to ensure the health of their offspring.

In some ways the language of the 1978 Pregnancy Discrimination Act (PDA) by treating pregnancy and maternity as temporary disabilities, like those affecting male workers instead of unique conditions, made comprehensive change unlikely. While working women in firms with good disability and health insurance policies were covered, the PDA did not require employees to establish such policies. Therefore, Congress failed to mandate sickness or disability benefits, instead opting only to require firms already providing such coverage to extend it to women disabled by pregnancy. Furthermore, only those five states that already mandated temporary disability insurance (TDI) programs were required by the PDA to extend coverage to women workers during pregnancy and childbirth. (When Rhode Island passed the first TDI in 1942 it included pregnancy as a covered disability, however as the costs grew it restricted coverage of pregnancy. On the basis of Rhode Island's experience, other states excluded pregnancy from the outset.) The remaining states were not required to institute mandatory state programs, and to date none have. The most immediate benefit of the PDA was that employers providing health insurance were required to include coverage for maternity care. Gold and Kenney (1985) report that as a result 89 percent of employees with medical insurance had maternity care benefits in 1982 compared to 57 percent in 1977.

The five states with TDI programs are California, Hawaii, New Jersey, New York, and Rhode Island. All states but California allow a maximum leave of twenty-six weeks, while California has extended leave to thirty-nine weeks. The benefit is usually offered with minimum and maximum caps and replaces between 50 and 66 percent of the wage of an average employee. Except in Rhode Island, where employers must buy into the state plan, employers are free to self-insure or purchase private insurance as long as they meet at least the minimum requirements of the state plan. Despite the PDA, however, "Fewer than 40 percent of working women have income protection at the time of maternity that will permit them a six-week leave without severe financial penalty" (Kamerman and Kahn 1987:56).

In several instances the language of the PDA led employers to challenge the legality of state pregnancy statutes mandating special treatment to pregnant women. In *Miller-Wohl v. Commissioner of Labor and Industry* (1984) the Montana Maternity Leave Act (MMLA), which, among other things, mandated job-protected maternity leaves and disability benefits to pregnant workers, was challenged. The Miller-Wohl company filed suit against the state after the commissioner of labor and industry ruled that the company had violated the MMLA by firing a pregnant worker for missing work. The company argued that the MMLA violated Title VII by treating pregnant workers differently than other similarly disabled workers. The Montana Supreme Court rejected the argument and held that the statute furthered the state's interest in promoting the health and welfare of its citizens and sexual equality in the workplace (at 1255).

In 1987 the U.S. Supreme Court ruled on a similar case involving a California statute mandating pregnancy leaves. In *California Federal Savings and Loan Association v. Guerra* (1987), the Court upheld a California law requiring employers to grant up to four months of unpaid leave to women disabled by pregnancy, even if similar leaves were not granted for other disabilities. Like Miller-Wohl, Cal. Fed. argued that the statute was preempted by the PDA, which specifically states that pregnancy must be treated the same as other disabilities. The district court agreed that the California law and policies of enforcement that require preferential treatment of pregnant female employees were preempted by Title VII and "null and void." The Ninth Circuit reversed the district court, holding that Congress intended to "construct a floor beneath which pregnancy disability benefits may not drop, not a ceiling above which they may not rise" (at 395). The Supreme Court affirmed, adding that the California statute "does not compel employers to treat pregnant workers better than other disabled employees. . . . Employers are free to give comparable benefits to other disabled employees, thereby treating 'women affected by pregnancy' no better than other persons not so affected but similar in their ability or inability to work" (at 289).

Despite Justice Thurgood Marshall's assurance that the California pregnancy leave statute was unlike state protective legislation of the earlier era, some women's rights organizations spoke against the California statute. Out of concern that any special treatment would ultimately lead to restrictions on job opportunities a coalition of women's groups led by the National Organization for Women argued that pregnant workers should not receive special benefits. As early as 1971 the Citizens Advisory Council on the Status of Women concluded:

> Childbirth and complications of pregnancy are, for all *job related purposes*, temporary disabilities and should be treated as such under any health insurance, temporary disability insurance or sick leave plan. . . . Any policies or practices . . . applied to instances of temporary disability other than pregnancy should be applied to incapacity due to pregnancy or childbirth. . . . No additional or different benefits or restrictions should be applied to disability because of pregnancy or childbirth, and no pregnant employee should be in a better position in relation to job-related practices or benefits than an employee similarly situated suffering from any other disability.   (1971:4)

Maschke (1989:59) contends that the Court's decision complicates the controversy between women's employment rights and the interest of the state and employer in protecting the fetus because the Court "blurred the distinction between special benefits and protection."

> In *Cal. Fed.* the Court legitimated [*sic*] that state's interest in protecting women on the basis of the 'uniqueness' of pregnancy. Thus an employer, or a state that requires employers to 'protect the woman to protect the fetus' could argue that women's unique reproductive capacity requires special treatment of women workers that may not be required for men.   (Maschke 1989:59–60)

Interestingly, eight days after the Court's ruling in *Cal. Fed.*, it denied by a unanimous decision (*Wimberly v. Labor and Industrial Relations Commission* 1987) an appeal to a Missouri Supreme Court decision rejecting a woman's claim that the PDA mandated preferential treatment for women on account of pregnancy. In the absence of a state law similar to that of California, the Court could find no reason to support the type of treatment of pregnancy they had validated in *Cal. Fed.* Clearly, the Court reiterated the tenet that the states, not the Court, have the power to extend the coverage afforded to pregnancy disability above the floor set by Congress in Title VII.

A related type of leave often confused with pregnancy disability leave is maternity or parental leave, which gives the mother (and possibly the father) time off from work to care for the new infant. As discussed earlier the European approach is based on paid leave while the dispute in the United States primarily centers on unpaid leave. Although federal legislation has been introduced over the last several years, it has yet to be passed. Even so, the concepts introduced by National Family and Medical Leave Act are very modest. For instance, the legislation proposed in the 101st Congress would have required some employers with more than fifty employees to provide unpaid, job-protected medical and parental leave to male and female workers. An employee would be able to take up to ten weeks of unpaid parental leave during any twenty-four-month period to care for a newborn, adopted, or seriously ill child. In addition, an employee with a serious health condition would be able to take up to fifteen weeks of unpaid medical leave during a twelve-month period with protection of preexisting health insurance, accrued leave, and seniority.

TABLE 7.3
Maternity and Parental Leave by State

State	Effect. Year	Coverage	Maximum Period Covered	Employees Covered	Job Protection
California	1980	Pregnancy disability	4 months	Over 5 employees	Yes
Connecticut	1988	Birth, adoption, or serious illness of child, spouse or parent	24 weeks in 2 years	State employees only	Yes
	1990	Birth, adoption, or serious illness of child, spouse, or parent	12 weeks in 2 years	Over 250 employees reduced in stages	Yes
Florida	1979	Birth	6 months	State employees only	Yes
Hawaii	1982	Pregnancy disability period	"Reasonable"	All employees	Yes
Iowa	1987	Pregnancy disability	8 weeks	Over 25 employees	—
Louisiana	1987	Pregnancy disability	4 months	Over 25 employees	—
Maine	1988	Birth, adoption, or serious illness of parent, spouse, or child	8 weeks in 2 years	Over 25 employees	Yes
Massachusetts	1988	Childbirth or adoption of child under age 3	8 weeks	Over 5 employees	Yes
Minnesota	1987	Newborn or adopted infant mother and father	6 weeks	Over 20 employees	Yes
Montana	1984	Pregnancy disability	"Reasonable" period	All employees	Yes
New Hampshire	1984	Pregnancy disability	"Reasonable" period	Over 5 employees	Yes
New Jersey	1990	Birth, adoption, or serious illness of child, parent, or spouse	12 weeks in 24 months	Over 100 to be reduced to over 50 by 1992	Yes

State	Year	Reason	Duration	Coverage	Law
North Carolina	1988	Pregnancy disability	—	State employees only	Yes
North Dakota	1990	Birth, adoption, or illness of spouse, child, or parent	4 months	State employees only	Yes
Oklahoma	1989	Birth, adoption, or care of terminally or critically ill child or dependent adult	—	State employees only	Yes
Oregon	1988	Birth or adoption of child under age 3	12 weeks	Over 24 employees	Yes
	1989	Pregnancy disability	"Reasonable" period	Over 24 employees	Yes
Pennsylvania	1986	Birth or adoption, pregnancy disability	6 months	State employees only	Yes
Rhode Island	1987	Birth, adoption, or serious illness of child	13 weeks in 2 years	Private over 50, local government over 30, all state employees	Yes
Tennessee	1988	Pregnancy disability	4 months	One hundred or more employees	Yes
Vermont	1989	Prenatal leave after childbirth, pregnancy disability	Total of 12 weeks	Ten or more employees	Yes
Washington	1984	Birth, adoption, or terminal illness of child	12 weeks in 24 months	One hundred or more employees	Yes
West Virginia	1989	Birth, adoption, or illness of spouse, child or parent	12 weeks in 12 months	State employees, schools	Yes
Wisconsin	1988	Birth, adoption, serious illness of child, spouse or parent, or general disability	Total of 8 weeks in 12 months	Fifty or more employees	Yes

Until that time when a national policy is implemented parental leaves will remain the responsibility of the individual states. Although this is less desirable than having a uniform national standard (see Sullivan 1987), many states have independently been making statutory provision for maternity or parental leaves. Table 7.3 demonstrates the confusing and varied combination of pregnancy disability and family or parental leaves in the twenty-plus states that have statutory-based leave policies. In all cases the leaves are unpaid. The most common coverage, variously worded in the statutes, is family leave for birth, adoption of a young child or baby, or serious illness of a child, spouse, or parent. The average length of unpaid leave is approximately ten weeks, and most of the statutes specify job and benefits protection. The state laws, of course, set minimum requirements that can be exceeded. Many large firms have relatively generous paternal leave policies, some with wage replacement. However, the vast majority of women, especially those in the service and retail sectors who most need the income, do not have access to paid maternal or parental leave.

8 | Building Rational Policy for Women in the Workplace

Women not only will remain in the workforce but will continue to move in greater numbers into jobs that were in the past male-dominated. Economic reality in the 1990s requires that most households have two incomes in order to raise and support families. Women contribute approximately one-third to one-half of family income in dual-earner households (Bookman 1991:71). For economic reasons alone married women—especially those from low and middle income families—need to work, thus explaining why by 1987 over half of all married women with children under one year old were in the workforce (Kamerman 1991:12). This economic need is reinforced by the social and psychological desires of many women to seek personal autonomy and make independent career choices. As women have fewer children in many ways pregnancy has become more of an interruption of career than a career itself (Murray 1984).

A second reason that an increasing proportion of women must work is because of the rapid growth in the number of households headed by women. Many women by necessity work because they are the sole wage earners and sources of support for themselves and their children. Currently, approximately 12 percent of all American households are female-headed–single-parent families and cannot afford any loss in income even for a short period (Bookman 1991:72). Furthermore, these women are disproportionately found in low paying, minimal wage level jobs and have the least adequate health benefits and leave opportunities. It is estimated that half of female-headed families live in poverty (Bookman 1991:72). To deny these women access to industry's better paying jobs for which they are qualified is to deny them the opportunity to support their children to the best of their ability.

The third factor increasing the number of women in the workplace is the result of decisions of a growing proportion of women to delay or forgo having children or families and pursue careers. Many of these women have specific career goals that entail entry into jobs that women in the past were denied. Frequently these women do not plan on having children—to exclude them from jobs in industries deemed hazardous to the health of fetuses because they are fertile is especially unreasonable.

Failure to Address Reproductive Health of Women

At the expense of equal employment opportunity and the economic need of many women to work, exclusionary policies still did little to protect either the reproductive health of woman or the health of their potential children. Because they were primarily applicable only to high paying industrial jobs, their impact was to force many excluded women to either take equally hazardous low paying jobs or to be unemployed. Furthermore, because FPPs did not usually address the contribution of the fertile males to the health of their offspring and thus also exclude fertile males from high-risk workplaces, they protected neither the reproductive health of males nor their potential progeny. Moreover, the reproductive health of the spouses of male employees was ignored, since they were not protected from hazards their husbands might bring home from the workplace.

More important, however, FPPs failed because they created a false dichotomy and forced opponents into an untenable dilemma. Although seldom explicitly stated the choice over reproductive health became defined as either:

1. Women's reproductive health should be protected from workplace hazards by exclusion, or

2. Women's reproductive health should not be protected from workplace hazards.

In other words, by shifting emphasis from protecting women's health to protecting fetal health through exclusion of women, attention was deflected from the core issue, ensuring women's health. By focusing on the danger of the workplace for the fetus, the health of the fetus, not the woman, received primary attention from the courts, employees, the media, and policy makers in the 1980s. Overlooked was the fact that in most instances maximizing the reproductive health of all workers in the long run would protect fetal health as well.

Similarly, the countervailing emphasis on the right of women to equal employment opportunity and job choice tended to overshadow an equally crucial right to be protected from exposure to work-related health hazards. Also lost was a focus on the interests of all workers to be fully informed of workplace hazards, to know what is potentially injurious and what is not, and to have unnecessary fears and anxieties allayed (Abdul-Karem 1984).

There are two critical dimensions of the concern over women's presence in hazardous workplaces that must be addressed. The first, which received almost exclusive attention over the last decade, centered on the controversy over exclusionary policies. As noted above the debate surrounding FPPs diverted attention from what in fact was the initial set of policy issues raised in the early 1970s—that many workplace settings are hazardous to the health of women and that steps should be taken to reduce the risks they bear. The Hobson's choice of protecting through exclusion or not protecting unfortunately tended to set the boundaries of the debate to the detriment of all workers.

Those groups most harmed by the resulting failure to address the core issue of reproductive hazards in the workplace were women in traditionally female jobs. Women of color and poor women are especially at risk for reproductive injury or disease. Not only do they often have the most hazardous jobs (most of which were never covered by FPPs) but also their low income forces them to live in inadequate housing and in neighborhoods contaminated by an array of environmental pollutants. Many work long hours in low paying jobs without benefits such as health insurance, maternity leave, vacation time, or even sick leave (Nsiah-Jefferson 1989:27). These women, particularly, have limited recourse when their rights are violated and are unlikely to initiate action for fear of losing their jobs, such as they are. The hesitancy of many opponents of FPPs to address these inadequacies in reproductive health, although understandable, is yet another tragedy of the inattention given the widespread problem of workplace hazards women face.

Another impact of the preoccupation with fetal health is found in the apparent reversal of the characteristic positions regarding risk assessment of industry on the one hand and labor and women's groups on the other (see Bayer 1982:651). Traditionally workers and unions have pushed for the most extensive reductions in exposure levels to toxicants, maintaining that uncertainty requires the most cautious assessment of potential harmful consequences. In contrast, industry has usually responded that risk-free work environments are impossible, uncertainty requiring toleration of levels of exposure that have not been proven harmful. As stated earlier, this industry position has led to conflicts with OSHA standards.

The debate over exclusionary policies designed to protect the fetus, however, forced labor and women's groups to take the cautious, more skeptical position regarding risk in the workplace. There has been a tendency of many opponents of FPPs to minimize the level of risk to the fetus through the mother and to favor less restrictive employment practices. Of course, to argue otherwise would be to give credence to the interventionalist strategies of industry, which adopted "an almost alarmist perspective" (Bayer 1982:652) regarding hazards to the fetus. While industries with FPPs contended that fetal protection requires absolute safety, which can only be accomplished by exclusion of all fertile women, workers' representatives and some feminist groups and political liberals argued that fertile women should be allowed to work in settings that may carry some risk of reproductive harm. Ironically, in the name of equal opportunity defenders of women's rights have resorted to demanding the freedom to share with men equal access to reproductive risks in order to improve or retain their earning capacities (Bayer 1982:654). This too is part of the legacy of controversy over exclusionary policies.

It is critical, then, that protection of women's reproductive health be conceptually distinguished from the issue of protection of fetal health. Even though the two are inseparable in practice, unless women's reproductive health is elevated to first priority it becomes easily lost within the controversy over fetal hazards. As argued earlier, the "solution" excluding fertile females from selected hazardous workplaces averted attention from the broader issue of maximizing the reproductive health of women workers in general. At this juncture, then, the pressing question is, What steps can be taken to ensure women's reproductive health?

First, considerably more research must be conducted to ascertain the causes of a full range of adverse effects on women's reproductive health and, by extension, that of men, since the two interact at least at conception. Although this book has focused on the impact of teratogens, chapter 3 demonstrated that women are vulnerable to a wide variety of reproductive injury and disease caused or aggravated by hazards in the workplace. With few exceptions, however, our knowledge of what agents cause harm at each reproductive stage and how they do so is inconclusive at best.

Second, a woman's reproductive health is a function of her overall health status. In the absence of a national health system that ensures access to high quality primary care for all women, it is imperative that employers accept heightened responsibility for providing such health care. This is especially critical for women because upward of 75 percent work in lower paying, nonprofessional jobs that are least likely to have adequate health care provisions. Although there have been many proposals recently to reform the U.S. health care system that include provisions for mandatory insurance coverage (for example, see Pepper Commission, *A Call for Action*, 1990), the outlook for a major reform remains unencouraging. Without such coverage, however, many women remain at risk—even if the actual workplace is not overly hazardous.

Third, in those workplaces that are potentially hazardous to the woman's reproductive health safeguards should be maximized. As discussed in chapter 7 preventive policies should encompass broad education and information programs so that all workers are aware of what the risks are, how to minimize them (i.e., through protective clothing and equipment), and what other less hazardous job options are available. Although many large corporations have well-established programs to accomplish these goals, many smaller firms and some of the larger ones do not. Short of making all workplaces free of potential toxicants, education, counseling, and full disclosure of potential risks at least allows a woman to make informed decisions and increases her capacity to maximize her reproductive health within the constraints of any particular workplace.

Finally, it is clear that policy incentives encouraging employers to reduce reproductive harm to both female and male employees have been inadequate at best. As chapter 6 concluded, current compensation systems are inadequate to deal effectively with reproductive injury and disease caused by workplace conditions. Workers who suffer reproductive injury that might in some cases be transmitted to their offspring are harmed, even though they often do not meet the conventional definitions of disability. Also, because job disability leaves are difficult to secure for reproductive injury the result is that such workers must continue to work, thus risking even more extensive injury. It is essential, therefore, as evidence builds concerning the harmful effects of certain work settings on the reproductive health of women and men, that workers' compensation and disability leave plans be reassessed and revised to account for these data. Likewise, the courts, which have traditionally dismissed causes of action for reproductive injury, should reevaluate this position, especially if workers' compensation is not expanded to include coverage.

Protecting the Health of Children

Despite the controversy over women in the workplace and the growing evidence of potential adverse effects on unborn children, there is also evidence that the overall pregnancy outcomes of

TABLE 8.1

Percentage of Selected Infant Outcomes by Working Status

Outcomes	Working Status			
	No Work	1–8 Mos.	9 Mos.	All Workers
Gestational age				
<36 weeks	7.4	10.8	2.5	7.2
>42 weeks	12.9	18.5	18.4	18.5
Birthweight				
<2500g	8.3	11.2	3.0	7.7
Apgar 1 <6	7.2	10.1	5.0	7.8
Apgar 5 <6	2.2	3.2	1.0	2.2
Special care nursery	16.3	21.5	12.2	17.5
Prenatal death rate	1.1	1.7	0.2	1.1
Prematurity	5.8	8.8	1.6	5.7
Any malformation	9.1	9.4	8.0	8.0
major	2.7	3.0	2.8	2.9
minor	6.4	6.4	5.2	5.9
Neonatal infection	0.9	1.4	0.6	1.1

SOURCE: Marbury et al. (1984:418)

women who work during pregnancy are better than those who do not. A French study, for instance, found that working women are less likely to have low birthweight or premature babies than are nonworking women (Saurel and Kaminski 1983). The authors attributed this difference to the better socioeconomic conditions linked with employment. Similarly, a U.S. study by Naeye and Peters (1982) concluded that working had no effect on gestational age at delivery, although there was a slightly lower average birthweight of children whose mothers worked during pregnancy.

In a major American study comparing pregnancy outcomes of 7,155 women who worked one to nine months during pregnancy with 4,018 who were not employed, Marbury and associates (1984) found that women who worked the full nine months had a lower rate of adverse outcome than the nonworking group as well as those who left employment during the first eight months. Table 8.1 presents comparative data for these three groups of women for a range of pregnancy outcomes. The data show that for most indicators of problems—including prematurity, low birthweight, low Apgar scores, prenatal death rate, need for special care nursery, malformation, and neonatal infection—women who worked the full nine months on average had the lowest percentage of problems and those who worked less than eight months had the highest percentage.

Although these data do not suggest that women should work throughout pregnancy to ensure healthy babies, they illustrate that there are many other factors besides working that might contribute to adverse pregnancy outcomes. These findings also emphasize the point that simply excluding pregnant women from certain workplaces does not guarantee a risk-free pregnancy. Women who lose their jobs or who are excluded from being hired might as a result face unemployment, inadequate health care and prenatal services, and poverty-related problems. As discussed earlier, the alternatives to working in a high-risk workplace for a pregnant woman might actually be less advantageous for her and for her potential offspring. It should also be noted that the significant difference in outcomes between women who work to term and those who leave before eight months might reflect the fact that the latter are forced to leave *because* they have a problem pregnancy. The absence of automatic pregnancy leaves in the United States, in contrast to other Western nations, accentuates the proportion of women who leave work during pregnancy for health reasons because they otherwise would not be eligible. Considerably more extensive comparative research in this area is essential to conclusively answer these questions.

Preventing Fetal Injury

Whatever the actual number of children harmed by parental exposure to hazards in the workplace the evidence in chapter 3 demonstrates that the risk of harm is extensive. Risks in the workplace, however, must be placed within the context of the significant risks to the fetus outside the workplace (Blank 1992a). Exclusionary policies purported to reduce risk to near zero solely by excluding fertile women. The assumption of those policies was illusory, however, because it did not adequately account for the potential contribution of the male, or balance workplace risks against other risks that might heighten as these excluded women became unemployed or took lower paying but more hazardous jobs. In other words, while FPPs did reduce one set of risks, they did nothing to address many other sets of risks to fetal health.

Risk, then, is a fact of life in an industrial society that affects all potential children in many different forms. Although the risk of workplace hazards to the unborn child cannot be eliminated short of excluding all fertile women and men from all jobs with any potential risk, there are other strategies that can help reduce the risk to manageable levels. Within the legal framework of permitting women equal employment opportunities, a range of workplace policies in combination can work toward enhancing the health of children of all workers. The goal is to design a multifaceted program that although fitted to each particular work setting contains many common elements in a rational preventive approach.

In addition to the factors discussed above, designed to protect reproductive health of workers in general, particular steps can be taken to lessen risk to offspring. When temporary job modification of the work setting to accommodate the changing physical needs of women workers is impossible, temporary transfers to a safer job are a reasonable option in larger companies. Upon request women who are pregnant or who plan to be should have the option to be removed from toxic areas without economic loss. Although this may be impractical in some job settings, especially in smaller companies, if the risk to the developing fetus is deemed to be exceedingly high some intermediate arrangements might be possible to reduce the level of exposure, such as a shift to half-time or to some type of rotational system. Unless the transfer is accompanied with retention of salary, benefits, and seniority, however, many pregnant women may be unwilling to request these changes, thus undercutting the benefits of the program.

Access to quality prenatal-preconception education and care has clearly been linked to healthy pregnancies and children (Institute of Medicine 1985). It is especially important in a high-risk workplace to guarantee access of all pregnant women to prenatal classes and medical care. Although there are many ways of ensuring such access (i.e., paid leave time for medical appointments, on-site prenatal care, on-site education and classes), as discussed in chapter 7 there is evidence that these programs are cost-effective for industry and that they contribute substantially to the health of a woman and her child.

Although there is less conclusive data on the cost-effectiveness of paid pregnancy disability leaves and postbirth maternity or parental leaves, data from Europe demonstrate that they advance the birth and development of healthy children. Although paid leaves are preferable, it is unlikely that they will be forthcoming or widely implemented in the United States. Therefore, attention will focus on unpaid leaves. If the primary goal is to maximize the health of the fetus paid prenatal leaves in combination with unpaid parental leaves after birth (with retention of benefits, seniority, and job) would be a useful intermediary strategy.

There is evidence that the costs of implementing a national paid pregnancy leave program would not be prohibitive. Data from the five states that already mandate pregnancy disability leaves demonstrate that by requiring employers and employees to each pay one-half of 1 percent of salary we could provide an insurance benefit that would cover about 60 to 70 percent of salary for ten weeks (Kamerman 1991:20). Variations of the system could be established that would ensure full or near full salary for women on the lowest end of the pay scale with diminishing percentages for those at the higher levels. Similarly, the General Accounting Office (1987) concluded that an unpaid, eighteen-week parental leave policy for infants would cost American businesses no more than $340 million annually. Relative to what defenders of FPPs see as potential enormous costs of litigation, the combination of paid temporary disability leave during pregnancy and unpaid parental leaves after pregnancy would be a bargain. More important, this package of benefits would symbolize a genuine interest in the health of employees and their children.

It is critical, whichever of these approaches is taken, that the affected women have an active role in the process and constraints on their choices be kept to a minimum. Although in a few exceptional cases coercive measures will be necessary, the primary role of the employer is to provide opportunities for access and educate and encourage the pregnant women to take advantage of them, not dictate the terms of her pregnancy. In the vast majority of cases the goals of both the employer and the woman should be identical—to maximize the health of the woman and her child.

Creation of Accident Compensation Fund

In spite of all efforts to protect the reproductive health of workers, toxicants in many workplaces will continue to put some unborn children at risk for prenatal or preconception injury due to exposure of one or both of the parents. It is critical, therefore, to establish a system to compensate those children injured that has the effect of spreading out the burden of fetal risk beyond both the pregnant or fertile woman and specific industries. As discussed in chapter 6, neither the current workers' compensation schemes nor the tort system are sufficient to accomplish this end. Workmen's compensation statutes, at least as presently interpreted, usually do not compensate the children harmed prenatally through exposure of their mother or father to workplace hazards. Similarly, the tort system, despite industry concern, is unlikely to serve as a routine compensatory mechanism, particularly in light of the Court's dismissal of their likelihood in *Johnson Controls*. Furthermore, even if tort law did yield large settlements for fetal injury in a few cases where evidence was undisputable, the system would not provide relief for most injured parties. Tort law would be least likely to compensate victims of injury that resulted from the mother's exposure in traditionally female-dominated jobs, where evidence of fetal harm may be significant but less conclusive.

The most promising alternative to current options is the creation of an accident compensation fund (ACF) designed specifically to indemnify fetal harm. If threats to the health of the unborn are as insidious and widespread as industries have insisted when justifying exclusionary policies, it would seem that they should be willing or even anxious to help underwrite an ACF to cover such contingencies. The moral responsibility to protect the unborn exercised through FPPs could be redirected to include a similar responsibility to compensate fetuses undisputedly so harmed. An accident compensation scheme could also be constructed so as to eliminate the threat of suits under tort law and the attendant costs (economic and public relations) they bring, even when unsuccessful. Furthermore, a consistent, fairly administered ACF might be a positive influence on worker morale and decrease the conflict inherent to the current system.

The ACF could either be state-administered, with national minimal requirements, or administered by a federal agency. Although a state-administered scheme would be easier to implement because it could be linked to current workers' compensation systems, a national ACF is preferable because it spreads the costs of workplace risks across the largest population. A nationally administered fund, however, would be politically controversial if a large proportion of the payoffs went to a small number of states with concentrations of hazardous industries. Sor (1986–87) recommends the establishment of a national fund based on mandatory contributions from affected industries, which would be used to compensate infants born with injuries "conclusively" resulting from exposures to fetally toxic work environments. For the "need for such a funding process results from the virtual impossibility of tracing such an injury to a specific employer, especially where the employee has worked for several employers and was exposed to potential fetotoxic agents at each workplace" (Sor 1986–87:227).

Another advantage of instituting an accident compensation approach is that it would not distinguish between the female and male contribution to fetal harm. This would encourage more equity in the research effort invested in maternal and paternal exposures leading to fetal injury. In addition, it would have the advantage of including coverage from industries that although potentially hazardous did not have FPPs, i.e., female-dominated industries and small businesses where women are disproportionately represented.

The apportionment of contributions to the ACF required of each employer could be based on a number of factors including: (1) the number of workers employed; (2) a hazardous substance index score based on the known estimates of fetal hazards in each industrial category; and (3) cumulative data on ACF payouts of each particular corporation. The latter two factors would encourage employers to minimize potential reproductive hazards and do as much as possible to reduce the incidence of fetal harm through preventive measures, short of exclusion, so as to reduce their monetary contribution to the fund. Those industries that continued to score high on the hazardous substance index and have disproportionately high compensation payout rates would be penalized with higher premium costs.

Along the lines of existing workers' compensation procedures parents who felt that their baby's injuries were related to a workplace hazard could file a claim with the accident compensation commission. Either lump-sum or continuous payment schemes could be instituted to settle claims that are accepted by the commission. If the claim is rejected the parents could appeal the decision to an appeals board. Since the purpose of the ACF is to compensate victims of workplace hazards the rules of evidence should be set low. Payment could include medical expenses not covered by health insurance plans, special care needs, possibly limited compensation for pain and suffering. Although the ACF would be designed to preclude lawsuits, torts for negligence by a company would be allowed. Companies that withheld information about known reproductive risks from fertile employees, that failed to meet OSHA or other regulatory standards, or in other ways acted negligently could not use the ACF to avoid lawsuits.

Shared Responsibility and the Need for Action

Responsibility for protection of workers and their children from reproductive hazards ultimately must be a shared one. No single sector of society can either assume to have or have thrust upon them full responsibility for the health of future generations. In the 1980s some corporations tried to shift the burdens associated with childbearing in the workplace to women by excluding them from employment. Just as this strategy failed so any policy will fail that tries to place the entire burden of implementing the recommendations discussed here on specific industries. American industry must maintain competitive productivity in a highly competitive world. Although they have a responsibility to society to provide as healthy as possible workplace for all employees, there are limits as to how far society can expect them to go toward that end.

Many of the changes described here can and should be implemented by the appropriate industries as part of doing business with potentially hazardous substances, but it is unreasonable to put all the costs on industry, particularly those sectors that are highly vulnerable in the present economy. Although large corporations can probably bear the costs of these needed changes, many small and mid-size ones possibly can not. Workers who want the higher wages that go along with high-risk industrial jobs should be willing to contribute more to the costs involved through copayments and higher taxes. Workers in low paying high-risk jobs, on the other hand, cannot be expected to make similar sacrifices. Substantial governmental action and financial investment will be necessary to reach the goal of producing healthy children.

It should not be surprising that the countries offering the most generous paid leave policies and comprehensive health care for working women and men also have considerably higher tax rates than the United States. Other Western democracies have made a societal commitment to children and families and have backed up this high priority with varying degrees of public funding. If we really place high priority on protecting women's employment opportunities, the reproductive health of workers, and the health of our progeny, as a society we must be willing to pay the costs. This book has presented some policy recommendations for accomplishing these goals, which, hopefully, will motivate a reevaluation of how we treat women in the workplace. Although, upon deliberation, more effective strategies than those offered here might emerge, the important point is that action is urgently needed by lawmakers to address these issues and appropriate the funds and guidance necessary to balance out the many conflicting interests. Failure to do so suggests that our resolve comes up far short of our proclaimed interest in protecting the health of our present and future citizens.

Appendix

Court Cases

Albala v. City of New York, 78 A.D. 2d 389, 434 N.Y.S.2d 400 (1981)

Allaire v. St. Luke's Hospital, 184 Ill. 359, 56 N.E. 638 (1900)

Alquijay v. St. Luke's-Roosevelt Hospital Center, 9 A.D.2d 704, 471 N.Y.S.2d 1 (A.D. 1 Dept. 1984)

Ard v. Ard, 414 So.2d 1066 (Fla. 1982)

Atkins v. Children's Hospital of the District of Columbia, 261 U.S. 525 (1923)

Becker v. Schwartz, 46 N.Y.2d 895, 413 N.Y.S.2d 895, 386 N.E.2d 807 (1978)

Bell v. Industrial Vangas, Inc., 30 Cal.3d 268., 637 P.2d 266, 179 Cal. Rptr. 30 (1981)

Bell v. Macy's California, 89 Cal. Daily Opin. Ser. 6195 (1989)

Bennett v. Hymers, 101 N.H. 483, 147 A.2d 108 (1958)

Blankenship v. Cincinnati Milacron Chemicals, Inc., 433 N.E.2d 572 (1982)

Bonbrest v. Kotz, 65 F. Supp. 138 (D.D.C. 1946)

Bouvia v. Superior Court, 179 Cal. App. 3d 1127 (1986)

Bowen v. American Hospital Association, 106 S.Ct 2101 (1986)

Bradwell v. Illinois, 83 U.S. (16 Wall.) 1130 (1873)

Brennecke v. Brennecke, 336 S.W.2d 68 (Mo. 1960)

Briere v. Briere, 107 N.H. 432, 224 A.2d 588 (1966)

Burwell v. Eastern Air Lines, Inc., 633 F.2d 361 (4th Cir. 1980), cert. denied, 450 U.S. 965 (1981)

California Federal Savings and Loan Association v. Guerra, 758 F.2d
  39 (Cal. 9 1985), 479 U.S. 272 (1987)
Canterbury v. Spence, 592 A.2d 404 (N.J. 1972)
Chamness v. Fairtrace, 511 N.E.2d 839 (Ill. App. 5 Dist. 1987)
Cleveland Board of Education v. La Fleur, 414 U.S. 632 (1974)
Cole v. Dow Chemical Co., 315 N.W.2d 565 (1982)
Coley v. Commonwealth Edison Co., 703 F. Supp. 748 (N.D. Ill. 1989)
Commonwealth v. Beatty, 15 Pa.Super. 5 (1900)
Craig v. Boren, 429 U.S. 190 (1976)
Curlender v. Bio-Science Laboratories, 165 Cal. Rptr. 477 (1980)
D'Angona v. Los Angeles County, 613 P.2d 238, 166 Cal. Rptr. 177
  (1980)
Dietrich v. Inhabitants of Northampton, 138 Mass. 14 (1884)
DiNatale v. Lieberman, 409 So.2d 512 (Fla. 1982)
Dorlin v. Providence Hospital, 118 Mich. App. 831, 325 N.W.2d 600
  (1982)
Dothard v. Rawlinson, 433 U.S. 321 (1977)
Douglas v. Town of Hartford, 542 F. Supp. 1267 (D. Conn. 1982)
Dumer v. St. Michael's Hospital, 69 Wis.2d 766, 233 N.W.2d 372
  (1975)
Dunlap v. Dunlap, 84 N.H. 352 (1930)
Eisenstadt v. Baird, 405 U.S. 438 (1972)
Ellis v. Sherman, 515 A.2d 314 (Pa. 1986)
Evans v. Olson, 550 P.2d 924 (Ok. 1976)
Florida v. Johnson, Case No. E89-890-CFA (Seminole Cty. Cir. Ct. July
  13, 1989)
Florida Lime and Avocado Growers, Inc. v. Paul, 373 U.S. 132 (1963)
Geduldig v. Aiello, 417 U.S. 484 (1974)
General Electric Co. v. Gilbert, 429 U.S. 125 (1976)
Gleitman v. Cosgrove 49 N.J. 22, 227 A.2d 689 (1967)
Goller v. White, 122 N.W.2d 193 (Wis. 1963)
Grant v. General Motors Corp., 908 F.2d 1303 (1990)
Griswold v. Connecticut, 381 U.S. 479 (1965)
Grodin v. Grodin, 102 Mich. App. 396, 301 N.W. 2d 869 (1980)
Harbeson v. Parke-Davis, 98 Wash.2d 460, 656 P.2d 483 (1983)
Harman v. Daniels, 525 F. Supp. 798 (W.D.Va. 1981)
Harris v. McRae, 448 U.S. 197 (1980)
Harriss v. Pan American World Airways, 649 F.2d 690 (9th Cir. 1980)
Hastings v. Hastings, 163 A.2d 147 (1960)
Hayes v. Shelby Memorial Hospital 546 F.Supp. 259 (N.D. Ala. 1982),
  726 F.2d 1543 (11th Cir. 1984), rehearing denied 732 F.2d 944 (11th
  Cir. 1984)

Hebel v. Hebel, 435 P.2d 8, 14 (Alaska 1967)

Hewlett v. George, 68 Miss. 708, 9 So. 885 (1891)

Hornbuckle v. Plantation Pipe Line Co., 212 Ga. 504, 93 S.E.2d 727 (1956)

In re A.C., 533 A.2d 611 (D.C. App. 1987), vacated and rehearing granted, 539 A.2d 203 (1988), en banc, D.C. Ct.App. (April 26, 1990), reversed

In re Baby X, 97 Mich. App. 11 (1980)

In re Phillip B., 156 Cal.Rptr. 48 (1979), cert. denied 455 U.S. 949 (1980)

Industrial Union Department v. American Petrol Institute, 448 U.S. 607 (1980)

In re. President and Directors of Georgetown College, Inc., 331 F.2d 1000 (D.C. Cir.), cert. denied 377 U.S. 978 (1964)

International Union, UAW v. Johnson Controls, Inc., 680 F. Supp.309 (E.D. Wis. 1988), rehearing en banc, 886 F.2d 871 (7th Cir. 1989), reversed 89-1215 (U.S. Sup. Ct. March 20, 1991)

Jefferson v. Giffin Spaulding City Memorial Hospital, 274 S.E. 2d 457 (Ga. 1981)

Jehovah's Witnesses v. King's County Hospital, 278 F. Supp. 488 (W.D. Wash. 1967)

Johns-Manville Corp. v. Contra Costa Superior Court, 612 P.2d 948, 165 Cal.Rptr. 858 (1980)

Johnson Controls, Inc. v. California Fair Employment and Housing Commission, 267 Cal.Rptr. 158 (Cal.App. 4 Dist. 1990), cert. denied 1990 Cal. LEXIS 2107 (1990)

Kofren v. Amoco Chemicals Co., 441 A.2d 226 (Del. 1982)

Levin v. Delta Air Lines, Inc., 730 F.2d 994 (5th Cir. 1984)

Lochner v. New York, 198 U.S. 45 (1905)

Logan v. Reeves, 209 Tenn. 631, 354 S.W. 2d 789 (1962)

McKelvey v. McKelvey, 111 Tenn. 388, 77 S.W. 644 (1903)

Mandolidis v. Elkins Industries, Inc., 246 S.E.2d 907 (W. Va. 1978).

Matter of Danielle Smith, 492 N.Y.S.2d 331 (Fam. Ct. Monroe Co. 1985)

Matter of Gloria C. v. William C., 476 N.Y.S. 2d 991 (Fam. Ct. Richmond Co. 1984)

Mercer v. Uniroyal, Inc., 361 N.E.2d 492 (1977)

Miller-Wohl v. Commissioner of Labor and Industry, 692 P.2d 1243 (Mont. 1984)

Muller v. Oregon, 208 U.S. 412 (1908)

Nashville Gas Co. v. Satty, 434 U.S. 136 (1977)

Nelson v. Krusen, 635 S.W.2d 582 (Tex. 1982)

Oil, Chemical and Atomic Workers v. American Cyanamid Co., 741 F.2d 444 (D.C. Cir. 1984)

Parham v. J.R., 442 U.S. 584 (1979)

Park v. Chessin, 60 App. Div. 2d 80, 400 N.Y.S.2d 110 (1977), modified N.Y.L.J., Dec. 29, 1978, at 1 (N.Y. Ct. App.)

Payton v. Abbott Labs, 83 F.R.D. 382, 386 (D. Mass. 1981)

People v. Charles Schweinler Press, 214 N.Y. 395, 108 N.E. 639 (1915)

Peterson v. Honolulu, 262 P.2d 1007 (Ha. 1969)

Phifer v. Union Carbide Corp., 492 F.Supp. 483 (E.D. Ark. 1980)

Plumley v. Klein, 388 Minn. 1, 199 N.W.2d 169 (1972)

Procanik v. Cillo, N.J. Sup. Ct. No.A-89 (1984)

Radice v. People, 264 U.S. 292 (1924)

Reed v. Reed, 404 U.S. 71 (1971)

Reed Tool Co. v. Copelin, 610 S.W.2d 736 (Tex. 1981)

Renslow v. Mennonite Hospital, 67 Ill.2d 348, 367 N.E.2d 1250 (1977)

Roe v. Wade, 410 U.S. 113 (1973)

Roller v. Roller, 37 Wash. 242 (1905)

Rosenfeld v. Southern Pacific Co., 444 F.2d 1219 (9th Cir. 1971)

Schloendorff v. Society of N.Y. Hospitals, 105 N.E. 92 (1914)

Schroeder v. Perkel, 87 N.J. 53 (S.C.N.J. July 15, 1981)

Security National Bank v. Chloride Inc., 602 F.Supp. 294 (D. Kan. 1985)

Siemieniec v. Lutheran General Hospital, 512 N.E.2d 691 (Ill. 1987)

Silesky v. Kelman, 161 N.W.2d 631 (Minn. 1968)

Smith v. Brennan, 31 N.J. 353, 157 A.2d 497 (1960)

Sorensen v. Sorensen, 339 N.E.2d 907 (Mass. 1975)

Stallman v. Youngquist, 504 N.E.2d 920 (Ill.App. 1 Dist. 1987), reversed 531 N.E.2d 355 (Ill. 1988)

State v. Buchanan, 29 Wash. 60 (1902)

Streenz v. Streenz, 471 P.2d 282 (Ariz. 1970)

Sylvia v. Gobeille, 101 R.I. 76, 220 A.2d 222 (1966)

Taft v. Taft, 388 Mass. 331, 146 N.E. 2d 395 (1983)

Teramano v. Teramano, 216 N.E.2d 375 (Ohio 1966)

Trevarton v. Trevarton, 151 Colo. 418, 378 P.2d 640 (1963)

Tucker v. Tucker, 395 P.2d 67 (Okla. 1964)

Turpin v. Sortini, 31 Cal. 3d 220, 643 P.2d 954, 182 Cal. Rptr. 337 (1982)

Union Carbide Co. v. Stapleton, 237 F.2d 229 (6th Cir. 1956)

Union Pacific Railway v. Botsford, 141 U.S. 250 (1891)

United States v. Vaughn, 117 Daily Wash. L. Rep. 441 (D.C. Super. Ct. March 7, 1989)

Vann v. Dow Chemical Co., 561 F.Supp.141 (W.D. Ark. 1983)

Verkennes v. Corniea, 38 N.W.2d 838 (Minn. 1949)

Walker v. Railway Co., 28 L.R.Ir. 69 (1891)

Webster v. Reproductive Health Services, 57 U.S.L.W. 5023 (1989)

Wenham v. State, 65 Neb. 394 (1902)

West Coast Hotel Co. v. Parrish, 300 U.S. 379 (1937)

Williams v. Marion Rapid Transit, Inc., 87 N.E.2d 334 (Ohio 1949)

Wilson v. Kaiser Foundation Hospital, 141 Ca.A.3d 891, 190 Cal. Rptr. 649 (1983)

Wimberley v. Labor and Industrial Relations Commission, U.S. (1987)

Wright v. Olin Corp., 697 F.2d 1172 (4th Cir. 1982), 585 F.Supp. 1447 (W.D.N.C. 1984), vacated without opinion 767 F.2d 915 (4th Cir. 1984)

Woods v. Lancet, 303 N.Y. 349, 102 N.E.2d 691 (1951)

Zuniga v. Kleberg County Hospital, 692 F.2d 986 (5th Cir. 1982)

Bibliography

Accurso, Allison E. 1985. "Title VII and Exclusionary Practices: Fertile and Pregnant Women Need Not Apply." *Rutgers Law Journal* 17(1):95–134.

"Accutane Alert: Birth Defects." 1986. *The Harvard Medical School Health Letter*, no. 3, p. 1.

Adbul-Karim, Raja W. 1984. "Women Workers at Higher Risk of Reproductive Hazards." In Geoffrey Chamberlain, ed., *Pregnant Women at Work*. London: Royal Society of Medicine.

American Medical Association. 1990. "Legal Interventions During Pregnancy." Report of the Board of Trustees, Report 00.

Annas, George J. 1981. "Righting the Wrong of 'Wrongful Life.' " *Hastings Center Report* 11(1):8.

—— 1987. "The Impact of Medical Technology on the Pregnant Woman's Right to Privacy." *American Journal of Law and Medicine* 13(2–3):213–232.

—— 1989. "Predicting the Future of Privacy in Pregnancy: How Medical Technology Affects the Legal Rights of Pregnant Women." *Nova Law Review* 13(2):329–354.

Arditti, Rita. 1985. "Review Essay: Reducing Women to Matter." *Women's Studies International Forum* 8(6):577–582.

Armstrong, B. G., A. D. Nolin, and A. D. McDonald. 1989. "Work in Pregnancy and Birthweight for Gestational Age." *British Journal of Industrial Medicine* 46:196–199.

Ashford, Nicholas A. 1984. "Legal Considerations of Reproductive Hazards by the United States." In Geoffrey Chamberlain, ed., *Pregnant Women at Work*. London: Royal Society of Medicine.

Ashford, Nicholas A. and Charles C. Caldart. 1983. "The Control of Reproductive Hazards in the Workplace: A Prescription for Prevention." *Industrial Relations Law Journal* 5:523–563.

Ashford, Nicholas A., Christine J. Spadafor, Dale B. Hattis, and Charles C. Caldart. 1990. *Monitoring the Worker for Exposure and Disease*. Baltimore: Johns Hopkins University Press.

Atchison, C. J. 1983. "*Ard v. Ard:* Limiting the Parent-Child Immunity Doctrine." *University of Pittsburgh Law Review* 44:977–1003.

Axelsson, G., R. Rylander, and I. Molin. 1989. "Outcome of Pregnancy in Relation to Irregular and Inconvenient Work Schedules." *British Journal of Industrial Medicine* 46:393–398.

Baer, Judith A. 1978. *Chains of Protection*. Westport, Ct.: Greenwood Press.

—— 1991. "Beyond Rights: Fetal Protection and Sexual Equality." Paper presented at Midwest Political Science Association Meetings, Chicago, April 18–20.

Balisy, Sam S. 1987. "Maternal Substance Abuse: The Need to Provide Legal Protection for the Fetus." *Southern California Law Review* 60:1209–1238.

Barlow, Susan M., and Frank M. Sullivan. 1982. *Reproductive Hazards of Industrial Chemicals*. New York: Academic Press.

Baron, Charles H. 1983. "The Concept of Person in the Law." In Margery W. Shaw and A. Edward Doudera, eds., *Defining Human Life*, pp. 121–148. Ann Arbor: Health Administration Press.

Bayer, Ronald. 1982. "Reproductive Hazards in the Workplace: Bearing the Burden of Fetal Risk." *Health and Society* 60(4):633–656.

Beal, Ron. 1984. " 'Can I Sue Mommy?' An Analysis of a Woman's Tort Liability for Prenatal Injuries to Her Child Born Alive." *San Diego Law Review* 21:325–370.

Becker, Mary E. 1986. "From *Muller v. Oregon* to Fetal Vulnerability Policies." *University of Chicago Law Review* 53:1219–1273.

—— 1990. "Can Employers Exclude Women to Protect Children?" *JAMA* 264(16):2113–2117.

Bellin, Judith S., and Reva Rubenstein. 1983. "Genes and Gender in the Workplace." In Ethel Tobach and Betty Rosoff, eds. *The Second X and Women's Health*. Stanton Island, N.Y.: Gordian Press.

Bellinger, David, Alan Leviton, Christine Waternaux, Herbert Needleman, and Michael Rabinowitz. 1987. "Longitudinal Analyses of Prenatal and Postnatal Lead Exposure and Early Cognitive Development." *New England Journal of Medicine* 17(316):1037–1043.

Benirschke, K. 1981. "Anatomy." In G. S. Berger, W. E. Bremmer, and L. G. Keith, eds., *Second-Trimester Abortion: Perspectives after a Decade of Experience.* Boston: John Wright-PSG.

Berg, K. 1979. *Genetic Damage in Man Caused by Environmental Agents.* New York: Academic Press.

Biggers, John D. 1983. "Generation of the Human Life Cycle." In William Bondeson etal., eds., *Abortion and the Status of the Fetus.* Dordrecht, Holland: D. Reidel.

Bingham, Eula. 1980. "Some Scientific and Social Hazards of Identifying Reproductive Hazards in the Workplace." In Peter F. Infante and Marvin S. Legator, eds., *Proceedings of a Workshop on Methodology for Assessing Reproductive Hazards in the Workplace.* Washington, D.C.: National Institute for Occupational Safety and Health.

Blank, Robert H. 1988. *Rationing Medicine.* New York: Columbia University Press.

—— 1991. *Fertility Control: New Techniques, New Challenges.* Westport, Ct.: Greenwood Press.

——. 1992a. *Mother and Fetus: Changing Notions of Maternal Responsibility.* Westport, Ct.: Greenwood Press.

—— 1992b. "Politics and Genetic Engineering." *Politics and the Life Sciences* 11(1):81–85.

Bolognese, R. 1982. "Medico-Legal Aspects of a Human Life Amendment." *Pennsylvania Law Journal Reporter* 5:13.

Bookman, Ann. 1991. "Parenting Without Poverty: The Case for Funded Parental Leave." In Janet Shibley Hyde and Marilyn J. Essex, eds., *Parental Leave and Child Care.* Philadelphia: Temple University Press.

Breese, Kevin M. 1987. "Sunbeam's Prenatal Program." *Personnel Administrator* 32:40–42.

Brent, R. L. 1980. "Radiation-Induced Embryonic and Fetal Loss from Conception to Birth." In I. H. Porter and Ernest B. Hook, eds., *Human Embryonic and Fetal Death.* New York: Academic Press.

Briggs, Gerald G., Roger K. Freeman, and Sumner J. Yaffe. 1986. *Drugs in Pregnancy and Lactation.* Baltimore: Williams and Wilkins.

Brokaw, Katherine. 1989–90. "Genetic Screening in the Workplace and Employers' Liability." *Columbia Journal of Law and Social Problems.* 23:317–346.

Brown, Barbara A. 1985. "Pregnancy-Related Disability—The Scope of Permissible Coverage." *Employment Relations Today* (Autumn), 221–225.

Burton, Wayne N., Denise Erickson, and Jorgia Briones. 1991. "Women's Health Programs at the Workplace." *Journal of Occupational Medicine* 33(3):349–350.

Buss, Emily. 1986. "Getting Beyond Discrimination: A Regulatory Solution to the Problem of Fetal Hazards in the Workplace." *The Yale Law Journal* 95:554–577.

Carroll, Douglas E. 1986. "Parental Liability for Preconception Negligence: Do Parents Owe a Legal Duty to Their Potential Children?" *California Western Law Review* 22:289–316.

Centers for Disease Control. 1985. "Leading Work-Related Diseases and Injuries—United States." *Morbidity and Mortality Weekly Report* 34:537–540.

Chamberlain, Geoffrey. 1984. "Women at Work in Pregnancy." In Geoffrey Chamberlain, ed., *Pregnant Women at Work*. London: Royal Society of Medicine.

Chasnoff, Ira J. 1988. "Drug Use in Pregnancy: Parameters of Risk." *Pediatric Clinics of North America* 35(6):1403–1412.

Chavkin, Wendy, Ruthann Evanoff, Ilene Winkler, and Ginny Reath. 1983. "Reproductive Hazards in the Workplace: A Course Curriculum Guide." In Ethel Tobach and Betty Rosoff, eds., *The Second X and Women's Health*, pp. 101–129. Staten Island, N.Y.: Jordian Press.

Chavkin, Wendy. 1984. "Walking a Tightrope: Pregnancy, Parenting, and Work." In Wendy Chavkin, ed., *Double Exposure: Women's Health on the Job and at Home*. New York: Monthly Review Press.

Chavkin, Wendy, and S. R. Kandall. 1990. "Between a 'Rock' and a Hard Place: Perinatal Drug Abuse." *Pediatrics* 85(2):223–225.

Clement, Susan, Lori Goldstein, Lori B. Krauss, Duncan A. Maio, Steven Reske, Wendy Ravitz, Cheryl B. Schreiber, Thomas K. Schulte, Bruce Shapiro, Lisa A. Sheeler, Robert Whalen, and Jean Zoubek. 1987. "The Evolution of the Right to Privacy after *Roe v. Wade*." *American Journal of Law and Medicine* 13(2–3):368–525.

Cohen, Ellis N. 1980. "Waste Anesthetic Gases and Reproductive Health in Operating Room Personnel." In Peter F. Infante and Marvin S. Legator, eds., *Proceedings of a Workshop on Methodology for Assessing Reproductive Hazards in the Workplace*. Washington, D.C.: National Institute for Occupational Safety and Health.

Cohen, M. E. 1978. "*Park V. Chessin:* The Continuing Judicial Development of the Theory of 'Wrongful Life.' " *American Journal of Law and Medicine* 4:217–262.

Coleman, Linda, and Cindy Dickinson. 1984. "The Risks of Healing: The Hazards of the Nursing Profession." In Wendy Chavkin, ed., *Double Exposure: Women's Health on the Job and in the Home.* New York: Monthly Review Press.

Committee on Education and Labor, U.S. Congress House of Representatives. 1990. *A Report on the EEOC, Title VII, and Workplace Fetal Protection Policies in the 1980s.* Washington D.C.: U.S. Government Printing Office.

Condit, Deidre Moira. 1991. "Constructing Fetal 'Personhood': An Examination of Law and Language." Paper presented at the Midwest Political Science Association Meetings, Chicago, April 18–20.

Corea, Gina. 1985. *The Hidden Malpractice: How American Medicine Mistreats Women.* 2d ed. New York: Harper and Row.

Corey, Lawrence. 1982. "Dx and Rx Changes in Primary Care for Genital Herpes." *Illustrated Medicine* 1(2):1–8.

Council on Scientific Affairs. 1985. "Effects of Toxic Chemicals on the Reproductive System." *JAMA* 253(23):3431–3437.

Crocetti, Annemarie F., Paul Mushak, and Joel Schwartz. 1990. "Determination of Numbers of Lead-Exposed Women of Childbearing Age and Pregnant Women." *Environmental Health Perspectives* 89:121–124.

Davis, John A. 1976. "Teratogenic and Subtler Effects of Drugs in Pregnancy." In A. C. Turnbull and F. P. Woodford, eds., *Prevention of Handicap Through Antenatal Care.* New York: Elsevier.

Devore, Nancy E., Virginia M. Jackson, and Susan L. Piening. 1983. "TORCH Infections." *American Journal of Nursing* (December), pp. 1660–1665.

Dixon, Robert L., and Carlton H. Nadolney. 1985. "Assessing Risk of Reproductive Dysfunction Associated with Chemical Exposure." In Robert L. Dixon, ed., *Reproductive Toxicology.* New York: Raven Press.

Doudera, A. Edward. 1982. "Fetal Rights? It Depends." *Trial* 18(4):38–44.

Duncan, Allyson K. 1989. "Fetal Protection and the Exclusion of Women from the Toxic Workplace." *North Carolina Central Law Journal* 18:67–86.

Eisenstein, Zillah. 1988. *The Female Body and the Law.* Berkeley: University of California Press.

Elias, Sherman and George J. Annas. 1983. "Perspectives on Fetal Surgery." *American Journal of Obstetrics and Gynecology* 145(4):807–812.

—— 1987. *Reproductive Genetics and the Law*. Chicago: Year Book Medical Publishers, Inc.

Equal Employment Opportunity Commission (EEOC). 1988. "Policy Guidance on Reproductive and Fetal Hazards." 193 *Daily Labor Report* D-1.

—— 1990. 18 *Daily Labor Report* (BNA) D-1.

Erickson, J. D., W. M. Cochran, and C. E. Anderson. 1979. "Paternal Occupation and Birth Defects." *Contributions to Epidemiology and Biostatistics* 1:107–117.

Erickson, A., B. Kallen, O. Meirik, and P. Westerholm. 1982. "Gastrointestinal Atresia and Maternal Occupation During Pregnancy." *Journal of Occupational Medicine* 24:515–518.

Everson, Richard B. 1987. "Review of Approaches to the Detection of Genetic Damage in the Human Fetus." *Environmental Health Perspectives* 74:109–117.

Feinberg, Joel. 1984. *Harm to Others*. New York: Oxford University Press.

Field, Martha A. 1989. "Controlling the Woman to Protect the Fetus." *Law, Medicine, and Health Care* 17(2):114–129.

Fletcher, John C. 1983. "Emerging Ethical Issues in Fetal Therapy." In Kare Berg and Knut E. Tranoy, eds., *Research Ethics*. New York: Alan R. Liss.

Friedman, J. M., B. B. Little, R. L. Brent, J. F. Cordero, J. W. Hanson, and T. H. Shepard. 1990. "Potential Human Teratogenicity of Frequently Prescribed Drugs." *Obstetrics and Gynecology* 75(4):594–599.

Funes-Cravioto, F., C. Zapata-Gayon, B. Kilmodin-Hedman, et al. 1977. "Chromosomal Aberrations and Sister-Chromatod Exchange in Workers in Chemical Laboratories in a Roto-Printing Factory and in Children of Women Laboratory Workers." *Lancet* 2:322–325.

Furnish, Hannah A. 1980. "Prenatal Exposure to Fetally Toxic Work Environments: The Dilemma of the 1978 Pregnancy Amendment to Title VII of the Civil Rights Act of 1964." *Iowa Law Review* 66:63–129.

Gallagher, Janet. 1987. "Prenatal Invasions and Interventions: What's Wrong with Fetal Rights." *Harvard Women's Law Journal* 10:9–58.

Garrett, Patricia, Sally Lubeck, and Dee Ann Wenk. 1991. "Childbirth and Maternal Employment: Data from a National Longitudinal Survey." In Janet Shibley Hyde and Marilyn J. Essex, eds., *Parental Leave and Child Care*. Philadelphia: Temple University Press.

Gelb, Joyce, and Marian Lief Palley. 1987. *Women and Public Policies*. 2d ed. Princeton: Princeton University Press.

General Accounting Office. 1987. *Parental Leave: Estimated Costs of H. R. 925, Family and Medical Leave Act of 1987*. Washington, D.C.: General Accounting Office.

Glass, Bentley. 1983. "Concluding Reflections." In A. Edward Dondera and Margery W. Shaw, eds., *Defining Human Life*. Ann Arbor: Health Administration Press.

Gold, Rachel Benson, and Asta M. Kenney. 1985. "Paying for Maternity Care." *Family Planning Perspectives* 17(3):103–111.

Goldberg, Susan. 1989. "Medical Choices During Pregnancy: Whose Decision Is It Anyway?" *Rutgers Law Review* 41:591–623.

Goldman, A. S. 1980. "Critical Periods of Prenatal Toxic Insults." In R. H. Schwartz and S. J. Jaffe, eds., *Drug and Chemical Risks to the Fetus and Newborn*, pp. 9–31. New York: Alan R. Liss.

Gonen, Julianna S. 1991. "Women's Rights vs. 'Fetal Rights': Politics, Law, and Reproductive Hazards in the Workplace." Paper presented at the American Political Science Association Meetings, Washington D.C., August 29–31.

Grobstein, Clifford. 1981. *From Chance to Purpose: An Appraisal of External Human Fertilization*. Reading, Mass.: Addison-Wesley.

—— 1988. *Science and the Unborn: Choosing Human Features*. New York: Basic Books.

Hanson, James W. 1980. "Reproductive Wastage and Prenatal Ethanol Exposure: Human and Animal Studies." In I. H. Porter and Ernest B. Hook, eds., *Human Embryonic and Fetal Death*. New York: Academic Press.

Harrigan, J. 1980. "Prenatal and Obstetrical Factors in Mental Retardation." In M. K. McCormack, ed., *Prevention of Mental Retardation and Other Developmental Disabilities*. New York: Marcel Dekker.

Harrison, Michael R., N. Scott Adzick, Michael Longaker, et al. 1990. "Successful Repair in Utero of a Fetal Diaphragmatic Hernia After Removal of Herniated Viscera from the Left Thorax." *The New England Journal of Medicine* 322(22):1582–1584.

Hatch, Maureen. 1984. "Mother, Father, Worker: Men and Women and the Reproductive Risks of Work." In Wendy Chavkin, ed., *Double Exposure: Women's Health Hazards on the Job and at Home*. New York: Monthly Review Press.

Hatch, Maureen, and Zena A. Stein. 1988. "Reproductive Disorders." In Barry S. Levy and David H. Wegman, eds., *Occupational Health: Recognizing and Preventing Work-Related Disease*, pp. 415–429. Boston: Little, Brown.

Hauth, John C., Jane Hauth, Richard B. Drawbaugh, Larry C. Gilstrap, and Wayne P. Pierson. 1984. "Passive Smoking and Thiocyanate Concentrations in Pregnant Women and Newborns." *Obstetrics and Gynecology* 63(4):519–522.

Heinonen, Olli. P., Dennis Slone, Samuel Shapiro, with Leonard F. Gaetano. 1977. *Birth Defects and Drugs in Pregnancy*. Littleton, Mass.: Publishing Sciences Group.

Hemminki, K., and M. L. Niemi. 1982. "Community Study of Spontaneous Abortions: Relation to Occupation and Air Pollution by Sulphur Dioxide, Hydrogen Sulfide, and Carbon Disulfide." *International Archives of Occupational and Environmental Health* 51:55–63.

Hemminki, K., and M. L. Niemi, P. Kyyronen, I. Kilpikavi, and H. Vainio. 1983. "Spontaneous Abortions as a Risk Indication in Metal Exposure." In T. W. Clarkson, F. N. Gunnar, and P. R. Sager, eds., *Reproductive and Developmental Toxicity of Metals*. New York: Plenum Press.

Hemminki, K., P. Mutanen, I. Saloniemi, and K. Luoma. 1981. "Congenital Malformations and Maternal Occupation in Finland." *Journal of Epidemiology and Community Health* 35(1):5–10.

Hemminki, K., P. Mutanen, I. Saloniemi, M. L. Niemi, and H. Vainio. 1982. "Spontaneous Abortions in Hospital Staff Engaged in Sterilizing Instruments with Chemical Agents." *British Journal of Medicine* 285:1461–1463.

Hoff, Rodney, Victor P. Beradi, Barbara J. Weiblen, Laurene Mahoney-Trout, Marvin L. Mitchell, and George F. Grady. 1988. "Seroprevalence of Human Immunodeficiency Virus Among Childbearing Women: Estimation by Testing Samples of Blood from Newborns." *New England Journal of Medicine* 318:525–530.

Holden, Constance. 1991. "Probing the Complex Genetics of Alcoholism." *Science* 251:163–164.

Howard, Linda G. 1981. "Hazardous Substances in the Workplace: Rights of Women." *University of Pennsylvania Law Review* 129:798–845.

Hook, Edward B. and Ian H. Porter. 1980. "Terminological Conventions, Methodological Considerations, Temporal Trends, Specific Genes, and Some Other Factors Pertaining to Embryonic and Fetal Deaths."

In Ian H. Porter and Edward B. Hook, eds., *Human Embryonic and Fetal Death*. New York: Academic Press.

Hubbard, Ruth. 1985. "Prenatal Diagnosis and Eugenic Ideology." *Women's Studies International Forum* 8(6):567–576.

—— 1990. *The Politics of Women's Biology*. New Brunswick: Rutgers University Press.

Huckle, Patricia. 1982. "The Womb Factor: Pregnancy Policies and Employment of Women." In Ellen Boneparth, ed., *Women, Power, and Policy*, pp. 144–161. New York: Pergamon Press.

Hunt, Vilma R. 1978. "Occupational Radiation Exposure of Women Workers," *Preventive Medicine* 7:294–299.

——. 1979. *Work and Health of Women*. Boca Raton, Fl.: CRC Press.

Infante, Peter F., J. K. Wagoner, A. J. McMichael, R. J. Waxweiler, and H. Falk. 1976. "Genetic Risks of Vinyl Chloride." *Lancet* 1:734–739.

Infante, Peter F. 1980. "Chloroprene: Adverse Effects on Reproduction." In Peter F. Infante and Marvin S. Legator, eds., *Proceedings of a Workshop on Methodology for Assessing Reproductive Hazards in the Workplace*. Washington, D.C.: National Institute for Occupational Safety and Health.

Institute of Medicine. 1985. *Preventing Low Birthweight*. Washington, D.C.: National Academy Press.

—— 1988. *Prenatal Care*. Washington, D.C.: National Academy Press.

Isaacs, Stephen L., and Renee J. Holt. 1987. "Redefining Procreation: Facing the Issues." *Population Bulletin* 42(3):1–37.

Jack, Brian W., and Larry Culpepper. 1990. "Preconception Care: Risk Reduction and Health Promotion in Preparation for Pregnancy." *JAMA* 264(9):1147–1149.

Jacob, Annamma J., Janet Epstein, David L. Madden, and John L. Sever. 1984. "Genital Herpes Infection in Pregnant Women Near Term." *Obstetrics and Gynecology* 63(4):480–484.

Johnsen, Dawn. 1986. "The Creation of Fetal Rights: Conflicts with Women's Constitutional Rights to Liberty, Privacy, and Equal Protection." *Yale Law Journal* 95:599–625.

—— 1989. "From Driving to Drugs: Governmental Regulation of Pregnant Women's Lives After *Webster*." *University of Pennsylvania Law Review* 138:179–215.

Journal of the American Medical Association (JAMA). 1984. "Syphilis—United States, 1983." *JAMA* 252(8):992–993.

Kamerman, Sheila B. 1988. "Maternity and Parenting Benefits: An International Overview." In Edward F. Zigler and Meryl Frank, eds.,

The Parental Leave Crisis: Toward a National Policy, pp. 239–255.
New Haven: Yale University Press.

—— 1991. "Parental Leave and Infant Care: U.S. and International
Trends and Issues, 1978–1988." In Janet Shibley Hyde and Marilyn
J. Essex, eds., *Parental Leave and Child Care*. Philadelphia: Temple
University Press.

Kamerman, Sheila B., and Alfred J. Kahn. 1987. *The Responsive Workplace: Employers and a Changing Labor Force*. New York: Columbia
University Press.

Kashi, J. S. 1977. "The Case of the Unwanted Blessing: Wrongful Life."
University of Miami Law Review 31:1432–1480.

Katz, Joni F. 1989. "Hazardous Working Conditions and Fetal Protection Policies: Women Are Going Back to the Future." *Environmental Affairs* 17:201–230.

Kelly, Rita Marie, and Jane H. Bayes, eds. 1988. *Comparable Worth,
Pay Equity, and Public Policy*. Westport, Ct.: Greenwood Press.

Kessler-Harris, Alice. 1982. *Out to Work: A History of Wage-Earning
Women in the United States*. New York: Oxford University Press.

King, Patricia A. 1980. "The Juridical Status of the Fetus: A Proposal
for the Protection of the Unborn." In C. E. Schneider and M. A.
Vinovskis, eds., *The Law and Politics of Abortion*. Lexington, Mass.:
Lexington Books.

Kolder, Veronika E. B., Janet Gallagher, and Michael T. Parsons. 1987.
"Court-Ordered Obstetrical Interventions." *New England Journal of
Medicine* 316(19):1192–1196.

Koos, B. J. and Lawrence D. Longo. 1976. "Mercury Toxicity in the
Pregnant Woman, Fetus, and Newborn Infant." *American Journal
of Obstetrics and Gynecology* 126:390–409.

Kotch, Jonathan B., Charlene C. Ossler, and Dorothy C. Howze. 1984.
"A Policy Analysis of the Problem of the Reproductive Health of
Women in the Workplace." *Journal of Public Health Policy* (June),
pp. 213–227.

Lagrew, David C., Terrance G. Furlow, W. David Hager, and Robert L.
Yarrish. 1984. "Disseminated Herpes Simplex Virus Infection in
Pregnancy: Successful Treatment with Acyclovir." *JAMA* 252:2058–
2059.

Lambert, T. F. 1983. "Law in the Future: Tort Law 2003." *Trial*
19(7):65–70.

Legator, M. S., and J. B. Ward, Jr. 1984. "Animal and Human Studies
in Genetic Toxicology." In Geoffrey Chamberlain, ed., *Pregnant
Women at Work*. London: Royal Society of Medicine.

Lenow, Jeffrey L. 1983. "The Fetus as a Patient: Emerging Rights as a Person?" *American Journal of Law and Medicine* 9(1):1–29.

Lipscomb, Jane A., Laura Fenster, Margaret Wrensch, Dennis Shusterman, and Shanna Swan. 1991. "Pregnancy Outcomes in Women Potentially Exposed to Occupational Solvents and Women Working in the Electronics Industry." *Journal of Occupational Medicine* 33(5):597–604.

Lipsett, M. B. and John C. Fletcher. 1983. "Do Vitamins Prevent Neural Tube Defects (and Can We Find Out Ethically)?" *Hastings Center Report* 13(4):5–8.

Locke, Nancy J. 1987. "Mother v. Her Unborn Child: Where Should Texas Draw the Line?" *Houston Law Review* 24:549–576.

Logan, Shelley Reed. 1983. "Adopting Fetal Vulnerability Programs to Title VII: *Wright v. Olin.*" *Employee Relations Law Journal* 9:605–628.

Losco, Joseph. 1989. "Fetal Abuse: An Exploration of Emerging Philosophic, Legal, and Policy Issues." *Western Political Quarterly* 42(2):265–286.

McGill, Linda D. 1990. "Reproductive Hazards and Sex Discrimination: A Delicate Balance." *Employment Relations Today* (Spring), pp. 15–20.

McKechnie, Sheila. 1984. "A Trade Union View of Reproductive Health." In Geoffrey Chamberlain, ed., *Pregnant Women at Work.* London: Royal Society of Medicine.

Macklin, Ruth. 1983. "When Human Rights Conflict: Two Persons, One Body." In A. Edward Doudera and Margery W. Shaw, eds., *Defining Human Life: Medical, Legal and Ethical Implications.* Ann Arbor: Health Administration Press.

MacMahon, B. 1985. "Prenatal X-Ray Exposure and Twins." *New England Journal of Medicine* 312:576–577.

McNulty, Molly. 1988. "Pregnancy Police: The Health Policy and Legal Implications of Punishing Pregnant Women for Harm to their Fetuses." *Review of Law and Social Change* 16:277–319.

McRae, Susan. 1991. *Maternity Rights in Britain: The Experience of Women and Employees.* London: Policy Studies Institute.

Manson, Rebecca, and Judy Marolt. 1988. "A New Crime, Fetal Neglect: State Intervention to Protect the Unborn—Protection at What Cost?" *California Western Law Review* 24:161–182.

Marbury, Marian C., Shai Linn, Richard R. Monson, David H. Wegman, Stephen C. Schoenbaum, Phillip G. Stubblefield, and Kenneth

J. Ryan. 1984. "Work and Pregnancy." *Journal of Occupational Medicine* 26(6):415–421.

Marx, Jean L. 1989. "The Cystic Fibrosis Gene is Found." *Science* 245:923–925.

Maschke, Karen J. 1989. *Litigation, Courts, and Women Workers.* New York: Praeger.

—— 1991. "The Ideology and Practice of Reproductive Freedom." Paper presented at Midwest Political Science Association Meetings, Chicago, April 18–20.

Mascola, Laurene, Rocco Pelosi, Joseph H. Blount, Nancy J. Binkin, Charles E. Alexander, and Willard Cates, Jr. 1984. "Congenital Syphilis: Why Is It Still Occurring?" *JAMA* 252:1719–1722.

Mathieu, Deborah. 1985. "Respecting Liberty and Preventing Harm: Limits of State Intervention in Prenatal Choice." *Harvard Journal of Law and Policy* 8(1):19–55.

Mattison, Donald R., Maria S. Nightingale, and Kenji Shiromizu. 1983. "Effects of Toxic Substances on Female Reproduction." *Environmental Health Perspectives* 48:43–52.

Mattson, L. P. 1981. "The Pregnancy Amendment: Fetal Rights and the Workplace." *Case and Comment* (November–December) pp. 33–41.

Meirik, O., B. Kallen, U. Gauffin, and A. Ericson. 1979. "Major Malformations in Infants Born of Women Who Worked in Laboratories While Pregnant." *Lancet* 2:91.

Mies, Maria. 1987. "Sexist and Racist Implications of New Reproductive Technologies." *Alternatives* 12:323–342.

Milkman, Ruth. 1987. *Gender at Work: The Dynamics of Job Segregation by Sex During World War II.* Urbana: University of Illinois Press.

Moelis, Lawrence S. 1985. "Fetal Protection and Potential Liability: Judicial Application of the Pregnancy Discrimination Act and the Disparate Impact Theory." *American Journal of Law and Medicine* 11(3):369–390.

Murray, Robert. 1984. "The Hazards of Work in Pregnancy." In Geoffrey Chamberlain, ed., *Pregnant Women at Work.* London: Royal Society of Medicine.

Naeye, R. L. and E. C. Peters. 1982. "Working During Pregnancy: Effects on the Fetus." *Pediatrics* 69:724.

National Institute for Occupational Safety and Health (NIOSH). 1988. *Proposed National Strategies for the Prevention of Leading Work-*

Related Diseases and Injuries. Part 2. Washington, D.C.: Association of Schools of Public Health.

New York Times. December 25, 1991.

Niebyl, J. R., ed. 1982. *Drug Use in Pregnancy.* Philadelphia: Lea and Febiger.

Nisbet, Ian C. T., and Nathan J. Karch. 1983. *Chemical Hazards to Human Reproduction.* Park Ridge, N.J.: Noyes Data Corporation.

Note. 1983. "Life with Mother: The Fourth Circuit Reconciles Title VII and Fetal Vulnerability in *Wright v. Olin Corp.*" *Alabama Law Review* 34(2):327–338.

Note. 1987. "The Evolution of the Right to Privacy after *Roe v. Wade.*" *American Journal of Law and Medicine* 13(2–3):365–525.

Note. 1988. "Maternal Rights and Fetal Wrongs: The Case Against Criminalization of 'Fetal Abuse.'" *Harvard Law Review* 101:994–1012.

Nothstein, Gary Z., and Jeffrey P. Ayres. 1981. "Sex-Based Considerations of Differentiation in the Workplace: Exploring the Biomedical Interface between OSHA and Title VII." *Villanova Law Review* 26(2):239–261.

Nsiah-Jefferson, Laurie. 1989. "Reproductive Laws, Women of Color, and Low-Income Women." *Women's Rights Law Reporter* 11(1):15–38.

Oakley, Ann. 1984. *The Captured Womb: A History of the Medical Care of Pregnant Women.* Oxford: Oxford University Press.

Occupational Safety and Health Administration (OSHA). 1987. "Federal Response or Legal Recourse Limited on Issue of Reproductive Hazards in the Workplace." 123 *Daily Labor Report* (BNA) A-11 (June 29).

—— 1990. "Occupational Safety and Health in 1990." 19 *O.S.H. Report* (BNA) D-4 (January 10).

Office of Technology Assessment (OTA). 1985. *Reproductive Health Hazards in the Workplace.* Washington, D.C.: U.S. Government Printing Office.

—— 1988. *Healthy Children.* Washington, D.C.: U.S. Government Printing Office.

—— 1990a. *Neurotoxicity: Identifying and Controlling Poisons of the Nervous System.* Washington, D.C.: U.S. Government Printing Office.

—— 1990b. *Genetic Monitoring and Screening in the Workplace.* Washington, D.C.: U.S. Government Printing Office.

—— 1991. *Medical Monitoring and Screening in the Workplace: Re-*

sults of a Survey. Background paper, OTA-BP-BA-67. Washington, D.C.: U.S. Government Printing Office.

Overall, Christine. 1987. *Ethics and Human Reproduction: A Feminist Analysis.* Boston: Allen and Unwin.

Parness, Jeffrey A. 1986. "The Abuse and Neglect of the Human Unborn: Protecting Potential Life." *Family Law Quarterly* 20(2):197–212.

Pastides, H., E. J. Calabrese, D. W. Hosmer, and D. R. Harris. 1988. "Spontaneous Abortion and General Illness Among Semiconductor Manufacturers." *Journal of Occupational Medicine* 30:543–551.

"Paternal-Fetal Conflict." 1992. *Hastings Center Report* 22(2):3.

Paul, Maureen, Cynthia Daniels, and Robert Rosofsky. 1989. "Corporate Response to Reproductive Hazards in the Workplace: Results of the Family, Work, and Health Survey." *American Journal of Industrial Medicine* 16:267–280.

Peacock, James E., and Felix A. Sarubbi. 1983. "Disseminated Herpes Simplex Virus Infection During Pregnancy." *Obstetrics and Gynecology* 61(3):13S–18S.

Pepper Commission. 1990. *A Call For Action: Final Report of the Pepper Commission.* Washington, D.C.: U.S. Government Printing Office.

Perkoff, R. 1970. "Renal Diseases." *Genetic Disorders of Man* 1:443–460.

Petchesky, Rosalind P. 1979. "Workers' Reproductive Hazards and the Politics of Protection: An Introduction." *Feminist Studies* 5(Summer):233–245.

—— 1980. "Reproductive Freedom: Beyond a Woman's Right to Choose." *Signs: Journal of Women in Culture and Society* 5:661–685.

Peters, Timothy J., Phillipa Adelstein, Jean Golding, and Neville R. Butler. 1984. "The Effects of Work in Pregnancy: Short- and Long-Term Associations." In Geoffrey Chamberlain, ed., *Pregnant Women at Work.* London: Royal Society of Medicine.

Phelan, Mary C., John M. Pellock, and Walter E. Nance. 1982. "Discordant Expression of Fetal Hydantoin Syndrome in Heteropaternal Dizygotic Twins." *New England Journal of Medicine* 307:99–101.

Phillips, Jimmie W. 1983. "Employment Discrimination—Fetal Vulnerability and the 1978 Pregnancy Amendments—*Wright v. Olin Corp.*" *Wake Forest Law Review* 19:905–929.

Pizzo, Peggy. 1988. "Uncertain Harvest: Maternity Leave Policies in Developing Nations." In Edward F. Zigler and Meryl Frank, eds.,

The Parental Leave Crisis: Toward a National Policy. New Haven: Yale University Press.

Proctor, Nick H., James P. Hughes, and Michael L. Fishman. 1988. *Chemical Hazards of the Workplace.* 2d ed. Philadelphia: J. B. Lippincott.

Public Health Service Expert Panel on the Content of Prenatal Care. 1989. *Caring for Our Future: The Content of Prenatal Care.* Washington, D.C.: Department of Health and Human Services.

Quinn, Margaret M., and Susan R. Woskie. 1988. "Women and Work." In Barry S. Levy and David H. Wegman, eds., *Occupational Health: Recognizing and Preventing Work-Related Disease,* pp. 479–499. Boston: Little, Brown.

Randall, Donna M. 1987. "Protecting the Unborn: Companies Are Responding to Possible Harm to Pregnant Workers." *Personnel Administrator* 32:88–94.

Rawls, R. L. 1980. "Reproductive Hazards in the Workplace." *Chemical and Engineering News* (February) pp. 28–30.

Remick, Helen, ed. 1984. *Comparable Worth and Wage Discrimination: Technical Possibilities and Political Realities.* Philadelphia: Temple University Press.

Ricci, Jean M., Rita M. Fojaco, and Mary Jo O'Sullivan. 1989. "Congenital Syphilis: The University of Miami/Jackson Memorial Medical Center Experience, 1986–1988." *Obstetrics and Gynecology* 74(5):687–691.

Rice, J. E. 1983. "Fetal Rights: Defining 'Person' Under 42 U.S.C. 1983." *University of Illinois Law Review* 1:347–366.

Risemberg, Herman M. 1989. "Fetal Neglect and Abuse." *New York State Journal of Medicine* (March) pp. 148–151.

Robertson, John A. 1983. "Procreative Liberty and the Control of Conception, Pregnancy, and Childbirth." *Virginia Law Review* 69(3):405–464.

—— 1987. "Gestational Burdens and Fetal Status: Justifying *Roe v. Wade.*" *American Journal of Law and Medicine* 13(213):189–212.

Rogers, T. D. 1982. "Wrongful Life and Wrongful Birth: Medical Malpractice in Genetic Counseling and Prenatal Testing." *South Carolina Law Review* 33:713–757.

Rom, William N. 1976. "Effects of Lead on the Female and Reproduction: A Review." *The Mount Sinai Journal of Medicine* 43:542–552.

—— 1980. "Effects of Lead on Reproduction." In Peter F. Infante and Marvin S. Legator, eds., *Proceedings of a Workshop on Methodology for Assessing Reproductive Hazards on the Workplace.* Washington, D.C.: National Institute for Occupational Safety and Health.

Rosenfeld, A. 1982. "The Patient in the Womb." *Science* 82:18–23.

Ross, Susan Deller. 1991. "Legal Aspects of Parental Leave: At the Crossroads." In Janet Shibley Hyde and Marilyn J. Essex, eds., *Parental Leave and Child Care.* Philadelphia: Temple University Press.

Ross, W. McL. 1972. "Environmental Problems in the Production of Printed Circuits." *Annals of Occupational Hygiene* 15:141.

Rothman, Barbara Katz. 1986. *The Tentative Pregnancy: Prenatal Diagnosis and the Future of Motherhood.* New York: Viking.

Rowland, Robin. 1985. Quoted in *New Birth Technologies.* Wellington, New Zealand: Department of Justice, Law-Reform Commission.

Ruddick, W., and W. Wilcox. 1982. "Operating on the Fetus." *Hastings Center Report* 12(5):10–14.

Ryan, Maura A. 1990. "The Argument for Unlimited Procreative Liberty: A Feminist Critique." *Hastings Center Report* 20(4):6–12.

Saurel, M. J., and M. Kaminski. 1983. "Pregnant Women at Work." *Lancet* 1:475.

Schardein, J. L., ed. 1976. *Drugs as Teratogens.* Cleveland: CRC Press.

Scott, Gwendolyn B., Margaret A. Fischl, Nancy Klimas, Mary Ann Fletcher, Gordon M. Dickenson, Robert S. Levine, and Wade P. Parks. 1985. "Mothers of Infants With the Acquired Immunodeficiency Syndrome: Evidence for Both Symptomatic and Asymptomatic Carriers." *JAMA* 253(3):363–366.

Scott, Judith A. 1984. "Keeping Women in Their Place: Exclusionary Policies and Reproduction." In Wendy Chavkin, ed., *Double Exposure: Women's Health Hazards on the Job and at Home.* New York: Monthly Review Press.

Sculnick, Michael W. 1985. "Update on Pregnancy Leave." *Employment Relations Today* (Winter), pp. 351–353.

—— 1986. "Sex Segregation in the Work Place." *Employment Relations Today* (Spring), pp. 3–10.

—— 1989. "Key Court Cases." *Employment Relations Today* (Spring), pp. 75–79.

Seksay, E. H. 1983. "Tort Law—Begetting a Cause of Action for those Injured by a Drug Prior to Birth." *Suffolk University Law Review* 17:257–268.

Sever, J. L. 1980. "Infectious Causes of Human Reproductive Loss." In I. H. Porter and Ernest B. Hook, eds., *Human Embryonic and Fetal Death.* New York: Academic Press.

Shaw, Margery W. 1980. "Preconception and Prenatal Torts." In Aubrey Milunsky and George J. Annas, eds., *Genetics and the Law, II.* New York: Plenum Press.

Shepard, Thomas H. 1989. *Catalog of Teratogenic Agents.* 6th ed. Baltimore: Johns Hopkins University Press.

Simon, C. A. 1978. "Prenatal Liability for Prenatal Injury." *Columbia Journal of Law and Social Relations* 14:47–90.

Simon, Howard A. 1990. "Fetal Protection Policies After *Johnson Controls:* No Easy Answers." *Employee Relations Law Journal* 15(4):491–514.

Smith, J. M. 1977. "Congenital Minimata Disease: Methyl Mercury Poisoning and Birth Defects in Japan." In E. Bingham, ed., *Proceedings: Conference on Women and the Workplace.* Society for Occupational and Environmental Health.

Sor, Yvonne. 1986–1987. "Fertility or Unemployment: Should You Have to Choose?" *Journal of Law and Health* 1:141–228.

Southgate, D. A. T. and E. Hey. 1976. "Chemical and Biochemical Development of the Human Fetus." In D. F. Roberts and A. M. Thompson, eds., *The Biology of Human Fetal Growth.* New York: Halsted.

Spallone, Patricia. 1989. *Beyond Conception: The New Politics of Reproduction.* Granby, Mass.: Bergin and Garvey.

Spielberg, S. P. 1982. "Pharmacogenetics and the Fetus." *New England Journal of Medicine* 307(2):115–116.

Stearns, Maxwell L. 1986. "Maternal Duties During Pregnancy: Toward a Conceptual Framework." *New England Law Review* 21(3):595–634.

Stetson, Dorothy McBride. 1991. "The Political History of Parental Leave Policy." In Janet Shibley Hyde and Marilyn J. Essex, eds., *Parental Leave and Child Care.* Philadelphia: Temple University Press.

Stoiber, Susanne A. 1989. *Parental Leave and "Women's Place": The Implications and Impact of Three European Approaches to Family Policy.* Washington, D.C.: Women's Research and Education Institute.

Stolz, Barbara Ann. 1985. *Still Struggling: America's Low Income Working Women Confront the 1980s.* Lexington, Mass.: Lexington Books.

Stone, K. M., C. A. Brooks, M. E. Guinan, and E. R. Alexander. 1989. "National Surveillance for Neonatal Herpes Simplex Virus Infections." *Sexually Transmitted Diseases* 16:152–156.

Strandberg, M., K. Sandback, O. Axelson, and L. Sundell. 1978. "Spontaneous Abortions Among Women in Hospital Laboratory." *Lancet* 1:384–385.

Sullivan, George M. 1987. "Pregnancy Discrimination: A State or National Policy? *Labor Law Journal* (October), pp. 665–671.

Sun, Marjorie. 1988. "Anti-Acne Drug Poses Dilemma for FDA." *Science* 240:714–715.

Susser, Peter A. 1986–87. "Chemical Hazard Disclosure Obligations." *Employment Relations Today* (Winter), pp. 301–308.

Swerdlin, Marcy. 1989. "Investing in Healthy Babies Pays Off." *Business and Health* (July), pp. 38–41.

Thompson, Elizabeth L. 1989. "The Criminalization of Maternal Conduct During Pregnancy: A Decisionmaking Model for Lawmakers." *Indiana Law Journal* 64:357–374.

Thorp, John M., Vern L. Katz, L. J. Fowler, James T. Kurtzman, and Watson A. Bowes, Jr. 1989. "Fetal Death from Chlamydial Infection Across Intact Amniotic Membranes." *American Journal of Obstetrics and Gynecology* 161:1245–1246.

U.S. Citizens Advisory Council on the Status of Women. 1971. *Women in 1970*. Washington, D.C.: U.S. Government Printing Office.

U.S. Congress, House Committee on Education and Labor. 1990. *A Report on the EEOC, Title VII and Workplace Fetal Protection Policies in the 1980s*. Washington, D.C.: Government Printing Office.

U.S. Environmental Protection Agency. 1986. *Air Quality Criteria for Lead*. EPA Report Number 600/8-83/028a F-dF.4v. Office of Health and Environmental Assessment, Environmental Criteria and Assessment Office, Research Triangle Park, N.C.

U.S. Food and Drug Administration. 1980. *Federal Register* 45(205):69823–69824.

Valentine, Jeannette M., and Alonzo L. Plough. 1982. "Protecting the Reproductive Health of Workers: Problems in Science and Public Policy." *Journal of Health Politics, Policy, and Law* 8(1):144–163.

Vaughan, Thomas L., Janet R. Daling, and Patricia M. Starzyk. 1984. "Fetal Death and Maternal Occupation." *Journal of Occupational Medicine* 26(9):676–678.

Vogel, Lise, 1990. "Debating Difference: Feminism, Pregnancy, and the Workplace." *Feminist Studies* 16(1):9–32.

Wagner, Eileen N. 1991. "Alcoholic Beverages Labeling Act of 1988: A Preemptive Shield Against Fetal Alcohol Syndrome Suits?" *Journal of Legal Medicine* 12:167–200.

Wentz, A. 1982. "Adverse Effects of Danazol in Pregnancy." *Annals of Internal Medicine* 96:672–673.

White, Heather M. 1988. "Unborn Child: Can You Be Protected?" *University of Richmond Law Review* 22:285–302.

Williams, Wendy W. 1981. "Firing the Woman to Protect the Fetus: The Reconciliation of Fetal Protection with Employment Opportunity Goals under Title VII." *Georgetown Law Journal* 69:641–704.

Wilson, J. G. 1977a. "Current Status of Teratology." In J. G. Wilson and S. C. Fraser, eds., *Handbook of Teratology*. Vol. 1. *General Principles and Etiologies*. New York: Plenum Press.

—— 1977b. "Embryotoxicity of Drugs in Man." In J. G. Wilson and F. C. Fraser, eds., *Handbook of Teratology*. Vol. 1. *General Principles and Etiologies*. New York: Plenum Press.

Winborne, William H., ed. 1983. *Handling Pregnancy and Birth Cases*. New York: McGraw-Hill.

Witwer, M. 1989. "One-Third of Infants Born to HIV-Positive Mothers Face Illness or Death During Their First Year of Life." *Family Planning Perspectives* 21(6):281–282.

Yazigi, Ricardo A., Randall R. Odem, and Kenneth L. Polakoski. 1991. "Demonstration of Specific Binding of Cocaine to Human Spermatozoa." *JAMA* 266(14):1956–1959.

Index

Designer: Susan Clark
Text: 11/13 Aldus
Compositor: Maple-Vail
Printer: Maple-Vail
Binder: Maple-Vail